Testimony Unveiled

KRISTINE DIXON

Kingdom Builders Publications LLC

E-Book ISBN – 978-0-692-79016-8
Paperback ISBN – 978-0-692-79226-1

Resources
Permission given to use NIV Scriptures by Allison McEmber of www.harpercollinschristian.com

Cover Designer
Kristine Dixon and LoMar Designs

Photographer
Michael Wanzer - Cover
Janice Bush – Author

Printed in USA

Go to these websites:
www.testimonyunveiled.org
www.kingdombuilderspublications.com

This Book Belongs to

Larry

To Someone
who always made
me smile. You'll never
know how much that
meant to me!!
"Pretty dopes"

DEDICATION

I won't think about what isn't, what can't, or what hasn't. I am concentrating on what will. I am a woman who continues to learn from this enormous lesson called life. I have surrendered to the One beyond all, the One where words have no description, whose abilities are unknown to the thought process, and the ultimate love of my being . . . God! God the creator of the universe has made some incredible wonders in my life: child birth, motherhood, marriage, self-discovery, friendships, and last but not least . . . LOVE. God knew my life story before I was even thought of. As incredible as that is, it is equally incredible to have a front row seat to how this gift of life is unfolding. Unstoppable growth, never-ending knowledge, understanding, and an undeniable scenery in every circumstance are the blessings I am witnessing. It has taken up till this moment for me to even have an inkling about LOVE. God loves me so much, He continues to open my eyes which has a domino effect to my heart and mind. Regardless of who I see in the mirror, God sees more. To give myself away means to give up control and let God have His way. Despite what life brings, I will always have power over it. The individuals and events that takes place are magnificent teachers. I thank God for loving me so! My life is dedicated to my Creator.

PREFACE

Going through life without understanding is a difficult task. We feel we are all alone, no one can relate, or we are helpless. Countless times I wanted to give up, but held on to that drop of hope I felt deep within. Despite the situation or how I felt, I continued on my journey. I made some very bad choices, yet they lead me to all the right places in order to find the healing necessary to move forward.

Without knowing it, God had me all along. To look back, I am able to see the miraculous triumphs that were overcome only by His grace and mercy. Never would have made it rings loud in my ear when I look back and realize what I did not have to be brought through.

God had a plan for my life and I know He has a plan for you too. I am called to share my journey with you in hopes that you are able to identify with the blessings in your life. Different situations, but same outcome . . . Testify about the goodness of God through Jesus Christ who left us with the Holy Spirit to help and guide us along.

TABLE OF CONTENTS

ACKNOWLEDGMENTS

Giving God all of the glory, it is my mission to inspire, minister, and connect to individuals through the testimony of my personal journey. Through the understanding I have gained, I am now able to share and continue to pray many will embrace for themselves what I have learned. I have found that individuals are able to gain strength and receive guidance through another's story. If I am able to impact one life, I have done my service.

Acknowledgement is an extremely vital component to growth. These stories and those to come would not be possible without the trials and tribulations of life, without those who have been a part of my life from afar, or without my close family and friends.

I acknowledge God as being the creator of my testimony. I thank Him for using me to minister to others through my story.

EARLY CONFUSION
Chapter One

SCRIPTURE

Psalms 119:169

*Let my cry come before you, O Lord; give me
understanding according to your word!*

Laying down in the bed as I did every early morning after my mother dropped me off at the baby-sitter's house, I began to fall back asleep. I faintly heard a creek in the floor but gave it no attention as I was drifting off. I felt the covers slowly being removed from my little, seven-year-old body, a rough touch, and a voice that said, "Shhh." I immediately froze because of the inappropriate circumstances. I felt my pants unfastening and beginning to drag down my legs as the cold of the air grazed my skin. In no time at all there was a grown, heavy man on top of me trying to jam himself into my innocence. I continued to lay there like a rock with so much wonder in my mind. It was finally over. He lifted himself up and covered me back up as if he were putting a baby down for a nap. Deeply confused, I pulled my pants up and closed my eyes.

I was awakened by my baby-sitter to get ready for school. As I rose up I realized I did not have a dream. Immediately I felt the pain coming from in between my legs. I quietly got up and went to the restroom to prepare for breakfast. Like nothing happened, I ate and left out of the house to catch the school bus. I went through the first part of the morning just fine, but by the afternoon I could barely contain myself. There were so many things going through my mind like a jigsaw puzzle; I did not understand. Making it through the school day was one thing, but I knew I could not make it any further. I would be seeing this man again once he came in from work. I began to fear the next meeting. I had a best friend at that time and I confided in her the happenings of that morning once we returned home from school. She looked at me with such concern and ran across the playground to inform my baby-sitter who was standing outside waiting on me.

Walking over to her had to be the longest stretch ever. She asked me one time with a very stern voice if it was true what my friend just told her. She told me to tell her, and I did. Unknowingly to me, he was around the backside of our apartments. Holding my hand tightly, she confronted him. He looked at me, then at her, and said nothing. She knew by the look on his face I was telling the truth. I am sure she was in total shock, but bared the pain in greater protection for me. I felt a sense of relief as if it were all over not understanding the effects that were to come. This was the beginning of life for me.

He was charged and the proceedings began. Probed by doctors and questioned by lawyers made me realize this was a lot worse than I thought. I could feel myself withdrawing a bit because I was the center of attention in an unfamiliar way. Sitting at a long, dark wood table while men and women in suits writing on pads every word I would say was very intimidating. Repeating this story over and over again as if they did not hear it correctly the first time. Even with my mother beside me I was so frightened. I remember wanting to cry. It was as if they did not believe me. By the time the big day in court came, I was too afraid to take the stand. I knew I would have to tell the story again in front of him. I did not like talking about it anymore and wanted it all to be over. My lawyer handled it without my testimony and that bad man was sent away.

Although I was very young, I could sense a change that was occurring. I could not explain it then, but I changed inside. There was a part of me that was no more. I knew I was different from other little girls. I did not speak about that incident, yet was very curious. I did, however, want it explained to me. I went through the motions of everything, but did not understand what had happened to me and why. What did I do? Did I make him do that to me? I thought he was a nice man. He played with all the kids, bought us candy, and let us ride on the back of his pick-up truck. I did not display on the outside the pain, discomfort, or confusion I was exploding with on the inside. Why is no one talking to me?

Instead of some counseling, special attention, or an explanation of what just transpired . . . we moved.

Because this was never discussed with me, I grew up putting things together from what I learned in the world. I was not sure what was correct and what wasn't. I just knew there was something not right about sex. From what I understood, only adults had sex. I was aware that there were "bad people" out there who did things they were not supposed to do to other people. What I did not understand was why. It was still a question deep inside of me wanting to know if it was my fault.

I steered away from boys for quite a while. I saw the way they would grab girls or touch on their bodies. It always made me feel a certain way when I saw that. I was unsure what it meant. It looked like they were being playful with the girls; but why was he playing with me like that? I did not understand what was okay and what wasn't so I avoided it altogether.

If you were to glance at me, you would have caught me in a wondrous stare. I often sat by myself very still and quiet in deep thought. No one spoke to me about it, so eventually I put it in the back of my mind. From time to time I would think about that incident over and over. Unable to figure it out, I would let it go again. This became the routine in dealing with that act.

It was difficult to have something rumbling inside me, and unable to settle it. For years there was an uproar within me. I did not know how to deal with it. Who would I tell? I did not trust anyone enough to talk to about it because no one cared enough to talk to me. I became angry and hurt at the same time. Being silent became my playing card.

Being withdrawn became a very lonely place. I had friends and participated in school activities, but was not close to anyone. I did not trust anybody. I always felt that in one way or another they would hurt me. If I did not get close, the opportunity was not there. The only closeness I knew that was safe was God; whom I learned about in church. So, I was saved in my adolescence.

As I grew older, my surroundings dictated what should and should not be for me. There was a voice inside telling me what was proper, but I wanted this pain to subside. The very thing that stole my innocence, lured me back. Having a desire to belong in a loving way, I fell for the boy's desire for me. Still feeling the effects of my love being taken, I somehow conjured up in my mind that someone wanting me could give it back. The unquenched, wanderings of my mind needed to be settled. It became confusing in another way altogether. How could I desire something that hurt me so? Could this be different because he asks me nicely and makes me feel comfortable first?

It was not about everybody else "doing it"; I could care less. I was already different from everybody.

Somehow, what scared me had me curious. When I gave in to it, it felt good . . . kind of. This was different because I went along with it. If I could just allow someone to get close to me, it will reverse these feelings I was having. I talked myself into what I know was against everything I knew. But again, who would I talk to about what happened. No one cared to talk to me, so I now do not care to talk to anybody. I just want to feel better. I knew God was there, but I was confused; He did not help me either (so I thought).

I went through years of trying to feel better. Nothing could remove the emptiness I had been carrying with me while lying next to the chosen "he." I grew restless in giving what I knew was precious away to those who knew not its worth. I realized what I had rumbling in me was not anger or hurt. I allowed myself to feel angry and hurt, understandably, because of what happened. I not only wanted more for myself, I also wanted more for the "he" I would ultimately be with.

A lifelong partnership is always what I was in search of. Each individual I gave myself to was in hopes that he could be the one to save me from the pains in my heart. I needed someone who would rescue me from all I had endured. But, it was not working out that way. No matter how wonderful he would be, he could never fill the void I had inside. There would always be something he could not settle for me. I was still yearning and I was unsure why.

Whenever I was alone, I would get closer and closer to something I was unsure of. It felt comforting. It was not frightening. I could be myself. This was unfamiliar territory. It was as if the goodness was too good to be true. I was alone and

I could not bear that. I felt I needed somebody there physically. When I brought the physical into the picture, it would damage what I was experiencing on my own. I began to desire the unknown feeling more so than the feeling I thought made me feel better. I found something that penetrates deeper than any man ever could.

When all was removed, I was there with my maker. I began to hear the sweet sound of His gentle voice. It was actually there the entire time. I kept bringing outside noise into our space. I could not do anything but answer when He called.

I attached myself to individuals I thought could do something for me. When in all actuality, I could not do for me. Until I allowed God to restore what had been stolen, hurt, misused, and disgraced, I was not any good to anyone. I was also very selfish. I wanted so much because of what was taken from me, I was not willing to give of myself fully. I came to a place where I was fulfilled and now had much to give. My cup is overflowing and I desire greatly to share.

When I gave myself time instead of a man, the confusion subsided. Through the darkness began piercing light shows. Conclusive answers appeared one by one and then two by two. All that I questioned throughout the years was standing in front of me. I was holding on to something that God had control over the entire time. I just would not let it go. And when I chose to latch on to someone, it was a man. As soon as I let that crutch go…. God swept me up into His wings! His arms were always open; I was running in the wrong direction.

It is a tragic situation when a child (or anyone) is sexually abused. It is not about the act itself but how I react now. God has provided me with the knowledge and the wisdom to overcome this seemingly damaging time. I have come to understand that it is not the situations that hinder us, it is our reaction to the unfortunate situation. I believe God takes every negative situation and enables us to use it to benefit others in many ways, shapes, and forms.

I understand the trials that result from sexual abuse, much more than I could describe to you in words. It leaves us feeling violated, destroyed, and unwanted among other things. No person is able to "fix" the pain. They can comfort you to the best of their ability, but that hurt remains until it is given to God. I looked to other people to soothe my pain and it brought more. It is difficult to face, but you do not have to face it alone.

He is the only ONE that can wipe the slate clean after we have reacted in ungodly ways to cover our flesh wounds. I now treasure myself like the precious jewel I am. A man has to ask God to take me out, otherwise aren't no happenings!

Because of interacting with many men, this has given me a sense of self. Like bumping your head, you know what you do not want to do. I am not who that first "he" made me to be. There is no question that I am still beautifully and wonderfully made. That man did not take anything from me. "He" gave me a story to share…and I came out VICTORIOUS!

INTRODUCED TO ABUSE
Chapter Two

SCRIPTURE

James 4:1-4

What causes fights and quarrels among you? Don't they come from your desires that battle within you? You desire but you do not have, so you kill
You covet but you cannot get what you want, so you quarrel and fight. You do not have because you do not ask God. When you ask, you do not receive, because you ask With wrong motives, that you may spend what you get on your pleasures. You adulterous people, don't you know that friendship with the world means enmity against God? Therefore, anyone who chooses to be a friend of the world becomes an enemy of God.

As I came in the house from playing outside I heard shouting. It was echoing down the hallway of our apartment from out of my mother's room. Through the opening of the door I could see her on the floor. I could not put a conscious thought to what I saw because I knew nothing of it. I was unsure what was going on. I could hear the silent moans from her wilted body as the door slammed shut. I stood in amazement and went into my room and listened. I was informally introduced to another kind of abuse.

From that time on I was afraid of that man. He was my mother's new boyfriend and was over quite often, so there was no avoiding him. He seemed very nice at times, but then a monster would form in a split second for basically nothing at all. I had never seen or heard someone talking or acting like he did. I would often ask myself why she was latched to him because he was so mean to her and her children. My question was answered after a period of time. He would be around for quite a while being my mother was having a child by him.

It seemed after the birth of my sister he became even more violent. Cursing and speaking very loud right in my face would bring tears to my eyes every time. It is extremely frightening to have a grown man with a deep voice using profanity right over top of your little body. "Why doesn't my mother save me", I would wonder to myself, "doesn't she love me anymore?" It was as if he was turning her into him. What used to be a loving atmosphere became a minefield. I never knew when I would get blamed for something, screamed at, or hit.

This went on until my mid-teen years. Although I was used to it, my feelings were trampled on regularly. Once he left the household, he had done enough damage to my mother that she carried on his torch. When I went to school with shades on, my mindset was totally twisted. I had been to school with bruises and welts up and down my legs and arms that he left on my body. Feeling embarrassed to dress out for gym was part of my regimen. The difference with this time was the bloodshot, swollen, bruised eye that was from my mother. The school nurse notified her of the difficulties I was experiencing at school with the lights, stares, and questioning. The response the nurse gave me that my mother told her was, "I would be just fine."

Later that evening when I saw my mother she looked furious. All I wanted was for her to love me again. She made a comment that rang through my heart as she looked at my eye." You should not have made me mad." I received this bruised eye from a back-handed fist after leaving a relative's house because she did not like the fact that I asked if they had heard from my mother before she had gotten there to pick me and my sister up. I never thought that asking that question would make my mother hate me enough to hurt me like that. From that day on I looked at her differently.

A few years later, I received a birthday gift from a girl across the hall. It was a curling iron set. My mother did not like me putting heat in my hair, but I just knew she would let me keep a gift. I immediately began working on my hair. Once I finished, my mother told me to return it to my friend across the hall. I could not believe she was making me give it back. Upset, I packaged it up, and was walking toward the door to return it and my mother shoved me in my back as if I were not walking fast enough. I was furious. She told me to give it back and I was doing so. Immediately, I turned around and bucked at my mother. It took all I had in me not to hit her. I had been so fed up with being beat, hit, smacked, yelled and cursed at. I could not understand why she pushed me while I was on my way to return the gift. I saw the look in my mother's eyes... as if I were going to hit her. As angry as I was, I could not put my hands on my mother. At that moment I realized how angry, hurt, and tired I was from the abuse that had been seen and dealt with from the previous years. I developed a hatred attitude toward individuals who had a mean streak in them. I also knew it was nothing I could do.

I believe from that incident on, there was another change within our relationship. Although these are the years for a teen to find their individuality, I felt trapped. I wanted to let loose, but there was such a fear in me. I had so much talent and desire in me to be involved in so many activities, yet felt so separated from everyone. Even when I was around what I liked, I still felt withdrawn.

One afternoon I was in my house with a friend of mine. We were in my living room talking about 'whatever' when I kind of spaced out. I went into the bathroom and got a straight razor and returned to where she was. My girlfriend was looking at me with a puzzled face. Instantly, I began cutting my arm. Stroke by stroke the blood began rushing out from the keen gnashes I drew so effortlessly. She simultaneously yelled, "What are you doing!" She got some tissue and began placing it on my arm as she removed the blade from my grip. I looked at her and said, "I don't know."

Later that night my mother saw my arm and asked me if I was trying to kill myself? Not at all, I said quietly. She shook her head and left me alone. I am sure I looked a bit crazy to my girlfriend and now my mother. I felt so much pain and did not know how to release it. Instead of hurting someone else, I figured I would inflict it on myself. All I knew is with each cut, I felt a release. I soon did the other arm.

Cutting did not become a regular thing. I did it all of three times. I began to realize it was scarring up my body and I was way too beautiful to put marks on myself after someone else doing it for years. I found another outlet; boys. I had steered away from boys for years but made a U-turn. I needed to feel something other than the hurt and pain I was feeling. I was not able to talk to my mother or anyone else. I did not want anyone to know the horror I had endured; besides, what could they do about it anyway?

I would live in the moment as much as possible with a wall around me. You would only know what was going on right now. I did not talk about my family or my feelings. I only spoke on what was happening at the time. Until I felt very comfortable with you, I would not tell you anything I was harboring inside. All I was concerned with was feeling good right now so I would not have to marinate in the happenings of the past.

Staying busy became my focus. Singing, working, and boys kept me happy at the moment. Anything involving singing I tried to be a part of. This was something I loved since very young. Listening to music, singing in the school choir, or singing around the house became a release for me. I could sing my way to happiness until I began to feel the words of a song. Working was my other option. I only had a half of day at school and was able to work the rest of the day. This worked for a while until my hours slowed down. I had time to recall the past and began feeling again. I realized I had much free time to spend with the boys who could redirect my focus. Instead of the job being about financial independence, it became about sexually independence.

I had sex with enough people to realize I did not like it. It no longer made me feel better. It began to be a detour from my feelings. I could not bear that traveled road, so I continued on this path to avoid the pains of previous covered grounds.

I had failed several classes twice, gotten into fights, and encountered sexual relations almost a whole year before my mother sent me to live with my father. It was right before my sixteenth birthday that I was being flown away from the hell I knew at the time. My dad and I had a good relationship through the mail and over the phone. Because of the way he spoke to me and embraced me through his words, he had always been everything to me. The way he nurtured me on paper gave me hope that there was better out in the world. To go live with him and his family was not a problem to me. "I have finally been saved", I said to myself.

It was amazing initially. To be around people that were calm and embracing was comforting. We talked, laughed, and enjoyed each other's company. I had a sister I barely knew but enjoyed because we had the same father and he was not mean. My little brother was cute and smiled a lot, and again we had the same father. We had different mothers, but because she was not mine was all that mattered. She seemed very nice and listened to what I had to say. That was something I was not used to. I became happy with my new family. Going to summer school was also a breeze; I passed with A's.

After a month or so of being there I had been in a fight. It actually was not my fault. A girl thought I was looking at her man while my sister and I was at the movies. While on the pay phone after the movie calling my dad to pick us up, she approached me. I calmly hung up with dad, took off my earrings, and whooped that tail! With not a scratch on me, I put my earrings back on and waited for my dad to arrive. My sister and I got in the car as if nothing happened. The next day the girl was at my house apologizing as her mother demanded she should. Her face was battered allowing my father to realize what happened. He sighed and proceeded to talk with me. I knew I had a rage in me and did not want anyone to catch that wave. I found a new sense of courage and strength within.

I became very bold and out spoken. I liked being treated like a young adult. I met a young man who was quite the gentleman. My dad took an initial liking to him and allowed him to take me out. But then he started being very protective and leery of my "fast" ways around my younger sister. He stopped allowing me to go out with him. Feeling betrayed, I snuck out of the window and saw him anyway. Previously to that, I had written my mother a letter complaining about the way my father was handling things around the house. The next day after I climbed through the window, my dad flew me back to my mother in time for the beginning of the school year. I felt unwanted by the only man I looked up to. Needless to say, I was hurting again.

I remained filled with all of the hurts and pains of yesteryear until I did not feel any more. I became very numb and calloused to anything negative coming my way. Inside was a waterfall of emotions ready to burst out of the openings of the windows to my soul. It was too much to relinquish. I dreaded the outpour of feelings that had been held by a dam named Kristine.

Going through years of not feeling began to be unfulfilling. I tried to shut off any and everybody who tried to get close to me. I wanted the closeness, but feared the hurt that could stem from trusting someone. I am sure I hurt many people by pushing them away. When I began to care is when the pain begun. At times this was very lonely. It started to take a lot of energy to be upset. I was exhausted from harboring what was dying to get out.

I had spoken to my stepfather periodically throughout the years, but had never forgiven him for all the pain he caused. Years later, I was in town visiting and was invited over his house. While there, a discussion came up of some sort and I made a "smart" remark. He caught it and asked me to come and speak with him privately. A swarm of emotions came over me, yet I was contained. He asked me what that comment was about? I proceeded to inform him of exactly how he negatively influenced my life and how it continued to affect me. He looked at me and said, "I AM SORRY." He then told me he wondered about all of that and felt very remorseful. I never even thought he could have been hurting as well. Everything I felt towards him dissipated.

I soon understood that phrase "hurt people, hurt people." As soon as I took my eyes off of the abuse and looked at who was doing it, I saw someone rather than something. I also began to understand that my mother endured much as well. The pain he inflicted on her was then directed towards me. I came to his house feeling very defensive, but left feeling offended by my hardened heart. It is understandable why I carried these feelings for many years, but did not warrant the hurt I was bringing into other people's lives. With that weight full of hurt removed from my load, I could lift my head up a little higher than before and was able to see some light on my dark path. That dam named Kristine was cracking.

That dam cracked so much it was unable to withstand the pressures of nature. As soon as I felt for another, I began to feel my pain. I could relate to another even if they were the one who did the damage. I could understand because of the damage I caused myself, let alone anyone else. The "whys" did not matter anymore. All that mattered was the emotions shared between hurt people. The specifics no longer existed. It was all common ground.

As my wall came down I was able to allow feelings in. By going through those times, I know exactly what that energy feels like when it is present. I do not need to build anything around me. Ultimately, God protects me. Trying to keep out the hurt had me keeping everything and everyone out. It is not so much how we go through, but who goes through with us. When I changed the view I was looking from, I was able to see a lot more. God began showing me that although hurt and pain comes in many forms, it stems from pain in one way or another. When I recognized the lesson, I understood the school, the students, and the props that were used.

I was also able to see how God was there for me. With each incident that happened, I became stronger and stronger. At the time I was looking at that strength as a defense, when in all actuality it was God lifting me up as I was weakening. I knew I could handle a lot because of what I had already endured. I held on to that and continued to carry it with me. It did not matter about the angle I was looking from at that time because God already knew my view was going to change!

It is obviously not God's will for anyone to be abused in any kind of way. It is for us to acknowledge He is with us at those times of despair. The fact that I lived through those rough and tough times and did not give up on my life is proof enough that He lives within me. Feeling as I did, there is NO way I got through on my strength.

God used everyone involved for me to later see. God offered me that hope through my dad. He was there when I needed him. As soon as I began "acting out", I was removed. I can understand the negative influence I had on my siblings at that time. What I was doing was improper and not of God at all. I was complaining, sexually immoral, and dishonoring my dad and his household. I brought strife to myself and was not permitted to bring it on them. My dad remains to be that hope. Despite all that has transpired throughout the years, he has always been there when I NEEDED him. I realize God has allowed this to happen. This lets me know, just as God's Word says, He will provide all my needs.

A strong desire remains in my heart. With all that has transpired, I continue to know there is so much more. I will strive to get closer to God to cling to the strength He provides. I know that no matter what may come, it will not be for too long. God has seen me through before and will see me through again and again. I hold on to all that has been learned and look forward to what is to come. For in the times of struggle is when

I am able to lift my head high and know not how difficult the problem is, but how incredible my God is!

DISCOVERING TALENT
Chapter Three

SCRIPTIRE

Philippians 2:13
...for it is God who works in you to will and act in order to fulfill his good purpose.

I have been singing since I can remember. I would have my mother's records all over the floor going through album after album. I even would sift through the 8-track tapes. When I sang there was a freeness felt. No one else existed when I sang. It did not matter what they thought, were saying, or doing. When a song came on the radio, I had to sing it. I sang in the choir all through school. Every type of performance I was trying to be a part of. If someone told me to sing, I would sing with no problem. It made me happy and took me to an unknown place. There were no inhibitions, fears, or sadness...just pure joy. I remember my first duet performance with my brother's best friend. We received a standing ovation after having to sing acapella when the instrumental tape cut off on the boom box we were using. It was epic. That was the way we had been practicing!

Realizing I was able to draw came at an early age as well. I remember in the third grade I had drew some pictures and this boy said he wanted to buy one of my pictures. I thought to myself these must be pretty good. At that time, I could look at anything and draw it. I had not gotten into portraits yet, but knew it was possible. All through school I did well in art class and was even asked to join the special art classes. I did not think much of it, but was very enthused to be in a class where there were others who were talented like myself.

English was my best subject in school because of my love for writing. I was so intrigued with the ability to use words to express anything. The more I learned, the more creative I became. Writing letters to my father was extremely helpful as well. Although he would write things sometimes I did not understand, it increased my vocabulary. I might not have spoken a lot, but I sure would have written you a long, impressive letter. I used to enjoy writing stories, essays, or even the definitions of words in class. When I learned about poetry, I fell deeper in love. The way the words could dance around on the page, yet never leave the lines was so beautiful to me.

Each of these talents were lovely and I enjoyed very much, but it did not seem like anyone else cared as much as I did. Whenever I received a special award or a good grade for what I did, I did not get the reception I had hoped for. I wanted encouragement, guidance, or assistance like others that were talented received. Watching what was happening in other people's lives began to get me down because my household was such a mess. There was too much going on for anyone to care that much about what I was wanting to do or how good I was at any of these things.

If I could have had special training or was involved in more activities maybe I could really do something with these gifts. My school counselor asked me about entering a teen pageant. I told her "what for, nobody cared any way." She was stressing how this was a wonderful opportunity for me and that I was very talented. I realized all that but still felt it was pointless. Although I was gifted in many ways, I was losing interest in the very things that brought me so much joy. As I got older I discovered more talents I possessed. I was a hairstylist and began to recognize a gift of teaching. I had an encouraging way of explaining things to people. This was noticed by my school counselor as well. She asked me to speak with the underclassmen about teenage pregnancy. This briefly uplifted my spirits and put a fire under me. With my mind so focused on what was not right in my life, I allowed myself to be side-tracked by a young man and lost sight of everything.

Because of my ignorance, I had to notify my counselor that I would no longer be a good candidate to lecture anyone about teen pregnancy being I was now a part of those statistics. "What a waste", I thought to myself, yet at the same time, maybe this is my new talent . . . being a mom. It was my senior year and I would be giving birth to my first child.

Before becoming pregnant I was on a youth bowling league. I was pretty good at this as well. I continued to bowl throughout my pregnancy. In the later part of my pregnancy I competed in a scholarship bowling tournament. Another opportunity, is what I was thinking when I signed up for it. Even though I am pregnant there is still promise for me. I kept believing my talents would get me somewhere.

Toward the end of my pregnancy I left my mother's house and went to stay with my boyfriend at the time. Another incident transpired with her and me. I was not dealing with the fighting anymore. While at his house I was notified about the scholarship tournament results. I came in second place. I was extremely excited and then reality sunk in. First of all, I was not at home which meant I was no longer in school. Second, I just had a son and was unable to do anything at the moment. I kept hope in my heart and figured it was possible somehow. I had to give an answer immediately so I said, "I am unable to accept it at this time. You can present it to someone else. I hope they appreciate it as I would have." I was crushed. It seemed like every good opportunity was passing me by with a lot of gusting winds from my decisions. Again I thought . . . what a waste. If I did not already have enough emotional anguish, I just added more. I was a high school dropout with a baby living with my broke high school dropout boyfriend at his father's house. How talented were those choices?

I began to regret everything and hope at the same time. Because I had so much in me I knew something was still possible. I tried to come up with ways to better my situation and all I drew was a blank. I could not get myself back into school. I was unable to find a job. I did not know anyone where I was now living. And to top it off, he became a nightmare. What a talent I had in choosing a boyfriend.

Over the years, my talents remained, but were not utilized to my liking. My talent became taking care of the kids, husband, and the house. I tried being creative with my children as they continued to come and grow. I would draw symbols for them to learn their alphabet and numbers. Turning the music on and singing to them was very fun. I tried to stick my hair skills in to keep their hair healthy and neat being they were all boys. In several places we lived I had accumulated several hair clients. I tried to keep busy and stay stimulated at the same time. I grew further and further away from who I knew I was, wanted to be, or could be.

It appeared I was not going to be able to accomplish anything I wanted until someone my husband knew told him about a salon position. I was offered an assistant to the manager position . . . shampoo girl. I was elated. At least I was able to be out of the house and around something that I loved to do. As with my younger days, this job became an escape. It was horror at home and this took me away from it briefly. It seemed my "get away" had to be cut short after a year. I was talented at having children . . . I had another son.

When my youngest son was about two, I enrolled into a hair academy. I had connected with my mom again and was able to work out a travel schedule. I had someone to watch the kids and I had a way to get to and from school. After being cooped up for so long, I did not know how to act getting back into one of my talents. As excited as I was, it would be short lived as everything else was. Because of personal problems with my husband, I had to withdraw from school. I was weeks away from graduating. I attempted to use those hours accumulated throughout the years and was unsuccessful. Once again I was unable to accomplish a goal. After this incompletion, I gave up on everything.

My choices had lead me away from where my talent was once taking me. I had allowed my emotions to override what was good for me. I had become so good at masking my feelings, I was unable to see where I was headed. With each choice I made, the realer the effect played out. Although some things were out of my control, it was a result of where I chose to be. Making good choices was not a talent.

My marriage was over, the children had to be with him because I could not provide for them, no career, no job, and nowhere to go. Depending on my talents became obsolete. Nothing was working out for me no matter how bad I was wanting it. I tried everything; so I thought . . .

What I was not trying was God. I was trying to accomplish these things myself with the talent God gave me when in fact, He gives according to His will not mine. I was thinking of myself when it came to my talents. I thanked God very much for them, but wanted to use them to serve my own purposes. When I acknowledged and understood that it was not about me but about God, I was then able to tap into what God had for me.

Instead of chasing something to make myself look good, I needed to chase something to make God look good. Glorify the Lord with what He gave me. It is not always with what the obvious talents are either. There are talents hidden inside me that I did not realize were there. This is how I am positive. I am able to glorify God because it is something I had no clue about. God puts something on my heart that I feel compelled to do, and I do it well. That definitely is not me, it is the Lord!

I understand that God wants the talents to be used for His good and not mine. His good meaning my talents are to praise His name and what He makes possible. Lift my voice and sing praises in church to those in the pews so they can hear and feel the joy coming from the sweet melody God put inside me. Draw in hopes to allow someone to see the beauty in something I was able to relay creatively using the many shapes, sizes, colors, and dimensions God has designed in this world. Use the ability God gave me to take someone's hair and change the dynamics of how they view themselves because of the new outward appearance that enhances the inner beauty that has BEEN radiant but overshadowed by low self-esteem. I am now able to pour my heart and soul out to everyone through the swift arrangement of fragments distributed strategically to amplify the very beating of my pulse as I encourage this language of universal love.

Utilizing my talents now goes much further than myself. I was always out to assist another person, but to make myself look good. Using what I am able to do well with purpose is much more fulfilling. I am moved out of the way, someone else received a wonderful gift, and God was glorified the entire time. It totally makes sense to do something for a purpose, with purpose. I have more desire behind my actions. My heart is filled with joy in knowing God is well pleased with me.

The Holy Spirit is amazing. The Holy Spirit will convict you very quickly when you are out of order with your intentions. Immediately I will feel a sense of guilt, ask for forgiveness, and change my approach. It is understandable to want to want to be used in a mighty way, accomplish magnificent things, and become successful at your heart's desire. The thing I acknowledged and realized first is that it is not of my doing. Because I surrendered myself to God, He provides everything I need in order to fulfill His will, directs my path, guides me along the way, strengthens me when I am weakened, sends the right people into my life, opens every door for me, removes what does not belong in my life, and answers any question I may have. I do not have to try to do anything.

God has placed everything inside of me that I will ever need. He also already has my life planned out. I just need to recognize, acknowledge, and allow God to work through the talents that I have been given. It is for me to draw closer to Him to hear the sweet whispers of His wisdom that leads me down the path of truth. I now discover talent every day!

When I make an unwise decision that leads me down a dark path, God is with me. While on that path I am being shaped and strengthened for what God ultimately has for me. He allowed me to go through the anguish of my choices. If God had turned every situation around for my benefit, I would have never learned that my talents were not for me. He disciplined me using what I chose to do. It all works for the good in the end. Ultimately, God has the last say. What I want may not be what

He has for me. It is not for me to understand His ways, but to surrender to them and relinquish the control I thought I had. I searched for what I could do with my talent, rather than asking God what was His desire for the talent He gave me.

It is such a relief to know that it is not for me to find the things in and of this world to fit into my life. It is refreshing to know that God puts the desires in my heart that compel me to strive for His approval. I had it so wrong in the beginning. I learned from so many that you have to work hard for what you want, get out there and get it, or fight to hold on to something. In all actuality, what is for me is for me. I do have to put forth effort knowing that God sustains me, not my efforts. I did not do or receive anything because of what I did. God blessed me with every moment, gift, and event. With the wisdom God grants and the truths learned through unwise choices I am able to discern what is proper and what is not. When something does not work out it is alright. It was not for me and God has something even better in store waiting for me. It is not about a wrong turn. God will lead me into a U-turn. My life is laid out and each moment is waiting on my arrival!

SEARCHING FOR LOVE
Chapter Four

Because of the previous abuse in my life, I had a warped sense of love. I was unsure what it actually was or what it meant. Those that I knew did horrible things to me. Everyone who inflicted sexual and physical pain on me, I knew. I was supposed to feel safe and special; instead I felt ambushed and worthless. As much as I wanted to "fit in", I did not feel comfortable anywhere for long periods of time. I would be alright for the moment, but then I needed something more.

I began my search of affection through a variety of people. Classmates, church members, family, and sometimes even strangers. At times, just a meaningful conversation was enough just so I could be heard without being judged or criticized. Sometimes it was as if I was not allowed to have an opinion or have an emotional reaction. So, for the most part I kept quiet.

When I became interested in boys, it was solely for the wrong reasons. I liked the attention no matter how negative it was. I was tough enough to take the bad with the good . . . so I thought. It was easy to be around someone and deal with the shenanigans as long as I did not involve my emotions. But as soon as my heart opened up, I was weakened. What was this feeling?

I cared for many people, but would not go that extra mile for all. The first extra mile I went was for my first real boyfriend, who ended up being my husband. I went out of my way to be with him, around him, near him, and yes sometimes on him. I put up with things I definitely should not have, but I felt I needed him. He became a part of my life in a needy kind of way. I needed him because I lacked fulfillment. Until I realized the kind of attention he was giving me was not warranted any more, that seven-year quest ended. That hole that once was filled was empty. I had to patch it up.

Continuing on my search I came across some "time beings." I knew it was not where I was supposed to be, but it suited me at the time. They took care of me enough to where I could tolerate the imperfections of the relationship. I desired something substantial, but it was not working out that way. Because of my previous quests, I became a bit calloused. Wanting the love, but not quite willing to give it. I would take what I could get.

It was when I was not looking did I run into a different pursuit. A gentleman came along that had I actually rejected. I was very honest with him about everything, yet he continued to pursue me. I enjoyed this kind of attention very much, especially because of the openness we shared. I had never been so honest with anyone. Although I was very much intrigued, I still was a bit stand-offish. My heart was opening at the same time I was trying to keep it closed. I began wanting to go that extra mile, yet would only move an inch. I was in a huge battle with a force much stronger than I wanted to admit.

I had wanted something for so long and when it appeared to be, I was pushing it away. No matter how immovable I tried to be, he lifted every part of me. He did all the right things, said all the right things, and acted the right way. I still would not accept what he was offering me. I was amazed with his persistence. I was not purposely sabotaging this relationship, I feared it. It left me feeling a desire I was not familiar with.

This man influenced me to do things I had never done before. It was like he was purposely breaking the hard coating I had carefully built around me. He looked at me at times like he was looking right through me. I liked what was happening, but would rebuild that shell he was breaking down.

After a while, I did not feel like I was enough for him because of what I lacked. I wanted so much so bad, but did not know how to get it. He was offering me so much, but what did I have to give him? I began looking at what wasn't.

I could see the mental anguish I was causing him. Trying to fill something inside me was failing miserably. I had a wonderful man in my mist, yet still lacked so much. I soon realized it was not about the relationship with him and me. It was all about me. I wanted him to provide everything I had lacked for years. Me being me, wanted to see if he could. I required much attention and activity. He was pretty good at supplying all I requested. We became inseparable. I wanted to be where he was. I was allowing myself to feel all that he wanted to give.

He was my whole life. I was in a state where I had no family or long-term friends. The people I did meet were more of associates. I knew his immediate friends and they were very fun to be around. We hung out and enjoyed each other's company quite often. With all of the interacting we would do I thought I would become submerged in a sense of belonging, but that was not the case. I needed more.

He even went as far to relocate me to the beach area; right on the water. I wanted a change and he gave it. He tried providing me with a beautiful, soothing atmosphere where I was able to collect my thoughts and find some peace. Because I loved the water this was ideal. A perfect view, extraordinary scenery day in and out, and a caring man should quench my desires. I was falling into a heavenly place until I began to think again. Whenever I was left alone, I began pondering on what was lacking . . . again. His attempts seemed to never be enough.

It became regular that I was left alone. Because of this time, I was able to feel more than I did when he was around. I was unsure if this was a good thing or a bad thing. I wanted to feel what I wanted to feel. I did not like for memories of yesteryear to trickle themselves into the present spaces of my thoughts.

I needed to keep busy so I began to watch Joel Osteen and Joyce Meyers on television. It was interesting because every time I would watch them, they spoke on something that was relevant to my life. This became routine for me and soon it encouraged me to read my Bible. The more I yearned for attention and affection, the more I read my Bible. I wanted him around, but began feeling a bit satisfied. Yet, as soon as he returned, I missed that kind of affection and attention and collapsed into him again.

This cycle went on for several months. Again, I needed something more . . . lack had resurfaced. Why was this feeling thing so hard to maintain? We enjoyed each other and communicated well. But something was still missing. I allowed this emptiness to draw a wedge in between us and began withdrawing. It was time to build that structure around me again. Once I did that, he stayed away longer and longer. Without thinking about it, sex between us diminished.

Here came the feelings creeping up from behind me. I became very angry and argumentative. I did not quite understand it.

All I knew were overwhelming sets of emotions were trying to display themselves and I was not having it. All I wanted was to feel loved, and that was it. All of that other stuff was extra and I wanted no parts of it.

I began to realize whenever I would read my Bible and watch Joel and Joyce, a calmness would come over me. Interesting enough, I did not yearn for his affection. This began to confuse me. I thought that is what I wanted. I used to want him day and night. What was happening to the "love" we shared?

I fell into my Bible all day every day. The more I read the Word, the more I began to feel. The emotions came rushing me at once and could no longer contain myself. I exploded with anger from years ago. I projected that eruption onto everyone I encountered. I never felt so lost in my life. Regardless of the unknown territory, I was willing to go in deeper and did not know why. I wanted that pull we had toward each other, but something else had a magnetic force I could not deny.

For months I had been threatening for him or me to leave. That day came when I was forced to see what was holding me. When the "love" we shared ceased, it took everything else we had along with it. What we shared was not strong enough to hold the passion within our bodies. There was so much dysfunction in our functioning that what was built was not solid enough. The passion rang true, but the purpose did not ring as loud.

How could I love anyone else when I did not know how to love myself? As long as we were intertwined, I felt a part of something. Whenever I was left alone, I would fall apart. I needed to be willing to accept the love given before I was able to receive it. When I began reading and listening to God's Word is when I found what I was searching for. I was reaching for love, when I actually needed to be touched in a way no man could ever reach. Until I was able to acknowledge and accept that; I was not able to receive it.

I now know that I am already loved and do not need to look to anyone to fill a void. I have no voids. I am a complete package as I am. God made me to be full from the start. The only need from another is to complete the task that God has for us to do. The search is over! I have found what I have been in route for through many years. I am grateful for the lessons that have been learned, the strength that has been gained, and the wisdom I now possess.

It is a blessing to not be afraid of feeling. Having to feel meant a reaction was anticipated very soon after that was uncertain because of the loss of control I never had. God will see me through any kind of pain imaginable and I need not be concerned with how. I know He is able to mend all the mishaps of my life. Knowing I am loved that much allows me to endure the unknown. Blind faith all the way through my life is the way I travel now.

Love has been found and a new search has begun. I now search for His face . . . I now look to Him for everything . . . I now look for His guidance daily. I look for love in all I do. I look for purpose in everything. I look to receive His love. I look for many blessings to be distributed throughout the world. I look for God to use me in a mighty way. I look to please God! I have found love in God who lives within me!

The "love" I was seeking was an unknowingly diversion from that ultimate love of God. I was running from it for years. I did not realize it, but that emotion I kept pressing down was God loving me. I did not feel I was able to withstand those turbulent winds. I did not consider God and His extraordinary power. I only considered me.

I was expecting that man and the ones before him to replace what was missing. I was trying to cover up the pains behind me with a very much desired love from a man. I realized he was not able to give me what I ultimately needed which was to deal with my past in order to accept my present to receive my future. Those feelings I stuffed down needed to be confronted.

When I let go of the concept of a man filling a void and understood my emptiness, I became open to love. God's love. He is my healer, comforter, and number ONE lover. I need not search any more for I know the ultimate love is inside of me. I am filled with more love than anyone could ever try to give.

Beginning with love personally will be an asset to joining with another who wants to share in it.

BATTER UP
Chapter Five

When we first met, we had a familiar connection which gave me much comfort. He grew up in an abusive atmosphere as well. I knew he would protect me for sure because he knew the effects.

As if I did not know already from my childhood days what anger looked and felt like, I would see more. He said he loved me and I believed him. He had such passion about being with me; that had to mean something. I felt I was tough enough to deal with his yelling, pushing, and shoving. I should have considered this relationship just a bit further when he knocked me around on the stairwell and fractured my arm while I was in the early stages of my first pregnancy. I left him alone, but not long enough.

He said he was sorry. I made him upset was his reasoning. I had indirectly participated in his conception of uproar. I found that very hard to swallow, yet he said again he loved me. I needed to hear those words and he said it often. Again, so much passion it must mean something. I know I did not do anything to make him act this way, but . . . he would say what I needed to hear.

Once I left home, 18 in my senior year, and moved in with him at his dad's house I just knew all my troubles were over. My house had been so full of hurt I dreaded being there. Now because of us being in the same place, our lives should be full of the love he expressed regularly. I held on to those thoughts until I was slammed up against the wall. I called my brother, he came over, and spoke with the two of us. I actually expected him to stick up for me and knock him around a bit, but not even close. I felt at that very moment, no one had my back. The "sorry" came again followed by my needed "I love you" and another scar was covered up.

We relocated to the Midwest and I was expecting my second son. I thought maybe things would change a bit because we were in a brand new place other than our own. It was only a matter of time. The cursing and loud talking became more frequent. I just did not understand how I ended up here. I swore I would not end up in a situation like my mother. There was a difference. He was not going to hurt my children. I could take it, but NOT MY CHILDREN.

There came a point where silence was in the house. The only sounds were the children and the television. By this time, he had begun a habit of leaving out of the house and staying out. Picking a fight and walking out became a routine that I was numb to. While preparing to walk out the door, I followed lagging a bit behind. "Well let me lock the door behind you" is what I said under my breath. As I came closer I saw his foot turn quickly, his body soon followed and it was like I was hit with a bat. I felt the next worst pain I ever handled in my life. It hurt so bad I did not make a sound for a few seconds. I fell to the floor and let out the most awful sound. He had punched me in my face! I do not know what happened right after that. When I regained focus, I felt his arm slide from across my back and I saw his feet walking toward the bathroom.

Trying to comprehend what just transpired, I was holding my pulsating face in pure silence. The next sound I heard was him in the bathroom crying "I am so sorry . . . what did I do . . . I am sorry!" Neglecting my own pain and disbelief, I went to the bathroom door to comfort him. I told him I was alright and to open the door. I really could not believe what I was doing. I felt as if I were a puppet being guided by strings. Why in the world was I concerned with his feelings? He punched ME in the face! Feeling delusional, I was the one who left the house that night and returned a little while later. I lied about my black and swollen eye and never told a soul. If anyone knew, they sure never said a word.

As more children came, more abuse came. We had moved several times and with each I hoped for the best. The apologies moved up to flowers and gifts. I was beginning to get fed up, but did not know what to do. I did not feel I could get any help from my family and I did not have any close friends. I truly felt very alone in a twisted, fearful, trapped situation. I remembered how my mother stayed. Calling the police was pointless to me because my stepfather was an officer and he was the abuser. I was bias toward them. I always said my family will not be what mine was growing up . . . it was very close. He still had not hit the kids, but they did witness me being beaten. That was just as bad.

He was really deranged. He would come home and accuse me of having someone in the house. He once said he could see footprints in the carpet. I am pregnant with kids all on my ankles; really? It seemed anything he could conjure up; he would use to start something. By this time there had been witnesses to the abuse, but of course no one cared enough to help. A watchful eye is all I received from the crowd.

It got to a point where I had bruises on top of bruises and I NEEDED to get out. I was a cosmetology student by this time who finally had a brief escape. My mind was tired, my body was sore, and my soul cried out. Being in school made me realize I was in a crazy situation. I was around some very strong women who began to rub off on me. Throughout the years I gained a very low self-esteem and felt worthless. He had degraded me so much I lost sight of reality. I began to regain a sense of who I was and recognized once again the potential.

Choking me on our apartment floor was another incident that happened in front of our children. I thank God for his mother living underneath us because out of nowhere she grabbed him off of me. As I caught my breath, I ran out of the door to her apartment and hid in her closet in her room. May of 1997, in the same week of Mother's Day, was the very last time he put his hands on me.

After taking pictures of me, the school suggested I resume my classes at a later date because of him attempting to see me at the school. Sorry was not going to cut it this time.

After staying with my girlfriend from class with my boys for almost a week, I had to take them back to him. It became very difficult for her to make several trips to numerous places throughout the day and no one worked. I totally understood, but dreaded the choice I made. I asked my mother at that time could we come and stay with her and she told me NO. My life was crushed even lower. I now had nobody and nothing. I did not care anymore.

I never wanted things to end up this way, but I could not bear any more fighting. How much was I supposed to take? I thought I stood for a lot, but that did not even matter. I said for better or worse; wasn't that the worst? I continued with questions and rationales for years. The more I questioned it the angrier I became. The angrier I became, the more I needed to numb it.

I pushed that pain down for years with Jack Daniels and "Mary Jane."

Would I ever trust again? I sacrificed my life and that was not even enough. What did I do to deserve this? I did not know how to live without them, they were my life. My life was over. I thought of taking my life several times, but never came close. It remained in the forefront of my mind.

I used alcohol and "trees" for many years to drown my sorrows. I took my feelings out on everyone around me . . . near and far.

I lost sight of everything I once believed in. My trust was diminished with everyone. I did not care about other people's feelings. I only cared about mine. Everything was everybody else's fault. I played the blame game for years. All I saw was the negative side of everything. It was only positive when it benefited me.

I was unable to function daily and think about my children. Out of sight, out of mind. I went into solo mode and did what I wanted to the fullest. I pushed those thoughts aside and began a new life in a new place. I missed my children tremendously, but could not continue this way.

I did not speak about my life previously when I met new people. I told them I had four sons, I was separated, and relocated . . . that was it. If I did not talk about it, it did not exist at the moment. I carried an attitude, but did not display it on a regular. It took a lot to get me upset, but when it happened it was not pretty. I had so much built up in me I did not want to be known. I did not want to feel.

A shell was around me most of the time. I would allow some people in, but as soon as they displayed a familiar behavior, I was done. I may have continued a relationship, but I was not fully committed. I did not want to fall back into the kind of mentality I had while with him. If someone did something to me, no matter what it was, it reminded me of something he did or said. I tried to protect myself by avoiding issues. There was so much stuffed down inside me. I began to fall apart.

I did not realize how bad I was affected until I was in a relationship with a gentleman and I could not be happy. It was time to confront my issues. I called my dad and . . . he drove for miles and picked me up from where I was. I had spoken with my dad throughout the years about the way I felt. He received the brunt of a lot of my anger. I stayed with him at his house for a couple of days and then he flew home to my mother. I was not happy about this situation, but knew it had to be done. I had been on a rampage for years and something had to change.

My mom had been attending a church in the area and began taking me. I was very leery initially, but continued to go. On a particular Sunday, this service would be different than any service I ever would attend. The choir sang several songs that morning that rang through my soul. On one of the songs, the lead singer came and stood right in front of where we were sitting. I looked at my mother and like a little girl grabbed her arm. An uncontrollable feeling developed as I wondered what was happening. I was not able to suppress these emotions as I had in the past. I was losing control.

We were at the end of the alter call prayer getting ready to return to our seats when the prophetess speaker of that morning who just delivered the prayer told everyone to wait. She closed her eyes and was waving her hands as if they were wands and said "right here . . . you." The crowd spread and a pathway lead to me. With a puzzled look on my face, she continued and said, "God said let it go"! I was truly amazed but knew instantly what it meant. She added a few more words to the message that was directed to me from God as I stared in pure amazement. "He is watching me", were my thoughts as I walked back to my seat. I looked at my mother and began to weep.

When they asked if anyone wanted to come and give themselves to Christ, I made a dash to the front of the church!

After accepting God in my life so many emotions were let go. Everything did not vanish instantaneously, but God removed a large portion of it. I had been baptized as a child, but did not really grasp the concept. Nevertheless, I was already a child of God who had made a wrong turn into darkness. The hatred I had for my ex-husband was gone. I realized God brought me through it regardless of the suffering I endured.

God began to show me through His Word that everyone goes through tough times and that happened to be mine. I did make the choice to be with him even after he put his hands on me the very first time. Because I made those ungodly choices, I had to suffer the ungodly consequences. Although it was very painful, God enabled me to handle all of it. It did take me quite a while to get to the mind frame I am at, but it is all due to God. Slowly but surely, He reveals the truths of life to me that puts it all into proper perspective.

It is not my ex-husband's fault per say. He had a darkness in him that heavily influenced him to act in the ways he did. It does not make any of that okay, but it explains the evil that was displayed. God allows things to happen in our lives for different reasons; His reasons alone. I realize that was my life, but is no longer. It had me bound for years I am not able to change. I am able to use those years as strengthening tools and most of all evidence of God's love for me. Never would have made it without Him!

I look back on the times I was comforting my ex-husband after he abused me. I acknowledge that as the God in me because that was not me. Instead of having me full of rage at that time, He had me showing compassion to the "Judas" in my life. I never wanted him locked up nor did I ever want to hurt him. I merely wanted the abuse to stop. Through those times I see how God was there. He was the one withstanding all those blows. He was the one showing love at such a dark time. I realize from no effort of mine; God was working through me. I was holding on to God and I did not even know it.

I will be alright with what has transpired because of where it has brought me to. I am able to encourage and inspire other individuals who are struggling with the effects of abuse. God allowed my life to partly serve as great purpose to others. I trust and have faith in God to know without a shadow of a doubt I was born to live through the trenches to witness the wondrous, most gracious, almighty God's love and TESTIFY . . .

THE WAY IT BEGAN
Chapter Six

⚜ SCRIPTURE ⚜
Proverbs 13:20
Walk with the wise and become wise, for a companion of fool suffers hard.

"I had a dream about you", was the first thing he said to me as he aggressively moved his way onto my bowling team. I thought that was a different approach and gave him my number. I was seeing someone else that went to my school, but I was not thinking too seriously at that time. We began talking quite often on the phone. Many times I woke up to the sound of the phone being off the hook because I fell asleep while talking to him. He did not live in my area, so I did not see him daily. I could not wait until the weekend to bowl so I could see him again.

It appeared we had so much in common as we were able to discuss any and everything. We were the same age, 16, yet I was a couple of weeks older. Our birthdays were in the same month, but I am a Gemini and he is a Cancer. In those days everything was fate if it was alike. Except for how short he was, he was perfect. His bowed legs and well-toned physic made up for his height. He did have a rough edged kind of way about him, but it seemed very mild.

My mother bowled on Saturdays as well, but in the evening. With us getting better acquainted, I asked my mother if I could go over his house while she bowled. We had it all planned out so that his brother could bring me back by the time she finished. His mom would be home so all should be well we thought. With the okay from my mother, it was a go. I was so excited. I had a boyfriend that my mother actually knew and kind of liked so far. Life was looking up.

With us spending so much time together, I tapered off of seeing my other friend. Every Saturday became a routine. I would go over to his house while my mother bowled. It was pretty cool over his house. His mom was very cool and down to earth. I could tell their household was a little different from mine but I loved it. He had his own room with his own television. We would play cards, laugh, and talk.

Trying to find something on the television was difficult but this time it did not matter. We both had that look in our eyes and was drawn closer to each other. He leaned in like a pro and kissed me. I was a little shocked but loving every minute of it. We went from sitting up to laying down in no time. Lost in the moment, we did not realize someone was knocking on the door. Being that we took too long to open it, his mother opened the door and said, "What are y'all doing!??!" I had never been so embarrassed in all my life. "Get up from there. Kristine has to go now." We looked at each other with that same passion as if she said nothing, kissed and then proceeded to get dressed. When we came out of the room we could barely look at her with a straight face. We giggled and went outside to wait by the car. She never said anything else about it.

I had seen my other friend a few more times, and then tapered off. I am sure he wondered what the issue was, but I did not know what to say. He did not know about the other, and the other did not know about him. We had one last rendezvous one day before I went to work and then that was it with him. I figured we were young; it really did not matter.

Several months after we began seeing each other, I found out I was pregnant. A thought crossed my mind, but then vanished immediately. My other friend knew already because he was the one who took me to be tested. At that time, I totally felt my friend I saw on a regular was the father because of all the times we had been together. It was so much more than my other friend that I figured there was no way it was possible for him to be the father.

Pulling up from the clinic, I saw my friend in my apartment hallway window as I leaned over to thank and kiss my other friend good-bye. As I walked into the building I felt my stomach do a flip. He immediately was upset at what he just witnessed. Trying to calm him down, I tried to explain the situation. He began to yell and cuss so I left out of the building and began walking toward another one. I understood the reason for his anger, but did not agree with the way he was acting. Following me into another building and not letting me leave back out, he held me down against the stairwell. With more and more force, he ended up fracturing my arm.

We broke up for a while after that incident, but shortly rekindled our relationship. He forgave me for my youthful freedom and I forgave him because I felt partly responsible. I also told him I was not sure, but thought he was the father of my son.

Several years later after obvious reasons, we had a blood test done. My first son did not look like my second son at all outside of the features that were from me. He began being very mean to everyone except my second son. Something had to be done. My mother knew of this situation and suggested my son go live with her and she would raise him. Feeling the blame for all this chaos, I agreed. I felt I was protecting him and offering him a better situation than I was in. I could endure the abuse he dished out, but not my child. I was torn but did not know anything else to do.

The results of the test came back negative. He received the results before picking me up from work, the salon where I was working at the time. Because of the results and his obvious anger, I had left him and took my kids and went to my mother's house. He had come to retrieve me the next day stating he did not care if he was his or not. I believed him and went back with him. My mother was upset because of my choice.

My oldest son remained with my mother and I remained in my abusive situation. Because of what I had done years ago being with him and my friend, at times I felt I deserved what I was dealing with. He had a hatred toward me because I had a son that was not his. It was my fault. I had to protect him somehow and my mother gave me a way.

I often wondered why did he come back and get us if he was going to still be mad. This was years ago and three children later. I bore him three sons. But knew I was missing one.

I was full of so much guilt, shame, doubt, and fear. What started out with so much passion was turning in to something so ugly. Was it my fault we were going to ruins?

I struggled for many years blaming myself for everything that was happening. This situation haunted me for years. He said he forgave me but he really did not. He said he wanted me no matter what but he really did not. Although I believed with all my heart I had to be there, I was being punished for cheating and giving my son to my mother.

The absence of one of my children and the aftermath of being with two guys at the same time is what I forced myself to deal with. All in good measure, I figured my heart was true so all would be well one day.

The birth of a child that wasn't his and three of his children, married at the justice of the peace while in my third pregnancy, becoming an abused housewife, and distant from my family were the highlights of my years with my once close friend. We eventually separated after years of abuse and I could not raise my other sons either. Everything I did not want to be, ended up being.

Much of my anger throughout the years stemmed from this relationship and I was not quite sure how to direct it. He blamed me and I blamed him. What I did, did not warrant what came in return.

Because of the duration of time before the blood test was administered, my son's father did not know until several years after his birth that he actually is his father. I believe their relationship thereafter was due to the unfamiliar territory. My son was still a child and had the mindset to adapt and draw close with his father, but for whatever reasons at that time his father did not encourage that to happen. A wedge is still in between them today.

For years I have carried the results of all this around with me and all because of the way it began.

It was many years before I was able to grasp the effects of my choices. When I understood the 'Serenity Prayer', I was okay with all my choices no matter how right or wrong. I could go on and on trying to find fault with myself and trying to justify my reasoning. The fact was it had already occurred. There was and still is nothing I can do to change the outcome. I have accepted that I am unable to change it. I was able to apologize to everyone involved at one time or another. To be able to confess to myself was one thing, but out loud to them was difficult yet very much needed. I had the courage to change the thing I could by admitting my wrongs and asking for forgiveness. There was and is a lot that is inside of the individuals involved that I am not able to do anything about. Those are their personal cases that they have to arrive to and solve. I have realized and understand the differences of what is possible for me to do and not.

I am totally aware of the individuals that were involved, but that era, circumstances, and situation is over. It is years later, 26 years to be exact. To continue to harbor anger, guilt, sadness, regret, or anything else for things that are no longer and out of my control are unnecessary. God saw me through my sins, and will continue. Knowing God still loved me no matter what I had done enabled me to let it go.

Life was a lot freer when I was able to accept what I had done. I also understood that my actions do not make anyone do anything. That is their personal choice to react in a particular way. It is not about the situation, but how you handle it. My choices were not the greatest, but children do childish things. I am now an adult and have definitely put away childish things. I pray constantly for God to open my eyes to see clearly and allow me to hear all I need to with my ears. This prayer is not for me to hear people around me, it is so I am able to see and hear Him in all that I do and say. Making Godly decisions in the beginning of a situation will determine the outcome. The way I would like to finish is the way I will begin.

From this situation and many others, I have learned to be very honest immediately. "It is what it is" is a familiar phrase that rings very true. It is that and is for the other person to decide what they would like to do. It is better to consider someone's feelings initially. Providing a choice is ultimately the goal and then it leaves the thought of you either like it or you don't.

Carrying fear and regret can hinder God's blessings in your life because you are not depending on His power to work in your life despite the circumstance. Nothing is too big, crazy, messed up, ugly, or damaged for God to turn it around. If I had faith like I did the way it began, I would have said all that was needed to be known.

All is well and will be well whenever and wherever God is concerned. There are not any mistakes in my life now, just "miss takes." I always am offered another opportunity to get it right!

SPOKEN WORD
Chapter Seven

Proverbs 18:21
Death and life are in the power of the tongue, and those who love it will eat its fruits.

From the time I can remember I usually do not say things unless I truly meant it. It could be cruel or harsh, but it would be the truth. The fact that I was so quiet made a difference to me when I would speak; it would mean I felt very passionate about what I said.

A thought in my mind would be so vivid as if it were right in front of me. It was not like wishing for something, it was knowing I would have it very soon. Not much thought would be given toward it. I would see it, desire it, and know it would be mine. Many things would not be desired by me. That thing would possess something unique that was just for me. I knew it when I saw it. It did not have to be common, popular, glamorous, or even expensive. A stimulation would run through me and I just knew.

While in my senior year of school, there were several of my peers that were pregnant. This was at the brink of teenage pregnancy. I remember being shocked every time I would see a young girl with a huge belly. Until there was one of those girls in one of my classes, I never gave it much thought besides "wow"! This young girl also worked where my mother and I worked. So I was familiar with her.

The entire class gathered around her one day as she began talking about her pregnancy. She spoke about how she felt and what it meant to her becoming a mother. Her age, status, or future was never discussed. The story began to have bells and whistles on it. I was so into what she was saying it did not look so bad any more. I looked at her stomach and thought . . . maybe. I made the comment, "I would not mind being pregnant." She looked at me and said, "Really?" and kept on talking.

Later that same day I was in the living room of my apartment with a girlfriend of mine chit chatting about who knows what. While conversing with her, I heard the keys at the door and realized my mom was home from work. We looked at each other and kept talking. My mother comes in and walked directly over to us. All of a sudden I felt a huge slap across my face. "What did you do that for?" I yelled at her. "You want to have a what!?!" she responded with such anger and disappointment. I just stood there in embarrassment as my girlfriend witnessed. Instantly I knew exactly what she was upset about. Apparently she ran into my classmate at work and was notified of my recent declaration. Needless to say, several weeks later I was pregnant.

Moving forward many years, two of my sons were living with me which turned out to be very briefly. They had gotten a bit rowdy over the years from living with the results of their father and me separating. Observing their behavior, I had been having many thoughts about their futures. After an incident I encountered with them I made the comment, "one of you is going to end up in jail and the other with babies all over the place." One of my sons said quickly, "Don't say that . . . then it is going to come true!" I looked at him in amazement and thought no more of it. Needless to say, a couple of years later one ended up in trouble with the law and the other has three children with one on the way.

There were many other incidences that played out to be so after I said it. I never felt I was saying anything wrong, just exactly what I felt whole heartedly. I was not thinking about God or His word, just what I felt so strongly.

I used to think it was the same way I had wanted to be rescued from the abuse of my childhood or the abuse from my ex-husband. I did want it, but my mind was not set on it because I never gave the feelings time to penetrate. When the emotions would come, I would press them down. Until I gave my feelings the attention and focus, I could not speak it.

Leaving my feelings bottled inside left a lot of negative thoughts trapped in my mind that eventually marinated in my soul. My life began to play out exactly what I felt. I did not have to say a word; it showed all through what I did. When asked what was wrong, it was N O T H I N G. That is what poured out of my heart as well . . . nothing at all.

If speaking out loud what I felt in my heart is what made things happen, then the thoughts I harbored on the inside are what made things happen as well.

Feeling defeated, low self-esteem, worthless, lonely, unloved, guilty, regret, anger, and hurt brought those very things into my life. I attracted just what I felt like. I acted out what I felt. I became just what I felt like.

Lost in my own world of unspoken words . . . pure darkness.

Because I did not take the time to deal with my emotions, I was unable to speak what I truly felt. It meant bringing that emotion up to the surface with those honest words and I could not bear the thought of it. It is not that I was not honest, I just never spoke on it. Not saying what I really felt kept me from freeing myself.

I got just what I wanted or just what I thought would happen. I would not say speaking the truth got me in trouble, it showed me what was really on my heart. It did not take much thought process; it was just known. Saying what I meant became very easy yet in spurts. There was not a specific reason, I just knew deep inside some things I should not say.

Say what you mean and mean what you say became very real to me but only because it meant a lot to me. It had nothing to do with anybody else. I knew I felt a particular way and that was it. I believed in what I said, and wanted to believe in what others said as well. I knew if they really felt it or not because it would show itself proven. When it did not happen, I waited on it . . . for a long time.

Releasing my feelings is what I needed to do in order to be whole again. I had used to say just what I felt but because of the fear of emotions, I would not face them. When I went back home to live with my mother I knew something was going to change one way or another. It took a while for me to let my feelings come to the surface, but when they did, it was all she wrote.

I started with honestly wanting the pain gone. It was like as soon as I said from my heart, "OKAY, let it rip", it did. All I had to do is believe it could be done, and let it happen. I had arrived back at the point I once knew . . . true feelings.

There was no way God was going to allow anything pure to come through all that negativity I was toting. Regardless of what I wanted, I could not have been honest about wanting anything because of what I was unwilling to do. How much faith did I have if I felt so bad? Although the pain is understandable, God allowed me to endure it until I asked for help. I chose to carry it. All I had to do was open my mouth. I now understand the connection of my words and their existence. It is always said that words are powerful. It is also said that words will never hurt me. The first saying should have rung true because "never say never." I knew from very young that I had a strong passion for things unlike the norm. I recognized I was different because people just did not understand me. I knew I knew and kept it at that.

God puts that desire in my heart. It becomes passionate to me because I feel the power of the emotions inside that passion. I began to realize when I hurt, it is alright to go through that pain because it is honest. It is from the heart . . . hints why it hurts. It is perfectly okay for me to feel upset, angry, or sad. God understands those emotions.

I was afraid of that passion for years, but only because I did not know what it was. Spoken words are passions said aloud. Of course, we speak every day but everything said is not necessarily from the heart. Some words are said with no purpose; an open end kind of thing. It comes out and evaporates into the air. Words have power. There is nothing wrong with being angry, it is an honest emotion. Keeping those unspoken words inside is what causes damage.

This is not to say that I am able to say whatever I want, that is not so. The thing I know is God knows my heart and whatever I believe within my heart will be. To keep something inside is pointless, when He knows it anyway. Why not express that feeling and remove it from your being; especially if it is negative. Thoughts are just as powerful. Anything truly felt, is heartfelt. The way I thought was the way I was. Spoken words through thought, although negative, very honest. I did not want to believe those things about me and did not believe them in my heart. God knew it all along, but I needed to know. Once I let the passion surface, I found out.

God understands all emotions. God is the one feeling it for me, removing it and allowing that to be the spoken word. It is a language that is reaching the ends of the earth. God spoke everything into existence. The spoken word can be felt in heavenly places as well as the dark ones. The spoken words are those very passions that are ultimately shared with God. God is that passion…He allowed it to be there. Speak . . .

IT'S OVER
Chapter Eight

I wanted my family to work. I thought I would be able to stick out the rough portion and arrive to the good part after a while. Because of the love I had, I would be awarded a prize of happy years to come with my husband and children intact. Realizing I did not want to indulge in the dose of whooping sauce he had for me softened the disappointment of losing my family.

I gave it everything I had. Putting up with craziness for years just to keep us as one unit. I did not want my children to come from a broken home. Trying to avoid that kept them in a violent atmosphere with half of a mother. It pained me, but I had to go.

I had moved away to the south and would come back to visit periodically. We had actually gotten back on speaking terms due to his grandmother taking ill. I was invited by his mom to ride with them to where his grandmother was being nursed since I was still family. I thought that was genius to ruffle his feathers. By the time we returned we were in an unfamiliar place with each other. I had been gone for almost a year and he was seeing someone else whom we both knew well. Even though we did not ride side by side, I think a bit of territory arose in both of us. We ended up in bed together that night with his "friend" knocking on the door. He let her knock.

That next morning when I woke up, he was not there. I searched the apartment and still could not find him. I had a funny feeling and went to "her" door and knocked. I ended up standing at the door just like she did the night before. I had played the fool again. I went to his mother's apartment and let her in on what had transpired. She went to the woman's door and banged on it. Yelling, knowing he was in there, she informed him how wrong he was to be with me and then run back to her. I followed her back to her apartment and realized for the second time, it was over. I should have known by the awkwardness of it all. I still wanted my family to be so again I was willing to do whatever it took to make that happen.

He never came out of her apartment until much later. I was in his apartment laying across the bed crying and feeling defeated. I was unsure what I was going to do, or how I was going to do it.

When he returned to the apartment, he did not have much to say. I really did not pay any attention to him, I was more upset with myself for choosing him again. I did not eat and was very silent for the next few days.

Once I acknowledged all that transpired and came to the conclusion for the second time that it was over, I decided to leave. It was difficult for me to leave my children after thinking I might have been back. I remember walking my children to school and my youngest to his class and him screaming for me to not leave him there. As I walked away, it was killing me, but I did not want to have to look at him and say bye. Leaving while they were gone was best . . . for me.

Dealing with this break-up was very difficult even though he was abusive. He was someone I loved and devoted my life to. I tried to do the best I knew how at the time, but was not good enough. I blamed myself in many ways, yet felt I suffered so much for nothing. Seven years and three children later it was all over.

There was a hole left inside me for a long time. I found myself gravitating toward those who were needy in some kind of way as well. I looked for that recognition of belonging to someone in some kind of way. Be it in a friend, relationship, or something I did . . . I needed it bad. I was looking for that satisfaction I once had, but as I thought about it, I was not satisfied then either. But I did have something.

I tried to deny the hurt that I had by covering it up every way possible for me. I drank, smoked "Mary Jane", and got plenty of attention from the men over the years. It all took up time, but did not fill the void I had within me.

I wanted to be loved, feel safe, and needed. I yearned for it terribly.

I became a very guarded individual who did not trust anybody. I did not care what you did for me, ultimately I felt something was wrong. I was very insecure within myself, therefore would push some wonderful people out of my life. I also was very needy with the ones that were in my life. I wanted so much from them but had nothing to give in return.

I was very selfish. I felt a lot inside but was so afraid of being hurt that I would not show my true feelings. I would accept everything and give nothing. Only when I wanted to continue to receive from you would I give. I would give just enough to continue within the relationship. As soon as more was wanted or needed, I was gone.

There were a couple who got past my defenses. It left me scared to death. Because I had no control, I feared they did not feel for me as I did them. I would end up sabotaging those relationships in the end.   I was left broken, lost, afraid, and troubled. I did not know what to do.

After being on my own for over 10 years, everything I accumulated would be lost. I ended up losing all I had and moved back home with my mother.

After I gave my life to Christ for the second time, the first being when I was around 9, I went on a two-day woman's retreat with my church. I was very unfamiliar with what it was about, but was on fire for knowledge. There were classes that we attended catered to married and single individuals. Although I was separated and lived as though I was single, I was still legally married.

In this class was a discussion about the woman and their marriages. They were going around the room, table to table, talking about how wonderful and lovely their marriages were. This was a beautiful thing to witness, yet I knew when it got to me, that would not be the case.

"Well, I am married but have been separated for over 10 years because he was abusive", I said reluctantly.   The entire demeanor of the room and the atmosphere changed. I started to get emotional but it dried up instantly as I felt a huge sweep of open arms. "I tried to divorce him initially but he would not sign the papers so I just left it and began to think because I left, I cannot divorce him. Isn't that what God says?"   One of the pastor's daughters was there and comforted me by saying, "At least you got out. We thank God for getting you out of there safely." She proceeded to search through her Bible and began to read aloud Mark 10: 2-5 and said, "oh no, yes you can "! From that point onward, I knew it would be over soon.

Several years after being told divorce is permissible by God, I filed. It is kind of funny how it played out. I always had a thought that it was wrong for me to divorce him; he had to do it. While in court I needed someone I knew for over four years to stand for me and be a witness. The individual I brought with me I only knew for three years. My motion was thrown out and my husband ended up using his witness, his fiancée. It turned out, he divorced me after all.

I was finally free. Although God had forgiven me for all I had done, I felt another sense of relief. I was no longer bound by the vow we once made, his last name, or a piece of paper. I could date people without feeling attached to another. A fresh start I felt and knew was in front of me. I had dreamt of this day for a long time. I was Kristine J. Bryant again.

I knew God had allowed this moment. The more I searched for answers, the more would be revealed to me. Once I acknowledged, accepted, and believed a positive change was possible, He allowed me to have it.

Although I wanted my family to work, I had already been rescued from my misery. I wanted a change deep in my heart and God brought that to provision. The change had already begun, yet once received it was difficult to handle. God allowed me to go through that humiliation to open my eyes to the truth. Not so much the truth of my ex-husband's foul ways, but for the truth of God. He gave me just what I asked for and then I did not accept it. I am sure God was not hurt by that, but would see to it that I would recognize when He shows me favor by letting me be hurt once again.

Dealing with hurt is difficult in any situation. I made decisions based on those feelings that were not the best. God knew my pain and understood it. I had to go through all of my actions of making horrible choices so I could recognize Him again later.

He was right there with me through all I was doing. When I was drunker than five sailors, higher than any kite can fly, and laying with the man of my choice . . . He was right there. He was there to guide me while driving intoxicated and not allow me to hit anyone or anything. He was there to allow me to sleep off the alcohol each time and wake up the next day. He was there to see to it that I came down off each one of those highs I was on and continue to be in my right mind. He was there while laying with each man as my protection in every way needed in that situation.

He rescued me several times over, protected me from many darts, and saw to it that I continued on the path He had for me. Life as I knew it was OVER!

MAKE IT WORK
Chapter Nine

✠ SCRIPTURE ✠

Ephesians 2:8

For it is by grace you have been saved, through faith—and this is not from yourselves, it is the gift of God—not by works, so that one can boast.

Within many things in my life, I have tried to make it work. From relationships, friends, jobs, and family to having something understood. Even rigging something in the house so that it would work. I believe I am a rebuilder. It is not so much changing something completely; it is adding to it so it works even better. When I see a problem I try and figure out the solution. The issue appears and my mind starts turning. It feels very natural to me. It is not something I try to do; it just happens.

As I child I tried to figure out ways to many things; although I had no real clue about what I was even doing. All I knew is I felt a specific way and it needed to change. I also would do things the adults said would work. I tried very hard, but it did not always work. I liked my way better.

Within my marriage I tried to make it work. Putting forth much effort to be the best mother and wife I could be under the trying circumstances. Everything was no near perfection and I suffered a lot, yet still wanted very much to figure a way for it to work. My efforts were useless.

Friendships throughout my life have at times been very difficult. Because of my "I can do it" attitude, I put up with many things most individuals probably would not. Regardless of the faults someone may display, I will overlook them and try to offer them another way. When my suggestions are not accepted, I will merely state my claim and continue to explain it until it is understood. Sometimes the person would understand and things would change, and many times it did not. It was not about me being correct, it was getting the other person to see my view other than their own. I had my faults too, but these efforts worked on others not myself. Because of my personal pains, making it work was suppressing my pain and assisting others with theirs.

On certain jobs there were many unfair situations that would transpire. Instead of me complaining and informing everyone, I would try and solve the issue. I believe my efforts were very noticed, but not wanted. At times were very effective, but again not wanted. Even though I would be shot down, I would keep my head up and know I tried.

Being understood was my main objective. Realizing the situation and understanding how a specific solution would be beneficial . . . in my eyes.

It became a bit frustrating knowing my heart was in the place, but not getting any reception for my efforts. It did not have to be my way, but couldn't my suggestions count for something? I began wondering why nothing was working out despite my efforts. I thought we were supposed to put our best foot forward and we would be rewarded for it. That seemed to happen to everyone else but me. Things would happen, but it would be when I was not even trying. "What kind of fulfillment for me is that", I used to ask myself.

I wanted a place in this world and wanted my opinions to matter. It was like the more I tried, the worse I would feel when nothing would transpire from my efforts.

At times, I believe, individuals thought I thought I knew it all. It was not that at all. When you sit back and look at things, you can see it from an angle maybe others do not see. I was trying to mend a situation, resolve an issue, or solve a problem. My heart was in the right place, but my efforts were not on time.

I wanted greatly to be of service and feel like I did something useful. Feeling rejected, it activated a defense mechanism within me.

I came to a point where I would look at others and wonder, why not me? When my mind was set on something, I would pursue it like nobody's business. Then I began to look at what I did not possess. Maybe I am trying to make it work with the wrong equipment.

I would always say, "I can do that too, with no problem. I am capable of that, with no problem. I want to receive recognition like them. I can make it work too if I was given the chance. "

Then I started looking at what these people had. Education, money, a strong family, lots of friends, and a strong sense of who they were. All things I did not have. I came to an assumption that although I strongly desired to make it work, I just did not have the right tools to do so.

I knew I had what it took, but I just did not stand up to what others displayed. That thought influenced me to doubt my efforts and who I was.

Not believing in myself despite my desire to help put a real chip on my shoulder. I would look at wonderful individuals with a crooked eye because I wanted what they had. I wanted to be a part of the team of efforts and be able to say, "I did that" or "because of my efforts look what happened."

I became very withdrawn and did not want to participate in anything. I did not want to give my all and then do not receive any credit for it. I did not want to try and it did not make any difference to anyone.

It was challenging knowing I had something in me that wanted to be noticed, but was unable to be. I wanted to help and make a difference somewhere, anywhere so bad. It seemed everything I tried either failed, did not matter, or went unnoticed. When was I going to shine? Something in me was shattered, but wanted to be together.

When I accepted God in my life, I began to see everything in a different light. I still wanted to know my place in this world. I still wanted to help. The effort changed.

I was searching for my purpose. "Father, what did you create me for? Everything I am trying to do is not working. I am trying so hard! What am I doing wrong?" was my plea. "You blessed me with this talent, I tried to capitalize on that it did not go anywhere. You blessed me with another gift and nothing panned out with my effort to do something with it. Nothing I am doing is working. What am I supposed to be doing!!!!?" I asked Him with much desire and anguish in my heart.

I was so through and tired of trying. Just when I wanted to totally give up, a strong sense in my heart said, "That is your problem. You are trying to do everything. When are you going to allow me to do for you? You accepted me into your life, yet will not give me the control." I began to cry. . .

For so long I have been wanting things for myself. I did not think it was wrong to want for myself. I wanted recognition for my attempts, ideas, and concerns. I wanted to be recognized for the efforts I put forth. I wanted to be noticed for trying to help a situation. I needed to fix something.

I, I, I was all I focused on. I was not allowing God to do just what He said He would do. When I realized it was not about my efforts and I could not make anything happen, my life changed. God makes all things possible, not me. God fills me with desire, it does not generate from me. I do not need to be recognized for anything but giving God all the glory!

My efforts were not going unnoticed; they just simply were not needed. That was not my place to try and do anything. My heart wanted to do, but it was working the wrong way. God works through me and when I keep taking over, He allowed me to see just what I was capable of. . . NOTHING. When I put God first in what I do, He will reward me. I do not need recognition nor is it warranted from anyone unless God authorizes it.

I wanted to be recognized for something God was ultimately responsible for. He definitely will not allow me to get credit for what He does. The desires I had were mine. To be noticed, recognized, or rewarded was very selfish and self-gratifying. Although it was about bettering a situation, the motives were all wrong. God is not going to mix His works with my self-righteousness.

Some things are meant to be broken. God does not need any assistance in putting anything back together; especially when He allowed it to break. My relationships, friendships, or family issues could not and will not be changed by anything past what I am able to do. I do not have the tools to make that work. Beyond my control is just that. . . Beyond!

It is truly a blessing to know I do not have to "try" and make it work. It is going to work if it is God's will. There is much stress and frustration off my shoulders being concerned about a drive inside that has nowhere to go. That burst of energy was God alerting me to let go of the wheel so He could shine. The light will radiate from me, yet seeing the beauty of Him shining through.

My mistake was trying to make things work. Whatever does not turn out as I expected, probably is not supposed to be, and if it is, God will turn it around. When I am needed to use my talents or gifts God has blessed me with, He will present that opportunity to me. I do not have to force my way into anything. When someone does not understand something, I will tell the truth and let it be. When and if God wants them to understand, He will open their eyes to it.

God has everything running smoothly. No tool belt of mine is necessary in what He has already done. It is a finished work! He is the Alpha and the Omega, the author and the finisher, the beginning and the end. God is the great I AM! His will makes it work.

ON MY OWN
Chapter Ten

SCRIPTURE

Isaiah 44:21
"Remember these things, Jacob, for you, Israel, are my servant. I have made you, you are my servant; Israel, I will not forget you.

I was in a lost place, gliding from one place to another. Friends became my new family. I never felt a part of a unit, yet thought persons were supposed to care for their own. No children, no family . . . just constant new friends.

I had been a very quiet person that became even more withdrawn while in my marriage. After leaving that situation and being by myself, at times, felt very freeing. I was able to do exactly what I wanted to do without the concern of anybody. No accusations, no arguing, and no aggravation. I was free to do as I pleased, whenever I pleased, with whomever I pleased. That was a new way of living for me. I was never able to do that before in any capacity.

When I was around other people's family, I would begin to get in my feelings. I wanted what they had. They had open conversations, laughed a lot, and was there for one another. It seemed as if I had stumbled upon an eye opening experience. I had been so secluded for so long, I did not even realize the possibilities of families or even life itself. At twenty-five the world had been opened to my every desire; a new way of living.

I did not have any close friends. I was not used to going out and really enjoying myself. I did not have any children around to watch after or hurry home to. I was amazed at all of the things that were now available to me. I had to get used to the freedom I now had to do whatever I pleased.

I became close with a young woman who went to the same cosmetology school as I. Once I left school, after leaving my husband, I went to live with her briefly. She was a real live wire, yet very, very fun. She spoke her mind and was very independent. I really admired her in that way. I had never been on my own and that aspect of her life was very attractive. We both enjoyed singing, laughing, and having fun. It was nice to be around someone who could break me out of the shell I was in.

She had a girlfriend that we went to see one day. She was a very good friend of hers so I was excited to meet her. We arrived and I introduced myself and began chatting. I had started smoking cigarettes by this time and drinking a little. We had a few beers and were listening to music. Her girlfriend had come out of the bedroom and lit up a very short cigarette. I soon realized that was an alternate to cigarettes; "Mary Jane" was its name. I passed on the invite to try it the first two times, but as I sat there something said, "why not, who do you have to answer to?" I sat up and said, "Give me that!" My girlfriend looked at me and asked, "Are you sure?" with a silly grin on her face.

I took a huge pull like I was smoking a cigarette. I waited a second and pulled again. I said to them, "This isn't anything special. I do not even feel anything." Eagerly ready to give it back, I stood up to return the short and began leaning very heavily to one side. I felt the effect as soon as I stood up. I got down on the floor and crawled to where they were in total astonishment of this new feeling. It was unlike anything I ever felt. I remembered a similar feeling during the labor of three of my children, but the thought process was different this time due to no pressured issues. As I sat there, I had escaped everything I had been secretly feeling. I was in a "right now" zone that was so welcoming to my circumstances. I had discovered a way out of my own.

It became a regular activity to embark on a mind diverter. It seemed like everywhere we went, everybody smoked "Mary Jane." Where had this been hiding all these years? I had never known of this until this point. I had been very sheltered and stayed away from the "troublesome" individuals so I was unaware of this kind of recess.

Wherever there was a group of two or more, alcohol and marijuana was lingering. Brown liquor, white liquor, beer, coolers, wine, champagne . . . you name it, it was there. When we went out, there was always someone who sponsored the evening being we were very attractive young women. I never had to worry about anything. This circle of friends and family became very cushioning to me. I fell right into the pocket.

When I had a chance to sit still, I would ponder about my past and what was lost. That would provoke me to put a veil over those thoughts. It came to a point where the cloudiness would begin first thing and would not end until . . .

I eventually added a male companion into the mix which encouraged the situation. He was a kind of man I had not been used to. He looked out for me, did things for me without a reason. He removed that worthless feeling I had and replaced it with priceless. I really felt on my own then. I was valued despite the damaged goods that was contained within me.

Spending more and more time with him, we became an item. Sooner than later I moved in with him and his roommate outside of the area I was living in. I was very surprised, but was riding the cloud I was on. We got along very well. He worked and I stayed at the house. There was not much for me to do, but I was just happy to not be in the situation I once was a part of. He was very nice to me and assisted in rebuilding my self-esteem.

Although I did not have anywhere else to go, I did not have any expectations with this relationship. I did not work, nor did I have any money. I had been taken care of since I can remember. It never crossed my mind that I had nothing; I had so much more than material things. I was enjoying my freedom and feeling nothing.

Lying next to someone who appreciated me and took care of me gave me a fulfillment at that time. We lived right outside of the area where we grew up, so we visited every weekend. Smoking, drinking, going out, sexing, and cursing became very regular and very familiar to me. I was on my own in a completely new way.

My behavior became more and more reckless. I had liked the fact that I was no longer being controlled by an abusive man and was able to do whatever I pleased. It was something I was not used to and felt a sense of power over my own life. Having this kind of freedom for the first time in my life provided me with a sense of self. I did not feel like an individual before. I always felt confined to something or someone in some kind of way as if I were trapped. I could not speak my mind without being condemned for it. I could not express myself for lack of significance. Who I had become was far from who I once knew, but I had been released from the chain gang.

The high I was on would eventually come down and I was left floating. I began to live outside of myself wondering where I was. I could see me laughing and seemingly filling myself, yet could see the empty space. What once was alluring, was becoming very dull and complacent. I was one who became accustomed to change and was desiring it once again. The high became lower and the alcohol lost its potion. The sex became a lonely act and a closing scene with no encore.

Freedom was liberating and allowed me to experience the world in a way I had no inkling existed. I was engulfed with the sweet scents of temptation in ways my strength could not bear. I was weakened to the degree of losing all sense of self.

The things I was doing that were once very fulfilling to me, became very empty. I was yearning for something my choices were not supplying. I developed a strong desire for change. I was void within relationships, no longer craved a high, and was not tempted by the thought of a man. I had tried chasing a high from my old friend 'Mary Jane', had depleted the taste of liquor, and required more than any man could do for me. There were no more people to run to. And the ones that wanted to rescue me were doing the very things I grew more and more tired of. I had been there and done that and it was not pleasing to me any longer. I needed more. I cried out. Doing what I wanted to do was not beneficial for me at all. On my own was not appealing any more.

I began reading my Bible. It was something I had once done, but was engulfed by the ways of the world. It felt just like it was my last resort. I had tried everything else and it was not working for me. I felt compelled to read. I did not know what I was looking for, I was just reading. As I read I became enlightened. It was as if God was speaking to me through each word. I no longer felt on my own, He was with me and had been the entire time.

My stimulation revolved around God once I gave Him some attention. I no longer wanted to be kept by anything of this world, I wanted to be kept by God.

I came to realize I did not want to be on my own because I did not know how to act. Because there is not any guidance, instruction, or anyone strong enough to assist me when I am weak on my own, I knew I needed something extraordinary. God is the only One powerful enough to provide everything needed. God is the One who created me for His divine purpose, not mine.

It was never for me to do things the way I wanted to. He allowed me to indulge in all the sins of the world I chose to get into while having full control to show me how out of control I was. Although everything I did while on my own was not sinful, it was my way in which lead to nothing. It allowed me to see I am incapable of being independent. I need and desire to be totally dependent on God.

In times of weakness, I will never be able to lift myself up. Help from my closest, dearest, most successful friend cannot give me the strength I need to move forward nor can tell me what I should do. I understand that I am not able to make it on my own and never will. I will always need assistance from God. I have given up control and have let God take the wheel.

Because of the mind frame I was in after being in a relationship that was abusive, confined, and lifeless, once I had the freedom to choose I went haywire. Not dealing with my feelings of being hurt left me angry and wanting to take control. At that time, just having a choice was liberating. Although my choices were not very wise, I had to prove to myself that I could do what I wanted now I was on my own. In doing that, it took me to a place outside of my own.

God allows things to happen in my life because of the choices I make. He already had His hand extended out for me to take, but I was in my feelings and wanted to prove myself. I ended up proving myself wrong. I was concentrating on what I wasn't able to do and the control someone else had over me that I indulged in all the improper things to show myself nobody could tell me what to do any more. I had to move out of the way and let God take over.

God opened my eyes yet again. Although I was by myself, I was never on my own. God allowed me to find out how useless it was to put things in me that were ungodly. Just telling me it is not good was not good enough. I had to experience the feeling of temptation, weakness, drunkenness, sexual immorality, and profanity to understand the fullness of my sinful nature. God allowed me to come to the end of myself in order to reach out for Him.

There is a sense of purpose in everything I do. Sinful nature is within me, yet does not lead me. Keeping God first in my life never leaves me on my own. There is a will, but not my own. I choose for God's will to be done. God has provided me with the Holy Spirit to lead, guide, and direct me in every way. I know I am lead by the spirit and not myself.

WHAT NOW?
Chapter Eleven

⁕ SCRIPTURE ⁕
Job 3:25

What I feared has come upon me; what I dreaded has happened to me.

It was very difficult thinking my life was going to be one way and it turned out completely different. I thought I would be married for years, raise my children until they were out of the house, and enjoy getting old with my husband. I never dreamt that I would have been in an abusive marriage, have to leave my husband and leave my children with him because I was not financially able to raise them, and have no family support. I had no clue what I was going to do.

I was in cosmetology school and had to stop due to the abuse. I was not working and had no money. I did not graduate from high school and had no job skills or training. I did not have any family that was able or willing to assist me at the time. I was totally lost.

Thank God for the girlfriend I met while in cosmetology class. I immediately did have somewhere to stay and food to eat. Friends became very important to me at that time. I was not one who was very open or engaging. I sat back and was very quiet. To be able to have a close person at this time in my life was a huge floating device. I had no clue where I was headed, but was holding on tight.

I found myself getting involved in things because I felt like it was what I had to do for the time being to get by. I believe my survival skills (I never knew existed) kicked in. I had always been taken care of so I knew nothing about the kind of life I was beginning to live. I do not blame anyone else for the decisions I made at all. Everything I partook in was solely my choice. But because of having nothing else, I almost felt like I had to. On the other hand, I needed an escape from my now reality. Everything I avoided in my life up until this point had become my involvement. If I wasn't participating, I was around it.

It seemed people would gradually wander into my life or I into theirs at a specific time I was needing. Ordinarily I would have feared these kind of individuals. There was a certain vibe about that person who was able to live on the dark side. I always felt I was not that person. I was not open enough, daring enough, or brave enough. I wasn't quite an angel, but I sure did not carry a pitch fork. I began to walk away from the light.

I was on the edge I knew this was not me, but it was me for now. I did not want to keep thinking about what I wanted being that I was unable to get it. I believed there would come a day when all would be well. I was just unsure of when that would actually be. I never had a plan or any kind of outlook on the future. I was in much pain, very broken, and extremely lost.

I was not trying to hear reason, what I needed to do, or where I needed to be. I had to carry the weight of my emotions minute to minute. I needed to be concerned with making it to the next day. I would wake up in a daze not knowing what the day would bring. I was comfortable around my new environment yet looked for the familiarity of my old one.

I kept feeling like I would get an answer soon. Somehow all this would be explained to me and life would be an awaited normal. The more I waited, the longer the days. I had to choose a side. I could not wait in the light without wanting to drain my anticipation with the darkness. I could not bear the pain of wanting any more.

Staying numb was very helpful. I did not have to feel or think about anything but that moment. That moment would last for years.

Although I was in unfamiliar territory, I was enjoying the newness of it all. I was seeing, hearing, and experiencing things I would have never fathomed. I only gave it thought briefly about what I was engaged in. I had fell so far into a pattern I was unnoticeable. I chalked it up as my life was this now and that was that. What else could I do?

It is interesting how when you think something about yourself, it actually plays itself out. I did not feel I was worth much, so I treated myself as such. I wanted so much more for myself, but felt so ruined I did not know how to rebuild. I was not quite sure if I even wanted to put forth that kind of effort any more.

Staying high, drunk, or laid up was taking up plenty of time. I had no real concerns and did not have to do anything but participate. I got to travel, meet some interesting people, and had total freedom from reality. Not having to worry about anything became very refreshing.

The individuals I was around were not always the safest, but I felt much protection. I was in some dangerous situations, yet was not afraid. They were not college graduates, but left me with a lot to think about. They did not always work, but we had everything we needed and some. Everyone stuck together, looked out for each other, and they made sure I was always alright.

Some things I saw were alarming but I always just understood. I do not know if I got used to my surroundings or just paid it no mind, but I did not see it as being the dark side any more.

I was already able to sustain a lot because of my past, but living life with no direction made me a bit bold. The once timid and quiet young woman became very witty and out spoken. I developed a backbone with a very cocky frame. I still had a calming spirit, but would bite if you toyed with me. My weakened demeanor was strengthened.

Gaining a sense of self, gave me a desire to want again. Doing whatever, however, whenever suddenly needed a schedule.

I still did not know what to do, but I knew I wanted something now. The search was on. Now that I was able to stand up straight again, it was time to look ahead. But where? I began to change the kind of individuals I was around, the things I did, and the way I dressed. I changed everything but my attitude.

My look changed, my conversation changed, but went back to my floating devices. I was in too deep of waters I thought. I felt the current changing but did not know how to ride with it. I had a broken spirit with a south paw defense that was attempting to mingle with high society.

As long as I had a desire, I began to feel a sense of hope I once had. I had an understanding that I needed to change my thought process. I had to confront those very things that I allowed to hold me down for years. It was not the drinking, smoking, or sex that held me back. It was the way I was thinking about myself. I felt I was unable because of my circumstances.

I was told by someone that I needed to forgive in order for me to move forward. I said, "I need to do what now?" It always seemed like it was something I had to put up with in my life.

But I had come to a point in my life where I had to do something because no one else could do this for me. As painful as it was going to be, I had to do it.

I also had to stand up to the hurt, pain, brokenness, anger, disappointment, shame, disgrace, regret, loneliness, frustration, and doubt. What now? God is now. As soon as I was willing and stopped running from the confrontation with myself, God stepped in. It was as if He said, "GO AHEAD KRISTINE, I KNOW IT HURTS BUT I WILL BE RIGHT HERE TO GET YOU THROUGH IT."

I knew I had a lot in me that was just too much for me to handle by myself. I felt it all . . . and then He removed it.

The very things that hurt me, I had to feel. I had not seen those feelings in a long time due to the years of coverage. But I was not that scared young woman any more. God had been shaping and molding me by the abuse of the past, the rawness of the world, and the courage of surviving. Each moment was a question to my character, but developed it all the same.

It was not as difficult as it used to be because what I desired became greater than the hurt. When God took the pain after I confronted it, He also left me with understanding. I was not angry at the situations, the people, or what I did not have. My focus became "what now" in a new way.

The more I grew closer to God, the more He would reveal to me. Although I made some crazy choices during this wandering time, God used each step for my good. I was a hurt little girl initially that was transformed into a healed, extraordinary, mature woman. The realness of the individuals that were sent to nurture me through my process could not have been any better. While strengthening me, it also allowed me to see others in a way I never had. I realized that we are all the same no matter what our circumstances are. Pain is hurtful to anyone. It just shows up differently on people.

What do I do with the knowledge I have gained was how I viewed things that were behind and in front of me.

God opened my eyes to more pain than myself. I saw pain through everyone I was around. "What now" was many people's question that they answered in their own way.

God gave me insight through their circumstances while I was struggling with myself. It was almost to say, "NOW THAT YOU HAVE SEEN THESE THINGS, WHAT NOW ARE YOU GOING TO DO ABOUT IT?"

I now believe that while we are wondering what to do, we are actually already doing it. Because I am able to feel my pain, I can relate to someone else's. The more I stayed away from dealing with my feelings, the more I was unable to see people for who they really were. God made me realize it was not about what I was going through, it was the wandering that enabled me to see what others were going through in the worst ways.

I am able to walk through those unknown times because God has an answer waiting for me in the end. I do not have to know what is going on exactly, but I know exactly who does.

THE INVITATION
Chapter Twelve

SCRIPTURE

Psalm 22:19
But you, Lord, do not be far from me. You are my strength; come quickly to help me.

I had been with a friend I met while living with my girlfriend for a few months. I moved in with him and was fairly enjoying it. I was not accomplishing anything but existing. I appreciated him greatly for lifting my spirits and making me feel wanted again. After leaving my husband and taking my children back to him, I felt very broken. This man gave me a sense of life again and I adored him for that. His invite to be with him was a huge boost for me, but I began to want more.

I was still unsure about how to move forward. I did not want to just get any job anywhere. Because I was totally dependent, I was unable to get around by myself. I did not drive. I really did not have much going on for myself except 1390 cosmetology hours which at the time did not mean much. I was becoming a housewife again. I did not mind taking care of him in a domestic way, but I just left this type of situation; there just wasn't any physical abuse.

I would call my mother periodically just to stay in touch. I was still upset with her for not allowing me and my children to stay with her, but wanted a point of contact. I would let her know how I was and what was going on; which was much of nothing. She apparently had been speaking with my oldest brother. He lived down south and I had not spoken to him in quite a while. We are the kind of siblings that even when a duration of time goes by without communication, we will pick up where we left off with no problem. There were no direct judgments nor criticism.

I spoke with my mother one day and she told me my brother wanted me to call him. As always, it was hey what's up? He said, "You should come down here with me." My mouth dropped and my heart melted. I instantly became excited. I knew right away that this was a fresh start. I was getting used to the idea of not having my family any more. Going to a new place would be just the thing; not to mention I would be with my big brother who I admired. I had been invited to live with him. We discussed the details and the invite had been accepted.

I told my friend and he was happy for me, but sad at the same time. It actually was perfect timing because there had been a discussion in the house with his roommate that I should leave. I had been affecting their "bachelor" living situation. I did not like the fact that I was being asked to leave, but being my brother has invited me to be with him, it really did not matter anymore.

My friend had gotten used to me being there. I had fell into a routine of cooking for him. If I knew he was coming home for lunch I would fix him a little snack. When he got home, I had dinner waiting for him. I guess it was a little satisfying to him to suddenly have these things after living alone for so long. It is a lot different from having company to having a live-in girlfriend. I enjoyed myself greatly, but felt the necessary changes had to take place.

I had gone from a housewife and mother to homeless living with friends. I was invited to stay with my girlfriend when I first left my husband. I received another invite from my friend to be with him. New doors were opening for me that I had no clue were even there. Here I was getting ready to walk through another.

Living with my friend at this time seemed to be an answer for me. I was unsure how it would all pan out. I did not see any direction and felt I had to stick it out as long as I could. He liked me and I liked him, so why not? I had nowhere else to go at the time and it appeared to be a step up from my girlfriend's house. Maybe that was the man I would be with. All I knew is I was taken care of, safe, and had some fun.

I was glad about my brother wanting me with him, but began to wonder. What would I do? I do not know this place or any people at all. At least where I was I had my friend and then his friends and family. There with my brother it would just be us. I had never been without a man before. I did not want to be alone. I did not want to leave my friend, my comfort, my floating device.

My excitement turned to fear in no time flat. I wanted something more, but it now was staring me in the face. I was getting used to making the choices. Although this was a choice also, it felt more like a command. I had wanted something very strongly, and here it was for me. It came from the heart. Just as things in my past when I wanted it, it came. This was one of those moments that I just knew it, but I was scared. I desired it greatly but did not seek it out, it came to me.

My brother who I adored invited me to be with him and I was afraid.

I tried to hang on to where I was. The date was set for when I would leave, but I tried to think of excuses why I could not. As the days got closer, the more afraid I became. The unknown became frightening. I had three changes in the past four months and was not anticipating another. My life had become a whirlwind. I did not know where I was or where I would be next.

I could feel myself latching on to my friend tighter and tighter. He became familiar to me. He brought me so far from where I was since we had met. Who would treat me like this now? I had found something soothing and I had to let it go. As difficult as it was to think about, I knew deep inside I really wanted to.

My brother wanting me with him was a shock to me. We had not been in the same house since he went off to college. I cried like a baby when he left then. I knew we would be fine, but my mind was shooting dice . . . crapping out every time. All these negative thoughts began to flow that we would not like each other now and I could not do what I wanted to do. I had gotten used to my freedom and did not want anybody instructing me on my behavior.

The "what if" game was next. I came up with so many scenarios that I almost changed my mind. My friend let me know I was being silly and popped all those crazy bubble thoughts. The invitation was still accepted.

I had been trying to get all my fun out of the way because I knew I would not be able to be entertained the way I had been since I would not know anybody. Because of my nerves, I believe I started drinking just a little bit more.

I had been informed that there was a party that was going to take place at the house. I was fine with that, as long as I had what I needed upstairs with me. I soon found out that it was going to be strippers there. I felt some kind of way at first, but soon was relieved because I would soon be leaving. I quickly saw how it was necessary for me to move on. Reason had showed up and gave me conformation and put an end to my negative thinking about leaving.

Positive thoughts began to fill my head and possibilities were on the horizon. I did not know what I would be doing or how I would be doing it, but it did not matter. I was happy about the opportunity to do so.

I began to look at where I was and how I got there. I had been asked to go many places since I left my husband. Some good and some not so good, nevertheless it was an invite. I did not have to accept them all but I did. In doing so, I had been taken care of, protected, and nurtured in the way I needed at the time.

Preparing to leave became fulfilling. The date came to pass and my friend drove me down to my brother's place. New place, new mind set, new beginning. I was further away from my children but figured it was better than being close. It would be easier for me to get myself together and then visit when I could. Out of site out of mind . . . for now.

I now lived in a very nice city in the downtown area. Tall buildings all around, walking distance of the football stadium, and access to everything. We lived in a brick low-rise building with lofts. It was a totally new vibe that had a classy feel to it. I looked at my brother and smiled . . . I am home!

With everything being in walking distance, I was able to get around and explore just fine. The curiosity of my new surroundings took away all the insecurities and I was ready. My brother insisted I go to the mall to seek out employment. I thought that was perfect. I would get a position in one of the stores and meet many people. All would be well.

I began working a couple of days after arriving. I was offered an administrative assistant position at a popular photography studio. It was just data entry, but I was ecstatic. I was the first person a customer would see when entering the store, the one who entered the data, and the one who made the transactions. I opened and closed, counted the money in the evening, and managed the store when the manager was not there. After having nothing for so long, I was given so much responsibility and I had just arrived. I was so glad I accepted my brother's invite.

There were many invites that came my way after leaving my husband that I did not accept. I desired deeply for help when I did not know what I was going to do. God allowed three invites to come my way at the opportune time. Regardless of what went on, once I opened the door, I was invited.

God provided a place for me within the choices I made. He made sure I was protected, comfortable, and in place for the next change. I had no clue I was being carried at that time. I did feel as if I were floating, but for other reasons.

There is a lot put into an invitation. The thought and that you are wanted to come is the biggest to me. God put on each of these individual's heart to care for me during this time in my life. He invited them into my life and I into theirs.

There was an invitation of love as well. He offered me something I asked for from within. I did not get on my knees and pray. I felt it through every bit of my being. It was embedded in my heart. When I was a little girl I accepted God into my life. Throughout everything I come up against, He is going to be there as soon as I receive Him again and again. When I am not even looking for Him, He will be there. I invited God into my life and without me giving it a second thought, He always invites me to be with Him. God's hand is always extended . . . the best invitation ever!

IN THE WORLD
Chapter Thirteen

Psalm 55:19

*God, who is enthroned from of old, who does not change -
he will hear them and humble them, because they have no
fear of God.*

The position at the photography studio was coming along well. I had fell into a routine and began feeling worthy again. I worked with a great set of people which made the day run smoothly. The staff consisted of a make-up artist and a photographer. Depending on the schedule the two of them would come in at specific times.

At lunch time I would usually walk around near the store watching the people move about in the mall. The photographer asked me one day what I was going to eat and invited me to go with him. I saw no harm and went with him. It appeared very innocent since we worked together. I did not have any intentions on my mind and actually never even looked at him in a romantic kind of way. He was very attractive . . . bald head, mustache with a trimmed go-tee, a physically fit body, and walked with a hint of a penguin toe . . . but I wasn't looking!

We began talking more and laughing more at work. We did not hang out afterward or call each other. It was pretty nice to have friend and not much more. I have to admit; I did look forward to coming to work. My focus began to shift, but not too much. I still loved my job; I just had another reason to enjoy it.

The manager of the store was acting very strange one day. He was a bit peculiar anyway, but this day was a little more unusual. All the employees noticed and we chatted about it for a while and thought no more of it. Closing time came and I was preparing the evening as usual. The gates to the stores in the mall go down at a specific time. I brought the gate down and then realized it was too soon, so I pushed it right back up. I closed out my register and by that time the gate was able to come down. I locked up and headed out as usual.

The next day the manager was in the studio a little earlier than normal. He stated he needed to talk with me, and immediately I knew it was about the night before. He informed me that the store was fined because I brought the gate down. I was very shocked being it was a split second before I pushed it back up. He said he understood, but had to let me go. I stood there in amazement. "Fired! I put it right back up. Isn't there someone I can speak with?" He said he tried and that was the conclusion. That was my last day. I had been there all of 3 months and was fired for a very quick mistake. I was furious and hurt at the same time. I went to the back of the studio to inform everyone and was heading out. I exchanged numbers with the photographer at that time and sadly went home.

A few days later my friend from the studio called me and wanted to meet up. I had been thinking of him along with the studio so it would be nice to see him and catch up. "The store is closing!" he said. My mouth dropped open. "He is on drugs, and they fired him. Now everybody has lost their job. He did you a favor." That is why he had been acting so strange that day. He said there were also some money issues, but with the drop-offs not within the store. I felt better about being fired, but still was saddened because I thought this was going to be something that lasted a while.

The job might have ended but my friend and I started hanging out more and more. He would hang out with my brother and me at the house, we would go out to eat, or just walk around town. It was refreshing again to have a close friend. There was nothing intimate, yet, but was still very nice. He was a very creative person as well. He sang, drew, and was outgoing just like me. I lost my job but gained a friend.

Although he was cool to be around, what was I going to do now?

I felt like I was on a roller coaster by this time. I had found a job instantly and was enjoying and doing well and all of a sudden another change. I just did not understand it. What was happening with my life? It seemed to be going further and further to the left.

My esteem was beginning to go up, but this circumstance brought it back down again. I was having such a difficult time understanding. My brother was working a lot, so I really had to deal with this on my own. He said I would be just fine, but I did not see it. Nothing was working out for me. The harder I tried, the worse things got.

My friend and I still hung out, but he could see that I was a bit depressed. He would have me with him a lot. Wherever he went, I went. So, I never was alone, he kept me near him. He did not have a lot of friends, just one who worked at the mall in a cafeteria. He was really funny, but I could sense something about him. He was my friend's friend so all was well. We all began hanging out more and more.

I finally spent the night at his place.

Spending the night with him felt very different. He was very caring and very gentle. He provided everything and made sure I had what I needed. That may sound simple, but it was something very different for me. He was not real aggressive and kept making sure I was alright. I glanced over at a little table and saw a Bible with paper sticking out of it. I knew there was something different with him.

He became a part of each and every one of my days. This relationship was unlike any other because it was not sexual. We did have sex, but not very often. He was more interested in me getting out and enjoying life rather than concentrating on what was not right with it. He did not have a lot of money, nor did he drive. We walked or caught the bus everywhere. That was interesting as well. I did not see it as a negative thing toward him because he was opening my eyes to new experiences. I was actually enjoying the adventure of roughing it.

He was showing me a new side of life. We sat in the park, his back to my back, and we sang. We ate out every day, all day. We shopped at thrift stores. We were out every day from the morning to the night. I became very attached to him.

One day he asked me if I smoked. Mary Jane was back.

Although Mary Jane returned, I did not feel any threat. I gave it a pass because we were so calm with it. It did not feel like an escape, it felt more like recreation. We began our day with it, traveled throughout with it, and went to sleep to it.

We had a routine going. We would meet up, go and get the trees, get some beer, and chill somewhere for a while. From there, go and get something to eat and then walk around sightseeing. It did not matter where we were going or what we were doing. I was just enjoying the freeness of it all. Doing so much of nothing. I was still bummed about losing my job and the new direction I thought I was going in, but did not care about the route I was on now. I was safe, with a beautiful man, and living a carefree life.

He would read his Bible at the end of the night and then we would listen to music and talk. I was not reading anything, but felt a sense of peace because he was. He did not know much about my past, so I decided to fill him in.

We would walk and talk, sit and talk, smoke and talk, and drink and talk. When I finally got it out, he just looked at me and said he could tell. I felt like he was my protector at the time. God sent me a true friend who did not want anything from me. What a change of pace.

I never had someone want to know so much about my life. He would encourage me to go visit my children. He would tell me how smart I was and what I was capable of doing. He could recognize the hurt in me, but did not take advantage of that. This was the first man I had been around that did not want a thing for me except for me to be happy. He would take up for me when someone was appearing disrespectful. He would acknowledge me around his friends in every way. He made me a part of things in a positive light. He was giving me something I never had and I was grateful.

Although I did not read the Bible, he did. He was getting the Word daily and in turn was able to minister to me in a positive way. He had issues too, but did not express them to me. It was all about me. God began to show me through him that everyone is not the same. God showed me through him that it is not about expensive things. God showed me through him the simplicity of life. God also showed me through him that every man does not take advantage of a broken woman. God began introducing himself to me personally through him.

God has, of course, been in my life all along. When I was younger I accepted the Lord into my life and was baptized and felt I have been covered from that day on. I allowed the awful things that transpired in my life to doubt the presence of God in my life. I still was not fully aware of Him or all that it meant to be saved, yet saw a glimpse from my view at this time in my life through my new friend.

Being away from what I knew as my world and having a dent in the start of my new world was startling initially. I believe God allowed me to meet my new friend at a place I was very comfortable just so I would have a cushion when it all fell through. Things were not going as I planned, but I was not so sad. I had not one clue what my future held. All I knew is I was with my brother safe and sound, had a new friend that was having a positive impact on me, and I was finding myself.

What would I do without God's love for me even while I am wandering freely in the world?

TRYING TO COPE
Chapter Fourteen

SCRIPTURE

Proverbs 1:8-10

Listen, my son, to your father's instruction and do not forsake your mother's teaching. They are garland to grace your head and a chain to adorn your neck. My son, if sinful men entice you, do not give in to them.

Living with my brother was encouraging in ways. He was striving for so much in his career field and that was impressive to see. He was very dedicated and had a passion for what he was doing. There are so many individuals who complain about work, so to see his work ethic was a positive force. I was still feeling a bit salty about losing my job, but enjoying each day to my fullest.

I was enjoying my friend, but began to think about my children quite often. Although I was out and about every day, I had a lot of time to think. I would wonder how they were, what they were doing, and how fast they were growing. I was missing everything. I wanted to be able to provide for them and now I did not even have a job. I was not able to contribute a dime. It only seemed to put a chip on my shoulder because it sure did not make me run out and look for another job. I felt warn out from trying and being let down. I had a plan and it fell through . . . again.

Continuing to smoke and drink, my friend introduced me to two homosexual friends he had. I immediately thought that was very strange, but then thought nothing of it. They were very sweet and very nice. They shared a condo uptown that was very cute. I could tell they had very good taste by scoping their place. Everything was immaculate from the furniture to the dishes. Neat, clean, and respectable flavor. I could not be upset with that.

We headed toward the back room where I could smell "Mary Jane." It was on and popping now. One of them did not smoke; he worked at the hospital. So when we began, he excused himself and we prepared for a smoke out. I noticed they were very hospitable and supplied everything. I instantly noticed the reasoning of this friendship . . . somewhat.

During the smoke-fest it was mentioned that my friend wanted to use the car to take me cruising around town being that we walked and caught the bus everywhere. He did not mind at all. As a matter of fact, he had insisted that my friend ask whenever he pleased because I was too pretty to be walking. I liked him even more after that comment.

So we were cruising all over the city. I had finally gotten a chance to see the city in a broader sense. It was actually pretty large. I started to see possibilities for me. The afternoon turned to early evening and we were riding down this one particular road that had strip clubs about every ten blocks. I had stated I had never been in one.

We stopped at a strip club and went inside. "So what's your name sweetie, you know its amateur night tonight?" The lady at the desk was waiting for me to give her a name. I looked back at my friend and said, "Oh NO, I am not dancing! I am watching"! He said, "Ok, but her name is BAMBI." The lady jotted it down and said, "Okay we'll see sweetie. Let's get y'all a table." I thought to myself, what in the world am I doing in here. My curiosity kept my feet walking inside without hesitation. My children were no longer on my mind. I was captured by inquisitiveness.

A waitress came over and said, "What would y'all like to drink; it's on the house"? My friend and I looked at each other and placed our order. I was out of my comfort zone, but did not feel scared. It was something I had never seen before. I was so green at this time; I was just so amazed. I had entered a whole new world.

After two shots of Jack Daniels straight with no ice, the lady from the front desk asked me again about being in the amateur contest. As we looked around I noticed we were the only African American individuals in this establishment. I could not believe it, but I was actually considering it. I told her one more drink and I would do it. My friend said he was all for it if I wanted to. I became very nervous and excited at the same time. I never dreamed of this. I always had bias toward people who did this kind of stuff and now here I am contemplating participating in a contest I know nothing about. I did not even have anything to wear.

I had on a jean jumper, a jean shirt, and my timberland boots. How in the world was I going to strip with no strip clothes? Next thing I know I am headed down some steps and one of the dancers was handing me a thong in a fresh sealed baggie. It was too unreal the way this was unfolding. Nevertheless, I continued on.

I was second to go on the stage. Feeling bold, I looked out on the stage as the first girl was dancing and that had my adrenalin going. It was soon to be my turn on the stage. That girl came off the stage and looked at me saying, "Go get 'em!" The music started and I stepped out on beat. I had my shirt unbuttoned to the fourth button, with a thong, and my timberland boots on! I strutted my sexy self out there and began dancing as if I were alone in my room. I could not believe I was out there on that stage in front of people I did not know grinding my hips, and shaking my tale. I was having a ball. On the second song my top had to come off. Liquid courage helped a lot because I just whipped it off like it was nothing. Dancing around in a yellow and white stripped thong with my timberland boots on was incredible. The customers seemed to really enjoy it. They were coming up and throwing money all over the stage. A few of them even put some money in my thong. I had never felt this feeling before. Frightened but excited at the same time was my new high. I had a ball!

By the end of the night I had entered another world. Counting my money, my friend and I laughed in amazement at what just transpired. We could not believe I came in second place. Making $100+ in about 7 minutes was incredible to me. I found a new way to cope with everything.

We had to brag to everyone about my new adventure. They could not believe my shy and timid nature went on somebody's stage, took off my clothes, and danced around sexually. I told them I was equally amazed, but enjoyed it thoroughly.

I had stepped way out of my comfort zone and was overjoyed about it. I had so much fun doing it. I did not think about anything or anyone while I was up there. I was in my own little world. I felt in total control. People were staring at me, liking what they saw, and giving me money. That was a power I never knew and was glad to have.

My friend and I talked about me dancing all the time. I was fascinated with the thought of receiving so much money at one time. That was for a few minutes; imagine all night. I would be able to do so much and could now help out with my children. It seemed to be a very good plan. We sought out a club and sat in the back of the club for a week watching the scenery.

I was scoping out the place seeing how things worked. I paid close attention to how the women were interacting with the men and vice versa. I watched how they danced on stage as well as giving table dances or lap dances as they are generally called. The girls appeared to be very friendly with one another and were having a good time. I knew there was probably more to it being so many women in one place, but felt I was strong enough to deal. Besides, it was not about anything else other than making money for myself and to contribute to my children's needs because I was not with them.

I did not see the dark side of becoming a part of this lifestyle. I did not know what it entailed and it did not matter. I was my own person and never followed the crowd. I drank and smoked "Mary Jane" and that was sufficient. I made my own choices and this gave me a sense of control. I called my own shots, set my own time, and decided how I would do things. All would be well. My friend would be with me every night looking out for me. I would learn to cope with my new surroundings.

I began to make a lot of money. I was able to do many things whenever I pleased. The choices within our lives were broader which appeared better. We were able to do just what we'd been doing, yet could do it better now. Eating at better places, buying more clothes, better liquor, and purchasing bigger sacks of "Mary Jane." I was able.

I called home and informed my mother what I was now doing. She did not necessarily like it, but could do nothing about it. She wanted me to be careful and be safe. I told her all about it and would see her soon. I was able to visit often and could bring gifts and drop off money. That felt so empowering.

I was able to do things I always dreamed of doing. With money being no option, life seemed so much easier.

Being able to give my children just what they asked for was joyous for me, but of course their father had a problem with it. What was wrong with me buying them what they wanted? It was Christmas and he was upset because I gave them just what they asked for. I knew it was something else in that so I did not let that bother me. I was able and he did not like it. He used to have control but not anymore. He hated it, but I loved it. I did not care that he knew I danced. I had the power now!

I thought being able to see my children often and buying them what they wanted would help the situation and alleviate some tension. It only got worse. He got to the point where when I came, I could not see them. One time I had brought a bag of clothes, and he would not let me see them nor would he accept the clothes I brought. He claimed he did not like where I got them from. If I bought my clothes from the thrift stores, what was wrong with them wearing them? They were very nice clothes that were clean. I could buy twice as many clothes as I would buy from the mall. If it was good enough for me, it was definitely good enough for my young sons that went through clothes like there was no tomorrow.

He was unable to cope with me being able. It had nothing to do with where the stuff came from. Money did not assist with me seeing my children. Not being able to bear the continuous rejection, I quit traveling to see them. My plan was not working.

Not being able to see my children really threw me for a loop. I had anticipated a major change of action being that I was making money and was able to provide more for them. I began filing that void with more smoking and drinking. I was now truly on my own and had no concerns whatsoever.

I was working at the club seven days a week from 9:00pm to 2:00am. I was the first one there and at times the last one to leave. I was making pretty good money and was able to do just about anything I wanted. I would give my brother money, not that he needed it, and buy whatever I could to help out. He was not all in my business and allowed me to do as I pleased. I loved him even more for that. I loved being there with him, but since I was able, I would rent a room from time to time for my friend and me.

My friend was not working so I took care of both of us. I did not mind at all because he was looking out for me and was at my side constantly. I needed that in my life at the time. He kept me strong and continued to encourage me to lift my head up and realize my potential despite my circumstances. Again, I could see the God in him, but would not embrace it fully because of the pain I was carrying. I was very grateful for everything he was doing for me and appreciated him very much. He took care of me and I took care of him.

I eventually got a room for us that rented out weekly. I would still visit my brother all the time, but was venturing out on my own. We had plenty of smoke, drinks, and everything else we needed. I was also able to fly my friend home from time to time when he wanted to go. I was not wanting for anything at the time except my children, but I was learning to cope.

I had fallen into a new world of desires. I had no idea what was ahead of me but was very excited about it nevertheless. I had no fear and felt protected always. God allowed this man to be in my life because of the road ahead of me. God knew I would go down this path and made sure I had the perfect person there for me at the time.

Although we were engaging in ungodly activity, God still had us covered. I needed him just as he needed me. Despite my choices, God knew my heart. I believe this is why I felt no fear, no doubt, and had no worries. I felt I was in control, but ultimately God was. He allowed me to have a shield of protection, a calming spirit, and a giving heart regardless of what was happening in my life. God knew I was broken and sent this man in my life to help rebuild my person.

Using the choices, God made them work for me. We did not argue, fuss, nor fight. We were there for each other 100%. God allowed me to see there was light. He provided me with a flashlight through this wandering stage in my new life of darkness.

I had stepped into an unknown zone in which I had no fear. It was not forced by anyone and did not feel wrong. I knew it was not a popular decision, but it was my decision at the time. It was liberating, strengthening, and built my self-confidence. God allows those things that are frowned upon to work for our good. He knew just what I needed to do in order to get to where He wanted me to be.

God made sure I had someone to go through this with. I did not go outside of my limits when it came to the dancing. I remained who I was and did not have to go further than that. I was committed to my friend and him to me. Our actions may have been incorrect, but our intentions were very much right. God knew our hearts at this time and allowed our path to be smooth.

My friend continued to read his Bible every night. God was not on my mind, but I was on His. My life at that time could have gone a lot different had I chosen someone else to cope with. Meeting him at the studio was God's plan. He was not just any man; he was a man seeking God daily. He too was trying cope, and sought out God to do so.

NIGHT LIFE
Chapter Fifteen

SCRIPTURE

Exodus 23:8

*"Do not except a bribe, for a bribe blinds those who see
and twists the words of the innocent. . ."*

I had now been in the club for almost six months and was pretty well known as "Bambi." My friend had given me that name when he had taken a picture of me while in the studio. He said that I had eyes like the deer Bambi. It became official when I did the amateur contest and came in second. Bambi was now a part of a popular club in a growing southern city.

The club was two levels with a circular stage. It was very roomy and held many people a night. I was very accustomed to the routine and the customers that came in. From time to time there were famous people that came through to patronize the establishment and its activities. I was never one to be star struck, so to me they were just more money coming through. There was nothing special about them while they were sitting in those chairs. "Want another dance", is what I would say to them. I could care less about the rest.

My birthday was coming up and I wanted to do something different. The girls in the club would all celebrate their birthdays in the club with some sort of party. I was not interested in a party, but wanted it to be known it was my birthday. I had accumulated a few friends while working at the club that I had become a little familiar with. One of the guys I knew came in with something around him that I wanted to use on my birthday night on stage.

He hinted that he had an interest in me but that was not an option being I had a friend, yet was very intriguing and I flirted a bit. Was he doing this favor for me only because of alterative motives? I brushed it off and proceeded to hook up the stage event. I invited some of the people my friend and I knew. I even told my brother about it, but did not think he would come . . . which was totally understandable.

My birthday night came and so did the excitement. Everyone was curious as to what I was going to do. Lights went dim, music came on, and I came out with a snake around my neck. It was a humungous albino python wrapped around my body from my neck to my legs. I was not a huge fan of snakes, yet had no fear. The guy was on the stage with me to make sure all went well. It was pretty alluring and a bit sexy. It moved with my every move. At one point in the act I stuck my tongue out at it and on cue it did the same. I got on the floor with it and rolled around with it. That had to be the highlight of my year. Everyone applauded and threw plenty of money. Happy twenty-sixth birthday to me!

My friend usually stayed until I left at closing but began leaving earlier which was alright because I would catch a ride with one of the security guards. We had been around for a bit so people were familiar with us and vice versa.

This night the guy who allowed me to dance with his snake stayed later than usual and was there at closing time. We were discussing the events of the night and he offered to take me home. I did not think it was such a good idea at first, but then thought my friend knew of him because of the snake so it would not be so bad. I accepted.

I always drank and was a bit buzzed by the time I left the club so when we pulled up to our room, I was giggling. My friend was standing outside waiting for me, and when I saw him my stomach went up to my chest and back down. I thanked the guy for bringing me home and proceeded to get out and head up the steps. I saw the look my friend's face and it wasn't good. I said hello and he just stared at me and asked, "Who is that", as he watched the car leave. I informed him that it was the snake guy. He was not happy at all that I allowed him to bring me home.

My intuition that I was feeling earlier was correct. I knew instantly I had messed up.

It became tense between my friend and I since that guy dropped me off. My friend said he wanted to fly home to visit, so I sent him. It was very different without him being around. I began to appreciate him again rather than the extra attention I had started getting. I had never been in a position where so many men were interested in me. I knew it had to do with the sexual desire I influenced at the club, yet was still flattering to receive so much attention. It led me to think differently of myself and my capabilities.

I began to look at my friend sideways at times because of what he was not able to do for me. Being around these other men in the club that were pretty stable in their careers kept me guessing about what was possible with someone other than who I was with. I did not sleep with another man, but the thoughts were there.

My heart was not fixated on my friend any more. I was getting caught up in the fantasy of the club. There was such a variety of men to choose from that were at my fingertips. They wanted me and I was excited about it. I started thinking I deserve more than what I have.

My friend no longer wanted to come to the club at all. I believe that is when my attitude began to change. I knew we felt comfortable about the club, but I felt in a way that he was not looking out for me anymore. My protection was not there, so he did not care. As soon as he faded, everyone else wanted to step up and take his place. He left me in the dark.

I was feeling alone again. My friend was not a part of my life as he once was. I was fine when he was right by my side, but as soon as he was not there, I felt lost. I was realizing I was not strong on my own. He meant more to me than just being my man. I actually needed him. I was a sheep wandering around with wolves and I could not take it.

It seemed the further apart we got, the more men would try and be with me. I wanted a closeness, but already had something with someone. I could see that they just wanted sex, so it was not that enticing. My friend and I were not having sex and this is what was pulling me toward the others. I felt unwanted by him.

I believe my friend knew my struggle but would just wait and see what I was going to do. He left me alone more and more. I could not help but to think about the time I allowed that guy to bring me home. I thought it was innocent, but soon realized it had much more power than I knew. The same way this night life was affecting me, it was affecting him as well. It was not just me needing him, he needed me too.

There became more and more flirting in the club. I knew I could not cross any lines, but was enjoying being on the edge. Something was missing from my life and I had to fill it somehow. My flashlight was gone and I needed something to light my way.

Although I was loving the attention from those at that club, I was missing my friend very much. What we had, these people could not give me. He knew me from the inside and I began to miss that. I regretted wanting anything from them other than their money. As soon as my desire turned to them, my friend turned from me.

I would work and come home like a robot. I was strictly work and that was it. I was not my playful self which in turn began to affect my money. I was unsure what to do. I did not want to lose my friend because I felt I needed him. What I became used to at the club was changing and I did not like that. I was accustomed to making a specific amount of money and it had dropped significantly. Here I am taking care of both of us, and making less. Something had to give.

I allowed the stress of money to draw a wedge between us. I wanted more but he was content where he was. He wanted me to be comfortable with where I was and enjoy it. I was not satisfied. What once was so easy became very complicated. The ease of our relationship had changed drastically. It went from men to money very quickly. I was not happy about anything anymore.

To keep the relationship on track I had to withdraw from the club. If I wanted more in my life, I had to make more money. I thought being with someone was important, but money became more important. I had to become a full fledge night lifer or I would not get what I wanted. My desire turned back to the club and we faded.

I knew I had to do what felt right. I felt compelled to let go of the grip I had on him and stand on my own. I had become very dependent on him in ways I should have depended on God. I still did not acknowledge God, but He was still creating a path for me.

I recognized what my friend had meant to me and did for me. Once I gained enough strength and confidence, it was time to move forward. It was not about another man; it was just the feeling of security with a man being there. I had not been alone and did not care to be, yet had to take a step. We remained friends. It was more for support. I did not see him for a while.

I had moved back home with my brother and was thinking about a place of my own. The "sweet" friend that I met who let my friend use his car told me about a vacant condo where he lived. It was a two bedroom with a den right underneath him. God allowed me meet this friend through my friend because that condo would soon be my home. I never would have known it when I met him months ago that we would soon be not only neighbors, but become very good friends.

I spoke to the landlord and told him exactly what I did for a living. He knew I was a friend of someone that lived there and trusted his word and now was trusting mine. The day after I saw the condo, I moved in. My night life afforded me to sign my first leased place of my own which was an uptown condo.

I appreciated, very much, all that my friend did for me. It does get confusing when my initial plan began to change even when I thought I wanted something so bad. I had come to realize that God allowed me to have what is necessary at that given time. I will always be protected for the duration of time He allows it for His ultimate plan.

When I initially met my friend, it was about having a close friend. It then turned into him helping me develop into a stronger individual. Because of that which was given from him, I did not want to let it go. I felt I needed him when in fact, he had already done what God assigned him to do. At the designed time God allowed these other temptations to come into my heart to lure me away from where I was. He allowed my desires to change just enough to go into the direction He would have me to go.

I was very curious as to why my friend knew this homosexual man, yet never thinking he would be a key person in my life to come. I was not dancing when I first met him. God knew I would be running into him very soon and set up our whole meeting.

I was believing my friend to be my flashlight, when God had already enlightened my night life.

UNCOVERING MYSELF
Chapter Sixteen

2 Timothy 1:7
For the spirit God gave us does not make us timid, but gives us power, love, and self-discipline.

From my first time on stage during the amateur contest I felt comfort. It was very strange, yet very daring. I had never been so open before. Even with a man sexually, I was not as open as I was dancing. It was something freeing about it that made me feel empowered. I did not think about my body, who was looking, or what they thought. I was totally caught up in the moment. I could feel each beat of a song as it cascaded down my every swerving curve. Gliding around the pole as if it were leading me in the dance. I would get lost in the words to the song and begin to act them out within the rhythm running through my body. Music was my first love and I had found it again in another fashion.

The shyness I once had was gone once I let the melody soak in my soul. I became alive and sensual. It was not an act; it came very natural. I laughed at myself at times when I caught my reflection in the mirror. "I see you girl", I would say as my hips swayed. When I was not thinking about it, this was very relaxing and extremely comfortable.

To think about it, I could not imagine myself sitting at a table talking with someone with next to nothing on. I really paid it no mind. I was very at ease in my skin and would get lost in the conversation rather than the sexual vibe that was escaping from my being. The song would come on, they said dance, and I would get lost until the last beat ended.

When I did not think about it, I was able to be me. It was not a character or an act. It was me 100%. A portion of me was being unleashed using my first love.

When I stopped letting go and tried to take control is when I felt uncovered.

When I began dancing, I did not set out to make a specific amount of money. I went in with a carefree attitude and would be happy with whatever I made. I was not concerned with how many people were there, who came in the club, or how acceptable my body was. No concerns and no thought process. I just danced. Coming in with this kind of attitude kept me level headed and very calm. I did not add any stress by being concerned with minute things. Yes, money mattered, but I was not going to worry about it. I always felt that I would be just fine, and I was.

I would notice the other females in the club talking about me. Whether it was good or bad that really did not bother me. This sure would not be the first time individuals would have something to say about me. I would think to myself, "I must be doing something right." I am making money and not having to do anything extra for it. I imagine that would make some individuals a little heated especially when they are breaking their backs to make it. I did not hang out with everyone. I was not best friends with anyone. I made my money and went home.

I did not talk much about myself in a personal way. I would speak more on a flirty level or we would talk about things going on in the world. I did not like talking much because then people would get to know me. I would lose my focus, begin to care about them on any level, and be uncovered.

It felt pretty lonely in the club at times because I was not partaking in the extracurricular activities, but I would still be able to make enough money to be satisfied. There were even times when I would make a lot more than I expected to. I would just shake my head and be appreciative.

As a year went by I became a little stagnated. I had met plenty of people, but still had not really opened up. I did not want to reveal too much of myself. I knew if I wanted to become a part of anything I would have to. I began to drink more than usual. I was able to contain my liquor so this was not an issue for me initially. Not having my friend around anymore meant I had to find my own supplier of "Mary Jane." I had to let go a little in order to get what I wanted.

It was not so bad developing some friends. I started hanging out with a group of people I felt comfortable with in the club. They smoked and drank after the club, so I decided to be with them. It was something to do, but I could see the harm in it. I hung out a few more times and then left that alone.

There were a few more sets of friends that I tried to click with. I just did not feel comfortable with everybody. I listened to my intuition this time. I found me a "Mary Jane" provider and left it at that. I was solo at my condo for quite some time. I was learning a little more about myself, however getting lonely. Once again I was craving a change.

Getting bored with the club I worked at, I was invited to work at another. It was so close to my house that I could walk. Being in a new spot, would allow me to come out of my shell a little bit more. Now, uncovering myself somewhere else.

I was able to reinvent myself at this club. Although I was reserved at the first club, no one knew me here. I had the opportunity to uncover myself all over again. With a sense of newness, I could keep in my zone without feeling as if I had to come out of it because of my boredom. I was realizing there was a pattern with my behavior. When things remained the same with little growth, I yearned for more. I did not feel a complete change was needed, but I needed something new.

With a new deejay, I could get into a completely different kind of rhythm. I truly loved being free, but loved the newness even more. The opportunity to meet more men and dance for them was exciting. Getting lost in a new atmosphere was very approachable. I did not want to know them, just wanted the opportunity to cross their path.

I would often be asked what I was doing in a place like that. I would say, "Do you not want me here?" I understood what they meant, but felt so different about myself when I was there. If only they knew what I was feeling. It would show in my dancing, "ready for your dance?" I would ask.

This was an older crowd than the other club which was a change of pace as well. The conversation was more mature and alive. I could sit and talk for hours with one gentleman and make a nice amount of money. I did not always have to dance to get paid which shocked me at times. My conversation was worth more than the dance. A lot was uncovered without taking anything off.

I was asked one time to become a madam to the young girls in the club. I thought that was a bit extreme and was not interested, but could understand where they were going with the thought. There was a lot that could be taught. Everyone had their own style and traits that the men desired and that was okay. Night after night I enjoyed getting lost into each melody that played on my own within my zone.

There was one night I had been giving dances since I stepped out on the floor. I had finally gotten a break and went to the bar to get a drink. There was a man there that was from the other club I worked at. It was really good to see him so I gave him a hug and we began to chat. He asked me how I liked it over here at this new club and that he missed me at the other. I smiled and proceeded to tell him how it was going. He interrupted me and asked me "how much do you want to make tonight?" I looked at him with a blank stare. I was not sure where he was going with this so I did not know what to say. He asked again, so I said "$500 more wouldn't be bad." This man went in his pocket and pulled out a wad of money. "Well I can do that, here you go!" I did not know what to say. He looked at me and said take care now. . .

From that point on I knew what I was doing could not be horrible. Who in the world else would allow that to happen but God! Again, I did not take a thing off for him and was given $500. I was worth more dressed God was revealing to me. My choosing to dance in the long run was not about the stripping at all. God uncovered many things about myself during this time. I went in blinded and remained that way for a long period of time. I had faith every night that I would be alright. I was not concerned one way or another. I was always okay with whatever I received.

The more I would speak to these individuals the more I would learn about myself. I was very intelligent and knew a lot more than I thought. I was very kind, respectful, and appreciative. I also realized how hurt I was from my past. I had a gift that was being developed and I did not even know it. I saw myself in so many individuals I spoke with.

I began to look at what I was doing in a completely different way. It became a learning device that I would take a front row seat to. I did not need to be careful, be concerned with the change of scenery, or be troubled with individual's comments toward me at any given time.

My eyes were opened in a new way and I became even more carefree. All eyes on me.

This was the first time I did not care at all what someone thought about me after being so concerned before. I was free to be whoever I chose to be. I still might have made some choices individuals did not agree with, but I was comfortable with every single one of them. God continued to reveal to me strengths I did not know I had.

God allowed me to wander this way and through it showed me many facets of myself. I had been told I should be ashamed of myself. I would think "for what?" For being brave, for overcoming fear, for being strong, for developing patience, for ministering to people, for showing initiative, for being confident, for building my esteem, for being bold, or for following my heart? Not a chance.

God knew it before I did it. This is the road that was needed for me to go down in order to fulfill what He has for me. Everything that was uncovered went way past what came off my body.

LOST
Chapter Seventeen

❧ SCRIPTURE ❧
Isaiah 41:10
".. So do not fear, for I am with you; do not be dismayed,
for I am your God. .."

Dancing in the club was exciting and new for me in the beginning. I was very sheltered and in a box personally previous to this experience. This allowed me to break free and interact with a variety of people. I had clientele from corporate America to the dude off the block. I was able to set my own schedule and make as much or as little money as I chose. I could take breaks whenever I wanted, arrive whenever I wanted, and leave whenever I wanted. It gave me a sense of independence as well. I learned how to manage my time and market myself. Once I was familiar with this "dance game", I began to book private parties. Private shows were bachelor parties, football parties, birthday parties, or just a regular get together. Whenever someone wanted a stripper, they could book one. Sometimes it was a one on one. I never could see the need for that. It seemed to me the two would end up having sex because of the arousal and lack of distractions around. Nevertheless, it was done for a price.

I had done several of parties and was accustomed to the process. I very seldom did them with other girls because of how explicit some would get. I would show them a good time, but there was a limit. There was a show I did with two other girls and one was not making as much as me and the other. She decides to get on the bed and reveal herself to those who would pay attention. That was quickly shut down by me and the party ended. That was my last show with anybody. Regardless of us being strippers that did not mean we would disrespect ourselves and become trashy to receive some money.

When I started, dancing seemed to be more of an escape for me. I could get lost in the music and take control for a few hours over many men's minds. It was also a creative way to express myself in a sexual way without actually having sex. It was liberating. With a lot of the girls at that time it appeared to be an art form. Of course it was all about money, but there were other personal pleasures too. From doing tricks on the pole, routines on stage, or extreme lap dances, it was a lot of talent in the room. Sexual intent was present, but not always the main focus . . . to me.

There came a point when it stopped being fun and became a need.

Going to the club became frustrating and tiresome. The vibe was changing for me. I was used to everything and needed something new. I had started saying I would not get close to the people in the club; those I danced for. That declaration ended when I became bored. I had always been asked to go out, but would always turn it down. No one could say anything about Bambi because I did not go out with no one. I did not attend different functions or gatherings in the area. I went to work and went home.

While working at the new club I had tried out near my house, I began messing with one of the managers. My focus quickly turned from boredom to curiosity again. This was briefly satisfying.

That club closed down and another opened up in the same building. I began messing with the owner of that one. Again, that was very brief. I am also sure I was making some kind of a buzz with the girls now that I began spreading myself around; and not with the little dogs either. I did not gain much from those relationships except seeing the business side of things. From that point on I looked at my dancing as a business. Getting to know people were for different reasons; mainly what I could get from them. I was going into unfamiliar territory, but enjoyed being lost.

I was not the type who wanted material things, I wanted your time. I needed something from them that they did not even know they possessed.

While traveling down this road of checkers, I was losing myself more and more. I was so far in that I forgot my purpose of being there. It soon became a means to no end. I showed up because that is where I was expected to be. I had no goal, no real focus, and no direction.

I began making the money and spending it just as fast as I made it. It may have appeared to everyone that I had a bundle of money stashed somewhere. I made quite a bit of money on a regular. I should have had some saved, but I did not bother. I wanted what I wanted at the time and did not think about tomorrow. Daily I would have a bulk of money on me, but by the end of the day I had just enough to make more.

I had my own place, the ability to make money, and the opportunity to build from it. I did not know what I wanted any more. I was lonely and missed my children.

A change was needed greatly in my life but I did not know exactly what. I only knew I was becoming very irritable, anti-social, and angry. I thought about my past a lot. The more I thought about it, the more I wanted to cover it up. Drinking day and night became a regular thing for me. Instead of coffee, I had a glass of Jack Daniels, Wild Irish Rose, or MD 20/20.

I drank before the club, at the club, and after the club. It did not matter what time, what I was doing, or where I was going. I had to have a drink to keep the high and remove the thoughts. It got to the point where I would catch a cab from a local bar to the strip club. I would have a buzz every time I arrived. Along with "Mary Jane", I would be pretty mellow on a regular.

I did not want to be home by myself, so I began to hang out. To do this I had to get close to someone. People became my crutch to escape my reality. I was also able to take my frustrations out on them as well. I developed a sense of control. I knew they wanted something from me and I wanted something as well. I did not care about anyone's feelings, I only cared about mine. They were there to serve a purpose and that was it. When I was through, it was on to the next. I was lost in this new world I created.

My conscious would not allow me to do that for long. I did care. I loved people and did not want to see them hurting or needing anything. I would assist anyone I could with whatever I was able. Reaching out to others gave me peace, but upset me still. I wanted this for myself and did not know how to find it. I was in a vicious cycle and did not know how to get out. Angry, upset, hurt, disappointed, needy, anxious, curious, yearning, high, helpful, desperate. . .

I was over my brother's house one day and went outside to smoke a cigarette. I would go and visit him from time to time to receive the love he always gives off when I am around him. As I am standing outside I see a man in the distance that looks like my friend that used to work with me in the studio. I had not seen him since we parted ways when I moved in my condo.

I was shocked but so very glad to see him. As he got closer, we both smiled and embraced each other tightly. We did not speak much on what had been happening in our lives, but seemed more excited about being together again. We spent time at my brother's and he went on his way. I mentioned to him where I lived and told him to visit. I felt like I had gained something back from seeing him, yet something was still missing. We did not say we were getting back together or anything, but it seemed like it would go that way.

He came by a few days later and brought me some snacks. There was something very different about him, but I could not put my finger on it. I had plenty of drinks and smoke to keep us occupied for quite some time. It seemed like old times. We walked the city as we used to and ventured the eateries. I got my friend back.

Several days later I received a phone call from my friend asking me to come down to the jail for a court date of his. What?????????????????

I showed up at his court date and was in amazement to hear what the charges were. Several nights prior, he broke in a pawn shop and burglarized it and then attempted to evade police when they arrived on the scene. He was caught in a ditch while trying to escape. My mouth was on the floor. I had been around this man day and night for a couple of years. I looked him in his eyes in the court room and could not see that person I just heard about. I was lost.

He needed somewhere to go once released temporarily. He showed up at my door days after that hearing looking very unfamiliar. I allowed him to shower and get comfortable. I knew he needed some time to get himself together, but I was baffled. I did not know who I had in my house. I continued to interact with him as usual, but was puzzled inside.

I continued to work as he stayed at my house. I felt as if I could trust him with my life and belongings, but was doubtful. I did not like feeling uncomfortable, but could not abandon him either. He would stay a few nights and then leave. This continued for several days.

One night while working at the club, I met this guy. He stood out from anyone else I had ever met in the club. He was very attractive and had a beautiful body. What captured me was his confidence. He had a debonair approach about him; something different than everyone else. We met after the club outside in the parking lot and chatted. He ended up giving me a ride home. The following day, my friend had returned to my house as he was doing frequently. He said he had not eaten so we went to grab a bite and got some drinks to take back to my house. When we returned to my house, the guy from the club was outside of my house. I was surprised to see him, but was happy he was there. He came to the door with my friend and me with no hesitation. Laughing to myself, we all went in. He invited me out for a drink, I told my friend I'd be back, and we left. Of course, my friend came up in conversation.

Upon my return home, I informed my friend he had to find somewhere else to go. The next day he left. This new guy was influencing enough to see that my friend was very lost.

I began in this club life with one objective that fell to the wayside. Although I still had no exact direction I could sense a huge change. God continued to protect me through my dark wandering through private parties and frequent rendezvous. I got involved in things just to take my mind of my personal affairs. I never once thought about my safety with the strangers, but doubted instantly once around an old friend. I thought I was the one lost, but apparently he lost himself as well. God allowed me to be there for him when he needed me. God also allowed me to see who had been with me the whole time. He had always been "that" man; just not with me. I had protection when I thought my friend was my protector. I was very lost.

How was I comfortable around people I did not know, yet so uncomfortable once I heard what he had done? The fear came when I thought about the possibilities. I did not think of the possibilities while in stranger's homes dancing half naked. It was at times five to ten men in the room. I felt totally safe. That was stepping out on faith and did not even know it.

God had me spend time with someone not knowing how dangerous he was or could be. I got to know him as a person and not for what he does. I would have never been around him had I known. I did love and care for him, but did not feel right after knowing his recent activity choices. Yet, as soon as I was aware, God allowed my eyes to see someone enough that he would move my friend out of the way. The path my friend was on was not the path God had for me, but He provided me with some light before redirecting my steps.

God has His ways of showing me I don't know what I think I do. I am often lost; however, He continues to show me the way . . . especially when I am not looking.

Why it is God allowed me to make such foul decisions sometimes, but not allow me to at other times? I believe some choices, although wrong, are very strengthening. Depending on the individual, certain situations are just right for them to see what is necessary. Because of what God has for me to do in this world, He will allow me to walk into situations blind-sided to learn exactly what He wants me to.

He continued to allow me to be in the club, I believe, to bring me out. Even though it is a very sexual and explicit place, I needed to know exactly what it was like in order to serve later in my life. Smoking "Mary Jane", drinking, and everything else I chose to do was necessary for me in the future. Who wants to speak with a straight laced individual trying to tell them about God saving them? I needed to have "been there and done that" in order to speak with the individuals God is going to have me speak to. I would look foolish telling someone I understand, but have never been where they are.

While I was venturing from one bad choice to another, God continued to put people in my life that would protect me, take care of me, or assist me in one way or another that was beneficial to my future He has laid out for me. I would also learn from individuals and my surroundings something I needed to take with me. He already had a plan for my life before I was born. No matter which way I go, I am traveling that road . . . lost and all.

THE EFFECT
Chapter Eighteen

❧ SCRIPTURE ❧

Isaiah 64:8
Yet you, Lord, are our Father. We are the clay; you are the potter; we are all the work of your hand.

A new adventure had started now I was seeing this new guy. He was a lot different from what I was used to. He exuded much confidence, was educated, and had a bit of a thug swag to him. There was just something about him that I fell for on the spot.

I had been wanting on a change in my life. I was getting tired of the club but needed to work to keep my condo. Everything was so right but so wrong. I had my independence and gained much self-esteem. I had my own place and was able to take care of myself. I just needed a personal life. Because I did not have the most respectable job, I felt a bit short of complete. I was totally comfortable with what I was doing, don't get me wrong, but I wanted more.

Once I started seeing this guy, I really wanted more. He had such aspirations and was goal oriented. I needed some of this in my life; finally, some direction. "He would be a wonderful influence in my life" . . . is what I often would think to myself. I had a real man in my life. He would definitely have an effect on my life.

He would come over quite often and spend pillow time with me. It was always an excuse about why it was always like this, but I did not really care. I was happy to have someone like him in my life. I was tired of the duds and those who were not very encouraging. I saw so much in him that I was enjoying the time I was getting. I did not speak much, but my heart was saying it all. I loved listening to him talk.

He told me that his aunt lived with him. This is why we would never go over his house. I had my own place so that was suitable for what we would end up doing anyway. That did not sit well with me initially, but I let it go. I wanted to believe his every word. I also did not want to mess this relationship up by bringing up past feelings about men. I gave him the benefit of the doubt and opened myself up to him. I dropped my guards and let him all the way in.

While working at the club one night, one of the bartenders told me that she had seen my guy at the mall earlier that day with another female looking very cozy. She informed me that she was positive it was him and it did not look appropriate. I waved it off and told her thanks for telling me. Not wanting to believe it, I assumed she was hating and brushed it off. I spoke with him a few minutes later on the phone and let him know what was said. He showed up later that evening to pick me up from the club. He swore it was not him and said she must be mistaken.

Several days later I received a phone call.

"You do not know me but I have heard about you", a woman's voice said to me. Instantly I knew what this was about. He lied to me after I opened my heart up again. I gave in again and played the fool. I thought he was different and really cared for me. I was crushed.

He came over my house attempting to explain himself. She was a roommate he was taking care of because they were going to be business partners and he felt obligated. I wanted to believe him so bad because of the way I felt about him. I figured I could not be going through something like this now that I opened my heart. I had fallen for him, and I could not let it end there. I was very doubtful, but remained a willing participant. He said it was nothing and I wanted to believe him. Why would he press so hard to apologize and make things right with him and me? He did not owe me anything, but made such an effort. I wanted more so I put my faith and trust in him.

It was like I was in a trance with this guy. I was hanging on his every word. No matter what was said or done, I was there. It was as if his wrongs were right. I already knew when I loved I loved hard, but dang. I was not ignorant to the facts. I wanted what I wanted and at that time it was him. I knew he was a liar and a cheat, but as long as I got what I wanted I did not care. He did not give me gifts or money. We did not go out very much. That did not matter to me. He offered me so much more than I could explain. This was someone I looked up to and admired. He was very good with people that were less fortunate. He had a very calming, comforting spirit about him. I enjoyed listening to him. He used to talk to me about going back to school and how he knew I was capable of more. He did not stress it, but it was to be admired.

As much as I cared for him, he still hurt my soul. I wanted to be angry, but I couldn't. Whenever he wanted to see me, he did. He made an impression on me that was lasting and immovable.

The effect this guy had on me was something I never knew. There was no way I was going to be faithful to someone and he not to me, and I knew it. I was very angry, but could not be upset with him. It was like I understood what he was going through. At one point, I figured she was not getting what she wanted either, so who cares. I cared about him and that is all that mattered. I did not go out of my way to find out about her.

I did not care. I knew I was on the fence, but he had me. I did not feel like the other woman, but I was.

I was getting what I needed at the time. I saw and spoke to him often enough where I was not lonely. I was sexually satisfied. I was not into receiving gifts and money from a man, so that was not an issue. I wanted him, not his money. I did want more out of a relationship, but did not feel I was ready. I wanted him no matter what.

Pondering on things he shared with me about bettering myself rang true to me. I wanted more for myself and I wanted to offer a man more. This is something I wanted for a while now but did not know what to do. It was on my heart to get out of the club and start working somewhere. I began thinking about it quite frequently.

Within a couple of weeks of me thinking hard about getting out of the club, I was offered a management position at a beauty supply store. My "sweet" friend upstairs from me told someone about me. I had spoken with him briefly about me doing hair in the past. He informed a colleague about me and suggested me to run a beauty supply store that recently opened. I went to the interview and was hired on the spot!

I was so excited. I could get out of the club, build employment history again, and become a working-class woman. My life was going to change once again. I told my friend and he was very happy for me. He knew it was possible if I just put my mind to it. I knew it as well, but a little encouragement never hurts. He gave me that.

Now having quit the club and working a 9am to 9pm schedule was a different pace. It was an incredible feeling to manage a store on my own. I had never been given this kind of opportunity before. There were no employees except me. The owner trusted me to open and close his store solely based on the word of my "sweet" friend who lives above me. I was so thankful and felt different as a person. Not being in the club was an awesome feeling. I was in there for so long it became a part of me. I was ready to move forward and my friend gave me the push I needed to change my focus.

My friend would come and visit me at the store periodically. It made me feel more attractive to be standing behind the counter of the store that I managed when he would look at me. My confidence was up and my esteem was higher. I was now a career woman. I was so proud to be working. It was a big difference from being in the club. I was hoping he felt that same way. Seeing him before work or after work became the plan. I was on a high, so at times it did not matter if I saw him at all. I was at his beckon call before because of the freeness of my schedule. Independence came in another form now and I was loving it.

The owner of the store asked me to come along on a merchandise run. He wanted me to select the items I felt should be in the store. This let me know he respected my opinion and made me feel a part of the business aspect of the store. I was fitting in very well. His wife would come in at times and help out. We became very friendly after a short period of time. I met their children as well; a boy and a girl. In no time we were a little family running the beauty supply store. My life was changing for the better.

I had asked my friend to put an outfit of mine in the cleaners. Wondering if he picked it up, I called his house. That was not something I usually did, but I felt bold. She answered and gave the phone to him. I simply asked about the dry cleaning and hung up. The funny thing was, I heard a baby crying in the background.

Later that same day, as I stood behind the counter in the store, I saw my friend drive up. He did not look as he normally does. He did not get out of the truck, so I went outside to him. He proceeded to tell me that he had something he needed to speak to me about. He would not tell me what it was about. I responded with ok and said I would see him later. I went through the remainder of the day wondering what in the world it could be. Is our relationship going further? Was it good or bad? Did I do something? I had no clue.

Later that evening he came over my house. He went straight to my room and sat on the bed. He put his hands over his face and let out a huge sigh. Curiously glancing at him, I went and sat beside him. As soon as I sat down he says, "_____ was pregnant and had a baby. I have a daughter." My heart sank.

"What!!!!!" I shoved him on his shoulders, looked at him with tears in my eyes, and went into the bathroom. I fell to the floor and cried. I was a fool to think he really cared about me the way he said he did. "I should have known" is what I said to myself over and over. I did not see this coming, but I did know there was someone else. Now I know it is much more no matter what he says. When I came out of the bathroom, he was gone.

I headed to the store to get a bottle of something to numb the pain.

I was not as joyous as I had been before the news of the birth of my friend's daughter by the female he said was just a roommate. My attitude was poor and I did not care anymore. I felt betrayed and was very upset about it. God allowed me to walk right into this. Yes, my friend was good for leading me into a better lifestyle, but once I knew about his affairs I should have walked away. I have to deal with whatever comes with it since I decided to stay with him.

I would drink before I came to work, but would lose my high halfway through the day. This gave the appearance of drowsiness and slurred words. The owner and his wife noticed a drastic change, but said nothing initially. Later in the day, I was called in the office and asked to go home and get it together. I continued to drink.

My job performance went way down. I began to open the store late, set off the alarm several of times, and did not take inventory as needed. The owner eventually hired a part-time worker, which made me part-time as well.

I called my boss one day and told him I would not be in that day. When asked why I could not lie to him. I was calling from jail. I had gotten a DWI charge early that morning leaving a party. I was driving a car my brother gave me, with no license, no tags, and no insurance. I became a hot mess. I was tired of trying and totally gave up.

God knew I would come to place of being broken-hearted again. He also knew I would have to come to him eventually and I was getting closer. I was able to see the possibilities that were given to me. I did not seek that job out, God brought it to me. Because I put all my trust into a man, God let me see exactly what I was trusting in. I was forewarned but did not take that exit out. God always provides an opportunity to get out of a situation.

Having a good job and being in that relationship allowed me to see what truly had an effect on me. I wanted to get out of the club, but more so for him. I enjoyed the job, but more so for him. As long as I had him with me, I felt whole. I let it all go because of the effect I allowed him to have on me. Now I was in jail. Not his fault, but my hurt knew no better.

Despite what my spirit told me, I wanted to follow my flesh. God showed me many times over why I should not continue the way I was. Opening new doors should have been enough. I had a change on my heart and a job opportunity came through. There was no way to mix the two together. One was of God and the other of deceit.

I realized I allowed my feelings to ride solely on him. Everything was only good in my eyes because he was there with me. He had encouraged me so much and offered positive information for me to move onward and upward with my life. I admired him so much for that, when in all actuality it was God. He only used him to direct me away from where I was. Anyone would not do, so He allowed this guy I would definitely look up to come into my life. God knows who will have an effect on you.

I will always hold near to my heart the way God lets things play out in my life. Even when something will hurt me, it is allowed in order for me to gain the lesson learned from the pain. My eyes were opened wider to those "red flags" that appear. They are there for a reason. I appreciate everything this guy did for me but I should have appreciated me more to not play second to anyone.

People affect our lives in many ways. They are used to serve more purpose than is realized. When pleasure was involved I was blinded and was not able to see the effect it was having on me until I had nowhere else to turn. I was in a cell by myself. God now had me to Himself. I never thought this would lead to the greatest effect of all …

PEACE BE STILL
Chapter Nineteen

SCRIPTURE

Psalm 46:10a
He says, "Be still, and know that I am God."

After my DWI arrest I was put on probation. I was able to sign myself out of jail because this was my first offense ever. I was shocked I had been arrested, but I was so far gone of caring it did not faze me yet. I had to report to my probation officer whenever an appointment was scheduled. This would have not been a problem, but I had a job and could not take off any more. I had been in enough trouble with my boss that I was surprised he did not fire me. Because of the part-time help in the store, I was able to make my first appointments.

I continued to drink and smoke. I had seen my friend several times, but was not wanting his company. While working at the store I began to meet plenty of people including men. Why should I be faithful to him, he sure is not faithful to me. I started going out with different guys I met at work. It was nothing serious, just a date or two. My mind was still on my friend.

Since my hours had been cut at work, this decreased my funds a lot. I could not take on another 9 to 5 job, so I resorted back to the club. I fell back into the routine I once had.

While at the club one night, my knee started to swell up. I attempted to continue dancing, but could not. One of the security guards carried me off the stage because I was in so much pain. Someone grabbed my things from the dressing room, I called a friend, and headed to the hospital.

I had an appointment with my probation officer but was unable to see her due to me being in the hospital. Our appointment was the same morning I was discharged from the hospital. I had my papers and was not too concerned with being in any kind of trouble for not showing up. I was walking with crutches and had an air-brace on my leg. I was unable to do anything. I could not go to work at the store and ended up getting fired. My life was beginning to slow down slowly but surely.

I received a phone call from my probation officer telling me I needed to get to her office immediately. A friend of mine drove me to her office soon after. As I swung through her door, she said I had to be arrested. I proceeded to show her my discharge papers I had stuffed in my brace and she refused to see them. She asked me if I could get to the station or does she need to take me. I could not believe it. This is now the second time I am being arrested. The officers at the jail informed me that she was a wicked, troubled woman who was known for being petty no matter what the circumstance. This felt unreal to me.

I called my guy while in there to see if he was able to help me out. He said he would take care of it for me. I was surprised, but very happy. I would not stay in the holding area long. A lawyer showed up to pick me up, and drove me home. My friend was there for me again. I began seeing him again.

The swelling on my knee had gone down and I returned to the club. On one particular night, one of the other girls and I were in her car getting ready to smoke a joint in front of the club. Right when I was about to light it, a woman knocks on the window and says to step outside of the car. "What in the world is going on?" I do not know where this woman came from, but she was part of the force that checks out clubs in the area. She wrote us both a ticket. The club was fined and I had to pay it. We were also supposed to go to some classes for a week and after receive a drug assessment. I did not do it.

Throughout all the chaos from the past months, I lost my condo as well. I was in a room with a friend when the police knocked on the door. As soon as I saw them, I knew they were for me. I was on my way to jail again.

This time I was locked up, booked, and had to change clothes. I knew it was a bit different because I changed into their uniformed orange top and bottoms. I began to feel a little funny. I had never experienced this before and it became overwhelming. I was taken to a pod with many other women in it, given a plastic case with a bunch of stuff in it, and was directed to my cell.

I looked around and thought, "I will not be in here with these people for long. I do not belong here." I began to settle in my cell by making my cot and putting the things given to me by the jail on a shelf made into the wall. One of the women came to my cell and introduced herself to me and gave me a miniature New Testament Bible. I thanked her, glanced through it and laid it on the table built out of the wall. I could not sleep that first night.

Looking at the walls around me and gazing at the light seeping through the little window, I wondered how in the world I ended up here. I could not understand what was happening to me. I never ever dreamed I would be getting arrested, let alone laying in jail in my own cell.

There was a counselor that came to see me in the pod I was confined to discussing my circumstance. She informed me that I needed to take a drug and alcohol class before I would be released that consisted of completing 30 days while incarcerated.

"30 DAYS!" I thought she was out of her mind. I did not have a problem like that, did I?

I resisted for one week and refused to admit I had a problem of any sort. I did not want to be the issue after everything I had been through previously in my life. It was because of those things that I even drank or smoked, but I did not want to disclose that information to anyone . . . let alone a drug class.

While waiting for this class to begin, a Bible study class was forming and I was invited. I was very hesitant to join. I had nothing else to do, so I went. I sat at the back of the room by the door on the end of the row. I could see and hear perfectly, but did not want to be visible to the leaders that facilitated the group. Prayer began and everyone bowed their heads except me. I was glancing at everyone around the room. I could sense how they held on to every word coming out of his mouth. It was actually pretty powerful. He did not say anything so elaborate, just heartfelt. It was just the thought that something was there everybody was adjoining to. I wanted that too.

The class had begun and I had my antennas directed to the front. As he spoke, it was as if he were speaking directly to me. Everything he was saying was scraping my soul. I could not understand what was happening, but I began to feel a release I was not releasing. Before I knew it, I had tears racing down my face that I could not hold back. Something was happening beyond my control very similar to my situation of being in jail. I continued these groups throughout my time there.

By the time the drug class began I had already been incarcerated 15 days. This was not an easy thing for me initially. I did not want to acknowledge anything was wrong with me or that I needed help in many ways. I tried to continue to be strong but was weakening each day.

It was very difficult conforming to the disrespect of the jail guards. I understand we were locked up for committing crimes, but we are still human beings. The language in which they used to speak to us was very degrading and uncalled for. I was already having a hard time because I had to confront my issues in a drug class and now I had to deal with rudeness as well. I was not having it.

All the inmates would have to stand in line for our new linen for the piece of mattress we slept on. Before receiving the new, we would have to first turn in our old ones. The guard pulled one of the sheets out of the cart. While we were standing in line, she made a comment about knots in the sheets and how we were responsible for them. Everyone remained silent as she ramped on with unnecessary badgering. I stepped out of line and said, "The sheets already have knots in them when we receive them." She proceeded to claim we put them there. I repeated, "The knots are already there when we get them." She carried on talking as she grabbed a clean sheet and unfolded it. To only her surprise did a knot lay perfectly at the corners of the sheet. I looked at her and said, "Wow, how did that get there?" Everyone leaned my way and said," Thank you."

The entire pod gathered together and wanted to write her up because of her deliberate attacks she displayed often. This was the first time someone stood up to her, I was told, and they wanted her gone. We all signed the proper paperwork and she was removed. From that moment on I realized the people that are incarcerated needed a voice. I looked at everyone differently. They were just like me . . . troubled.

I was silent in my drug class when it started. I did not want to participate and reveal anything about me. I did listen carefully and observed everyone including the counselors. I began to have a clearer view.

God slowed me all the way down by allowing me to be incarcerated. I was doing too much while not acknowledging what I was actually feeling. This situation forced me to look at things whether I wanted to or not. I was not willing to face what I needed to, and it was time that I did. Once I let go, all was well.

I gained a new sense of myself and others while incarcerated. Being forced to do what I did not want to was exactly what God designed. It also made me realize He was a part of my life. I began acknowledging Him more than I used to. An awareness that was not there before soon appeared. He has a way of allowing my faults to define my strength. Although I was in a low point in my life, I reached a high. When I stopped fighting the process, I was relaxed and felt a weight lifted off of me.

In the last week of the drug class, the counselor told me I had to speak or I would have to stay longer. I cried when she told me that because it was time to admit out loud my faults. What I grasped from that moment of me giving my very brief story is it was not about me. Telling my story and why I chose the substances I did opened a whole new line of discussion. I not only discussed the drugs of choice, I clarified why I did it. Narrowing it down to my past allowed the others to look at themselves in that very way. They then started identifying the issues of their childhood and past events that brought them so much pain. This provided a clear vision of why they were doing drugs in the first place. Dealing with the hurt assists with the actions that follow. The counselor commended me on speaking out to the class and I understood why. It did not just bring me peace, it brought them peace as well.

I saw how God used my situation to shine light on others'. I spoke from my heart, He poured out, and presented new direction.

Through all I was doing that was very inappropriate, incorrect, degrading, unhealthy, and just bad judgment, He used for my good. It served a purpose for where I was going and what I needed to do while I was there. I did not know it, but I was destined to be incarcerated to carry out just what I did along with preparing me for later moments in my life. It is not about what I was doing to get there. It is more about how what I was doing is going to be used later. That definitely is not the thought at the time, but as I grow in Christ, I am more and more aware of it.

When I look back on my life, I can see other times I was forced to be still. Each one of those times served a purpose. God will slow down the pace to get me to understand what is to be learned at that time. Many times I am doing too much to recognize Him when I need to. The more this happens, the more familiar I become of Him.

I am now tranquil by choice. I slow down so I can hear Him, see Him, and get to know Him better. I am sure if I get out of line or I need to see something immediately He will allow an unfortunate situation to redirect my steps and use me in the process to redirect others as well.

All in all, He can bring peace to any situation if we can only be still to recognize it. There is much beauty in chaos. Be still and see the peace within it and watch Him come through.

SOMEONE ELSE
Chapter Twenty

SCRIPTURE

Proverbs 23:7a
For as he thinketh in his heart, so is he.

While incarcerated, I began a process of change. My mindset was not as before. I believe attending Bible study while there for 45 days had a great deal to do with it. I accepted God into my life, yet again, with a better understanding, after many years of pain. His process had never stopped, but mine began again.

There was so much released from me through opening up to these women and to myself. I avoided this for many, many years and was finally face to face with yours truly. I could not run, could not hide, and realized I really had no control. Carrying around so much hurt for so many years was tiring and extremely heavy. Letting go of some of that load was refreshing and encouraging. I began to see the world in a way I never had.

Without focusing on all that was wrong, I recognized what was right. My talents increased tremendously while I was confined. It was like all my abilities displayed themselves to me in a way I never seen before. Critical thinking came naturally instead of speaking out of feelings. Understanding began to mean so much to me instead of not wanting to hear it. I believe I always paid attention to detail, but it was now amplified. Everything mattered in a new way; a positive way. I did not focus on the negative, but did recognize it. I was changing slowly but surely.

I was so apprehensive to the lesson I was supposed to learn in the beginning of this occurrence. Knowing there is a problem is considerably different from dealing with it. Once I stared that monster in the face, being locked up felt like I was in an overly managed retreat. The conditions were less than usual, but it did not bother me. I was comfortable with where I was and more impressed with who I was becoming.

Feeling the change during my time inside the jail was interesting enough. It became strange once I was released. My friend that had meant so much to me but had a child with someone else was actually the one who picked me up when I was set free. He put me up in a room for a couple of months. He came to visit while I was locked up which meant a lot to me. I cared no longer about what he had done or how I was hurt by him. I only cared that he cared enough to be there. Although this was all good, I began to see a problem with me dealing with him. A conflict began within myself.

I could still sense the desire to be with him, yet was able to resist. I did not yearn the same way I once did. I saw him as a man, but not as someone I needed like before. I did need his help, but did not have to ask. He volunteered his services and was there when I needed it. At this time, I did not require much . . . I needed a place to stay. I laid low for a few days in my room trying to situate the new view I had. I was in an unfamiliar place.

I needed to make money so I returned to the club. As strange as it was, it was effortless. I gave it no thought and just went through each night blindfolded. I was aware of what was happening around me, but it did not feel the same to me. I did not know these people any more. I did not see them the same. I was very critical of what I was doing and all that was transpiring around me. I became quiet and observant versus engaging and vibrant.

This did not seem right any longer. I kept thinking about the experience I just went through. I had found a new kind of high and I liked it much better than this. What I found while being locked up was comforting and reviving. I felt no pressure and had a huge sense of peace. Life on the outside was stressful and compact. I began to feel weight again and was not happy about it. I did not want to lose what I had found. But what was it? And how do I get that back?

Unsure of how to maintain the feeling I had come to know, I became frustrated. I did not know what to do any more. I wanted so bad to speak with someone who would be able to tell me what to do next, but there was no one. I began to reach out to individuals again as well as alcohol and smoking. It was nowhere near the same type of understanding I had come to know. Because of the lack of fulfillment, I did it even more. Totally aware of the harm, I had wished to be saved from myself.

It was, however, refreshing to know that there was a new height to reach. I knew it was attainable, it was just a matter of returning to that place. Instead of searching for it, I soothed my frustration with other things. My desires for the things of the past had lessoned, but were still present. It was very different though. I would have a strong sense of wrongness afterwards and sometimes while I was participating in the chosen act of sin. This made things even more difficult. Not only did I know it wasn't right, now I would have to feel bad about it too.

Feeling as if I were floating along, I left the room my friend was paying for and started living out of my suitcase. Whoever I was around that night is where I would end up staying. Every night almost felt as if it were planned. There were no problems, mishaps, or confusion. All of that was spinning around inside of me. It was not seen on the outside, but I was full of despair. I did not know what direction I was headed in. Something was happening that I could not explain.

I wanted to find what I found while incarcerated. All that I had collected was just sitting dormant inside of me. What was I supposed to do with it? I had nothing and nobody after coming from so much. It was a tug of war inside of me that I could not understand. While one part of me was surfacing, the other was defending her ground.

I was changing and did not know how to continue the metamorphosis.

I needed to be around the atmosphere that circumference me behind those bars. I longed for a friend that once asked me to go to church with her. I knew she would provide me with what I needed to hear to guide me in the right direction. I thought of the male friend I had who I gave up because of his choice to indulge in crime. Amazing I ended up in jail too. I wonder if these were the kind of feelings he had that lead him to turn to illegal activity. He would read the Bible all the time and had that sense of peace I had tapped into. He went from one person to another, just as I felt I was doing. Only I was turning toward the light.

I knew several people at the club that I had become pretty comfortable with. I had begun hanging around one particular guy who was much younger than myself. He had a baby that was several months old that he co-parented. We did not have a sexual relationship, although it went there a few times. We were more companions of the moment. He had a lot he was going through that I could assist with, and I had the means to keep us satisfied day to day. He stayed in a nice size house with a family member that was hardly home. This situation worked out lovely for the position I was in. It was not really discussed; I was just there.

Because of my "stripping" capabilities, we would throw house parties where I was able to bring us some funds whenever we felt the urge. Adding a little flare to the party was perfect at that time and served everyone well. We drank, smoked, and had much fun. My carefree attitude resurfaced for a brief period of time.

The yearning of peace could not leave me. No matter what I would do, it was not good enough anymore. Indulging in this kind of behavior became very displeasing. I was in the bathroom one day looking at myself in the mirror and began to see someone else. I was not that hurt little girl I used to see or that abused woman. I was a woman who had been through some things that hurt her. It was a big difference. I tilted my head to the side and looked deeper. I saw potential. How do I get from here to there? I shook my head and figured "what a nice thought."

As it would come to be, my conscience would not let me be. Once I would turn away from what I knew to be right, the pit of my stomach would do flips. I could not go on this way.

I called my mother as I did from time to time to check in and let her know I was still alive. She told me to call my brother. He had moved to another area and I had not spoken to him since before I went to jail. I could do nothing but laugh when he said, "Come here to live with me."

It was pretty clear to me that my time was up where I was. I felt as if I had been rescued. After a few days, I got on the greyhound and was on my way to him . . . once again.

God slowed my life down in order for me to see it. There was nothing wrong with anything that I had endured. It is all necessary in His ultimate plan for my life. Had I never been arrested, I would not have accepted who I was or was becoming. Having those memories made it possible for me to look back when I was moving forward in the wrong direction. I was only able to see someone different within myself because of what I had known from before. There had to be a time where I recognized I needed something other than myself or anybody else. I was exposed to God in jail. I would always know there is someone else and I could see it.

Being held down long enough to receive God enabled my spirit to guide me along thereafter. A quick change had to take place somehow, and it did while I was in that jail. Depositing what was needed to take along with me from that point on. I became aware of something changing within me. Although I would continue to make choices that were not the best, they were best for me to gain understanding while moving forward in my life. The exchange had taken place, now it is the manifestation that will follow.

I will always have what I do with me. That is what makes me. What I do in life is what develops me. Right or wrong I am not only able to see my mistakes, but learn that they are supposed to be in order to get me to the next phase of my life. Once I got out of jail I had a different perception of everything. It is not necessary to make immediate changes; it is only necessary to recognize something needs to be changed. God makes the changes. I only open my heart to it.

As long as I have the desire in my heart, God will do the rest. Acknowledging He is there is all He wants. Now I will let Him show me. I did not quite understand it at this time, but I was willing to be shown. I wanted to see that other person emerging.

When I looked in the mirror, I realized someone else was there. It is not me; it is someone else. Throughout this time of growth, I was evolving and not even aware of it. Going through these sets of events was not as frightening as moving closer to God. It is scary in a reverence kind of way; the unknown. I was traveling a road I knew nothing about, but was eager to go. I am always up for a challenge. The challenges I am willing to take is what changed.

Because I knew more I wanted to be more. I no longer felt like what I was surrounding myself with. I do not put those individuals down at all. I can say I understand them so much better. God has allowed me to go down some paths where I am able to see the other person as myself because I was right there with them. I had an inside peek of their lives because of the life I was leading. Once I let go of the wheel and let God take over, He guided me to Him to see something greater. The heights of that peace is impossible when attempting to get there yourself. That is recognized when you let go of Him. Finding Him would still be a struggle, but at least I had a sense of direction.

My grip was loose when I got out of jail, but my heart knew the strength of that grasp. Knowing was everything for me. Possibility stayed in the forefront of my mind. There will always be something greater that is within me. I felt it. I saw it. I knew it. Someone else existed that I desperately needed to become familiar with.

MOVING ON
Chapter Twenty-One

❧❧ SCRIPTURE ❧❧
Isaiah 43:18-19
*"Forget the former things; do not dwell on the past. See, I
am doing a new thing! . . . "*

Seven years had gone by while searching for my new life.
Learning to live without my children and husband had been
difficult; yet doable. I met many people and was involved in
much activity. There were a lot of firsts that happened for me
since being on my own. I tried 'Mary Jane' obtained an entry-
level job, had many firsts dates with men, stripped in a club,
managed a beauty store, recognized real love, got arrested,
attended jail Bible study, received the Holy Spirit, spoke in
tongues, discovered new talents, and saw the world in a new
light.

Although I was leaving to go stay with my brother again, I
was very apprehensive. I had begun to feel a change in my
attitude and had already reverted back to my old ways. Would I
lose what I had gained altogether? I was scared to fail. Would
God follow me to where I was going?

While riding on the bus, I could not help but to miss all that
had transpired. I had met so many people, developed
relationships, and lost much. With tears in my eyes, I
reminisced.

As I watch the scenery go by, I wondered what it would be
like where I was going. My brother always lives in a very good
area so that was not a concern. I was thinking about meeting
new people, where I would work, and what kind of men were

there. I was not trying to start a new relationship . . . just curious.

I tried to remain optimistic and believe all would be well. Keeping what I learned while in jail was necessary and it needed to kick in at this time. When I set my mind on God I was good, but from time to time my mind would wander. I could not help but think of the negative. What if I hate it? What if people do not like me? What if I cannot find a job? Questions just kept pouring in my head.

I had moved several times before so I knew how to adjust. I guess it was the thought of what happened in order for me to have to move this time that got to me so much. I had never messed up so bad. I now had a criminal record. I was not making the best choices. Whenever I would think of the past, I would seem to jump in some kind of hole. I had to rid of that kind of attitude and hopefully this move would be helpful.

I was given another opportunity for some reason. I would tell myself this over and over. It does not matter anymore what I did. I thought about God again and I felt better. I had to move past my past.

I had to come to a place where I not only knew what I had done had been forgiven, but I had to forgive myself. This would take longer than this bus ride, but I did acknowledge it. I was going through the motions, but had not allowed myself to move on from the events that had taken place.

During this trip it seemed I was dealing more of with what I was leaving behind rather than what was ahead of me. Holding on to these things would weigh me down; I know. I had just got rid of a lot of baggage while locked up. I did not want to start my move out by carrying more than I needed. I had toted around too much before. Keeping these things in the forefront of my mind would cripple me. I realized I was doing it to myself. I have to deal with it as it is and move forward.

I learned a lot from being in jail. I was able to face my truths and deal with some pains I had. I had a long way to go. Although I was not completely healed, it was so much better than the limp I had. I was able to handle my pain. I did not want to even acknowledge it before, which had me needing crutches.

Looking out the window with a smile on my face, I knew I was able. I thought of God and all positive thoughts came to mind. I can still get a job. I am not a felon. I made a mistake and paid my dues. "Yeah, that's right!" I thought to myself. I have my brother there to help me once again. So what I am having some trouble; God knows it!

I began to look at all the people on the bus and wonder about their lives. I was not the only one going through things. There are many individuals struggling with life and trying to find their way just as I am. I was very fortunate to have a big brother that God continued to use in my life. I realized I had to keep a positive attitude. If I thought negative my attitude would take a turn for the worst. I did not want to be that way. I wanted a change; not just for the better, but forever.

I looked at it as traveling the U.S. Many people cannot leave their hometowns, but I am now traveling halfway across the map. The more I thought of the goodness of God, the better I felt. I was learning at that very moment how to take Him with me.

God has been with me in every aspect of my life up to this point. It was me who allowed stinking thinking to hinder my thought process. With every incident that happens I have to become aware of how I am directing my attention. Am I looking forward or backward?

Looking in front of me is so that I will not trip on my troubles that are now behind. Stumbling from time to time is not the problem; not getting up from that fall is. God allows me to move on . . .

STARTING AGAIN
Chapter Twenty-Two

SCRIPTURE
Acts 8:22-23
.".. Repent of this wickedness and pray to the Lord in the hope that he may forgive you for having such a thought in your heart. For I see that you are full of bitterness and captive to sin."

I had moved from the east coast to the Midwest to live with my oldest brother. Once again he had invited me to stay with him as I traveled this road I was on. I appreciated him so much and still looked up to him. He was doing well, as always, and was wonderful to be around. He was a positive influence that kept me encouraged more by seeing him involved in such heart felt career choices.

I anticipated this new start and wondered what it would bring. What would I do in another new city? I did have a little more job history being that I managed that beauty salon. I felt I was in a better position than when I arrived with him last time. God worked it all out for me then and would definitely do it again. I had a positive attitude and knew it all would work out.

After a few days I began to feel a bit lonely. I had no friends again and knew of nothing. My positive attitude was slowly turning into misery. Yet, to look around at all the action around us was motivating. We lived near the Galleria area so there was much movement. I started taking walks to see exactly what was in the area. That was uplifting, but not enough to get me going. I made a phone call to my friend who I used to be in a relationship with and helped me after a got out of jail. I did not communicate with him before leaving, so he did not know where I was. Once I informed him, I believe he was relieved. He did not have to be concerned with me anymore. Any charade he was putting up could cease. It was closure for me as well. I let go of the past and looked forward.

My brother had hooked me up with a position at his old place of employment. It was a high-end store that sold furniture, household items, gourmet foods, and wines. I was excited. I had a job and was able to meet new people. Cashier was not necessarily my top choice, but I was in the center of a very popular area and was employed.

After working about two months, my brother and I began to bump heads a bit. I am really unsure why, but we started disagreeing a lot. Because of this, he found an apartment complex for me to apply to. It was funny because he wanted to co-sign and as it turned out, I did not even need one. I was able to get it in my name. I moved in immediately. My brother was wonderful. I came home from work one day and he had the whole front area of my apartment furnished. The bedroom was the only room unfurnished. I did not care because the couch was also a pullout bed. I was all set with a complete living room and dining room suit.

I was pretty nervous to be on my own and afraid of failing again. Being alone was not a good thing for me. I was able to do it for a while, but as soon as I met someone . . .

I invited him to my apartment. The funny thing was, I did not have sex with him. My body wanted to, but my mind would not let me. I felt like I had never been with a man before. I had changed and was moving forward in a positive way. I think that was the first test and I passed.

I was enjoying my place, but not enjoying being alone. I befriended a few people from my job and hung out occasionally.

I was apprehensive because I did not want them to know anything about me. They were cool to be around, but not really what I was looking for. I was moving forward but unsure how to do it and felt comfortable at the same time. Drinking flowed while gathering with my new friends which took the edge off. I began to laugh and share a bit about myself. I knew my past and did not want to fall into that hole again. I tried to limit myself and have fun in moderation.

One of my managers invited me to his home for dinner. It was a bit shocking, but nice at the same time. We talked and got to know each other better. He was a homosexual white male who was very laid back and down to earth. At the end of my visit he asked me something that opened my heart. "Would you like to go see Joyce Meyers with me?" he said. The inspirational speaker I have heard several times on television was about to be seen because of the invitation from my manager at my new job. I was overjoyed. He was spiritual. He knew the God I had found. I may have found my connection again. I was so excited. He also asked me to start coming over so we could have Bible study. He placed in my hands a new leather covered Bible he bought for me. My mouth dropped.

It was close to Christmas time, and I had no family to be around. My brother was still there, but was very busy. My manager invited me to his house for dinner. Spending this time with him opened my mind so much further and began satisfying a craving I was having. I was not sure exactly what it meant, but I loved what it was doing for me. Things were fine when we were together talking about God, but when I got alone, I did not know what to do. I would try and read the Bible, but did not understand it.

I started to get confused and could not understand the point. I would think of things I heard Joyce Meyers say when I saw her. Different things my manager said while we had Bible study would run through my mind, but I could not make them make sense in my life. What did all this mean?

From time to time I could not help but to think about the life I used to lead.

The holidays were over and I had been at my place for several months now. My manager and I were not hanging out as much anymore. It slowly tapered off. I am unsure why, but I could feel a change of some sort happening. I had just been introduced to how to connect with God and then left alone to figure it out. I was not one to ask questions; I let things fall where they may. Without that plug I felt detached. My spark was dying out and I needed energy. I was getting aggravated with trying to do something different and not knowing what exactly to do. I only knew one other way, and I knew it well.

While walking to the bank one day, an SUV stopped ahead of me and waited for me to come closer. The guy inside asked me if I needed a ride; I said no. He was persistent in receiving something from me at that time. I gave him my number and kept on walking. We spoke on the phone later that evening for quite a while. He made me laugh and I needed that. I invited him over two days later. He ended up being a pretty interesting character. We listened to music and had a few drinks. I had let him know about my past working in the club. He offered to pay me to dance. I denied, but was very enticed to do so. I had not felt that in a while and became very puzzled. He made a comment that if I was interested in making money I would have jumped on that offer. For some reason that sat in my head for a while.

Working at the store started becoming too regular. The thrill was gone and it became routine. I needed some excitement and was desperately seeking it.

I tried to be "good", but it angered me because I seemed to not do it correctly. I always did everything so well, and I did not know what to do when it came to God. Moving toward Him was hard.

Leaving the grocery store, a man stopped me asking for my number. I laughed and said, "Dang that was blunt." He said, "Why beat around the bush? I think you are cute and want to talk with you later." That made me laugh, so I gave it to him. He was an older gentleman, and that made me curious. We spoke on the phone that evening and he picked me up the next morning. He was a personal contractor that did all kinds of odd jobs. He could fix any and everything on and in a house. I thought that was so interesting . . . a carpenter. Wasn't Jesus a carpenter?

When I was not working, I would ride with him on his jobs. We were not intimate at all. It did not even come up. I could share things with him, and he with me. It was refreshing. Helping him paint, put in wood floors, or lay tiles seemed rewarding somehow. We would be all over town in all kinds of homes for all kinds of people. He became attractive in a different kind of way. I saw a provider within him opposed to his physical attributes I always saw in a man. He had so many qualities I would overlook in men. I am sure they were there, but I never took the time to move past the surface.

Things at my job became very disturbed. We had a promotional sale all the time on merchandise in the store. We received gift cards that contained a specific amount on them to give to customers at checkout. Some of the customers would decline the gift and would leave the card with me. I saw nothing wrong with this being it was given. I combined that with a store discount and my mind went to work. The furniture my brother put in my apartment was from that store that he purchased way before I even arrived. By working in the store, I had become hip to how to make exchanges and work the system so to speak. I wanted to change my living room to a new set we had come into the store. With the store credit I would receive and with the gift cards, I was able to make it happen with no problem. I did this throughout a two-week period trying to get all the little things to coordinate with my new look in the living room.

Apparently too much was going on because I was called into the office and asked how I was doing these transactions. I told them how and had to write a letter to Headquarters. I was told to go home because they were looking into this issue. "What issue?!" I was livid. All I did was use what all the customers did every day while returning and exchanging merchandise. The furniture was from their store, previously bought by my brother. The thing was those gift cards. It was the same as stealing. The gift cards were for the customers. If they rejected them, I should have turned them in and made it known. Otherwise it looks like I just took them. But wasn't that too obvious to do things that way. I would have furnished the rest of my place instead of exchanging what I already had. But I bit that bullet and said okay, I was wrong. I was fired. On to the next . . .

Now I was jobless. My brother went up to the store to try and rectify the situation, but nothing was overturned. He told me not to worry about it, and to move on. So I did, but I had a hint of anger in me. I tried, failed, and was called a thief.

I was still venturing with my new friend on his job sites and actually learning a lot about building a house. It was fascinating to see the different phases of a house being completed. From the foundation, to the framework, to molding, painting, putting in the floors and ceilings, along with the stairs to the higher levels, and incorporating water and electricity to bring it to function is really incredible . . . at least it was to me.

The thought of money began to creep in my mind now that I had no checks coming in. I often thought about what that guy said about me wanting money and what I would do if I really wanted it. I did not want to revert to my old ways and needed to keep looking forward. Losing my apartment was in the near future and failure set in my heart. My friend had a daughter that was moving into her own, so I donated my furniture to her. That was very difficult for me to do, and freeing at the same time. I was happy about helping someone else out who needed it, yet was saddened about not having anything anymore. I moved back in with my brother.

God showed me while working at that store that I can do anything at any level no matter what I am wanting. It was not about the job itself, it was dealing with the circumstances that came while working there. I was not paid a lot, but enough to maintain my household. I had the opportunity to be alone and see if I was able to uphold the values that were being instilled in me. Although I had difficulty, I was able to recognize it. God was preparing me. It was not for me to get all at once, only for me to see what was given.

Meeting my manager and experiencing what I did with him will always be a pivotal point in my life. It started a new thing in me. He served his purpose and added to my growth. I became frustrated because I was unable to carry on what he was starting, when in all actuality I was still carrying it within me. It would be there whenever another moment was ready to stir it up. More importantly, I was willing to be put in a position to move in that direction.

Working with my friend was volunteer work. I enjoyed the development and did not even think about money. I was happy to be a part of the process. To know when someone walked in their new or improved home and I assisted with what makes their life a little brighter, easier, or more comfortable was rewarding in itself. While building these homes, God was building my character. Making connections that I never knew were there, laying down surfaces for many to travel, and improving frequently used areas was life changing.

I became available for what was needed. Assisting with the homes was an attribute to many. That was something I did not turn towards in the past. It was all about what I could get out of it. Like at the store, I was trying to use what I had to get more. I should have been happy with what I had because it was new to me. I did not need anything else, but kept trying to get more. God showed me my greed and the direction I was headed in.

God exposes things to me in ways I do not think of while I am in it. I only know how I feel while doing it. I wanted to come to this area and become successful in one way or another. Successful meaning able to accomplish whatever I set out to do. At the time, I was unsure where it would take me. I simply wanted to understand while in the moment.

My brother had been an important part of that transition connecting me to the other side of these bridges I continued to cross. I was used to someone always being beside me. Through this I had no visual guide. I was learning to trust my instincts, but could not quite hold tight enough. Still in my mind, I was not moving far away from it. Not knowing, I was moving closer.

I was very disappointed in the current events that had taken place, but was more curious about what was to come. I was learning how to have faith and just go with it. I was through with badgering myself and downplaying my growth. Losing meant rising as well. I would not have known how much I changed had I not lived by myself in that apartment. Inviting men over was not bad in every sense because through them I saw the growth in me. I tried to revert back, but my mind had already started over and my body followed.

I did not see it clearly, but I was starting again successfully. God continued to flow through me and always had a place for me to land when I fell. It is not that things ended, it is the fact that it can start again.

WANDERING
Chapter Twenty-Three

SCRIPTURE

Mathew 15:14

". . . Leave them; they are blind guides. If the blind lead the blind, both will fall into a pit."

My brother knew a young woman who was trying to start up her own transitional home for women. He knew that was right up my alley because of my personal history and he thought I could add to her vision or at least assist her. I was introduced to her and we clicked instantly. I began volunteering any services I could offer her. She lived in the 13-unit apartment building, in need of serious work, where the clients would eventually reside. I could see the potential and respected very much what she wanted to do with that space. Because of my friend that did work on homes, I figured this was a match made in heaven. I saw nothing but good things coming from this and was headed in a positive direction despite my recent disposal.

I never thought I would be putting in work and not get paid for it. This was the beginning of God showing me firsthand what volunteering was about. I did not feel cheated because I was enjoying what I was doing. I was also learning how this type of establishment was developed. I met a new girlfriend who was into God and helping others in a positive way. Although this was a different kind of experience, I was excited moving forward with a friend like her. She offered to pick me up in the mornings which was very nice. It was quite a distance from my brother's place and walking would have been very long.

I was not sure what I would be doing for her, but I always looked forward to new challenges. Because of the newness, I had a little bit of uncertainty. It did not seem like she had it all together on the business side of things. I was not sure how this type of place began, but I could see confusion when it presented itself. It almost made it all the more fun because she was just as lost as I was.

She just received her 501(c) (3) status which was pretty exciting. This lets it be known that you are now established as a specific non-profit business. My only question was about the building itself. It was not in any way able to house anyone. It needed much work which would cost more money than she had. I did not understand the way she organized the importance of certain things concerning her business, but who was I. I was there to assist, but felt at times there was nothing to assist.

We were to go to a meet and greet type of deal where we would pass out our information and receive from others to begin a form of networking. This was exciting for me. I had the opportunity to see how these kind of functions worked. There were varieties of businesses and organizations representing all sorts of individuals. To see so many positive women in one room for a common goal was so uplifting and inspiring. I could not help to think I would do this one day for my own.

I was told to leave the table and go to others to collect their information and to discuss ours. I was not a big talker, and about peed in my pants. I made my way around like a little girl searching for her parents. It became easier as I conversed with more people. I was a fish out of water who was trying to breathe. Everyone was so friendly and made things comfortable when I approached them.

It was like everything I learned from watching my mother at work, during school, in church, and through working all came into play at that time. I was so nervous, but it played out smoothly.

Now her status was obtained and networking had been done. I still could not understand why these things were done before having the units ready to be occupied. What if someone had clients that needed housing? So, I asked my friend to come by and survey the building to see what he thought.

He bypassed the work needed to be done and went straight to her. He wanted to talk cost. Budget seemed to be more of concern than the issues the building had. I kind of understood his position, but wondered how he knew to ask that first. I was even more shocked when she said she wanted the work done for free or close to it! I thought she was pretty brave to assume that and even more so to say it aloud.

Embarrassed that I asked him to come by, I walked him to his truck apologizing repeatedly. I told him I had no idea that was what she was thinking. I did however know she had no money; but I did not tell him that. When I returned inside, I could barely look at her. I kind of shrugged my shoulders and sat down. She proceeded to scream about how he would charge way too much. All I could think of is the amount of work that needed to be done. It would definitely cost a lot no matter how you looked at it and no matter who did it.

Outside of this incident, there was a conference call that we were on speaking about some paperwork that was needed. The person on the other end suggested she have a particular folder together that contained specific information. My girlfriend said no problem, she believed she had everything. So to make sure everything would be accounted for, the woman on the phone went through everything expected.

I believe I about lost my breath when half of the paperwork was suggested, my friend did not even know what it was. My mouth dropped. My mind began to wander . . .

What had I gotten involved with? What was the purpose of me being here? It seemed she was very unfamiliar with starting a business. I was under the impression she knew what she was doing. The impression I came with began to fade as I saw my friend was not filled with all the knowledge to begin a non-profit organization such as this. I mentioned this to my brother and he just shrugged his shoulders.

Now I really was confused. If she does not know what she is doing, how will I? I did not mention this to her. I figured she kind of knew I thought something. I still respected what she was attempting to do. I only thought she knew what was required and had all that was needed to get this transition running. With no money to renovate and lack of necessary knowledge, I was unsure how this would turn out.

She then suggested that we make scented candles to come up with some funds. It would be like a fund raiser for a specific cause because non-profits cannot sell items. She proceeded to purchase the items we needed. We even had labels with the name and logo on them. I thought to myself, 'this is a pretty good idea . . . I think.'

I could not help but to have questions. How will we advertise? Who will we target? I did not want to rain on the idea, but I started thinking it would not be enough for what was needed.

As it turned out, there was not adequate advertising so many people did not even know. She made some money, but not enough to do any kind of work. She went shopping with the money.

When I saw that she made money for her business yet went shopping with those funds, I knew this place was not going to turn out as expected. There had to be something else in this experience for me. Here I was a lost soul trying to find my way and had been guided to someone who was misguiding me in many ways . . . so I thought.

She was a proclaimed Christian whose mom, a pastor, came and blessed the grounds of this nonprofit business. She was trying to start a housing ministry for those who were in need. She went out of her way to pick me up in the mornings so I could assist with whatever she needed. She fed me daily out of the food she had in her refrigerator and prepared herself. She was trying her best with what she had and knew. She had been feeling her way around this new experience for several months and was not very familiar with the particulars of beginning a housing facility.

When I sat and listened to her talk with me after feeling worn out from all of her attempts, I saw things differently. I saw a woman who had the courage to step out on faith and begin a huge project like this. Despite all of the failed efforts that are plain to see, I saw clearer the affect it had on me. She displayed great strength throughout this grueling process. I was the one looking at her sideways because of the lack of ability. Seeing her continue to push forward and think of new ideas was encouraging. Whether they worked or not, she was trying. I saw a woman in the flesh fighting a fight of her life.

As she was wandering around in her darkness, she brought me light.

God allowed me to view someone in training. Training in many ways. She was a Christian woman who cussed from time to time, drank, and smoked cigarettes. She angered and held grudges just like anybody else. But what stuck out the most to me, although these things could be discouraging to someone trying to learn the proper ways, was how she continued to have faith. She was always positive in that manner. No matter what, she was holding on.

My mind went all over the place during these beginning stages with her. I thought I was walking into a "professional business." I thought she had to have it altogether in order to be successful. My perception was all wrong. Being professional does not look as we think it may. It is not always clean, neat, and in place. Things can be very disgruntled and be very well together.

God not only was starting her off on this journey, He allowed me to go with her. It was meant for her to struggle the way she was. It was meant for me to see it. I saw more than a struggle. I saw a fight. She was building on her faith and I was beginning to have it.

It is amazing how God can show Himself in anything at any time. He allowed my eyes and mind to wander in every way humanly possible in dealing with the situation I was in. What I thought I saw initially was not what I ended up seeing. After a bit of blurred vision, He cleared my sight. Once I was able to see what was really going on, I understood a little better. I began to appreciate this opportunity that much more because of the hardship she was facing. I could see us coming together in facing the challenges to come. We were pretty much one in the same.

She had faith and I could see it which lead to my faith increasing beyond this situation. My mind now was able to envision the very best for my life past where I was.

It was God's intention for us to wander and feel our way around at the same time.

SPREADING MY WINGS
Chapter Twenty-Four

Proverbs 3:27
Do not withhold good from those to whom it is due, when it is in your power to act.

Assisting my new girlfriend in the beginning stages of the transitional living for women was encouraging. It was something I had thought of doing personally and now was a part of. Seeing how to obtain non-profit status, networking with other organizations, and coming up with ideas to bring in revenue was enlightening and educational. I was in a place I was unsure of how I got there. I had definitely reached another level even if I was just peeking in.

As time went on, I met her family and spent quite a bit of time with her outside of work. It had been discussed that I move into one of the units to be on the grounds to assist her further and to provide me a place of my own instead of paying me. I had no problem with that. I would have my own space again and I could be right there on the property whenever she needed me. I could see the start of something good.

She was not from where we lived, but had lived there for a while. My brother and she used to work with each other in the past. Because of their relationship, it made me less apprehensive to open up to her. We would talk about everything. She discussed her life and I disclosed mine. I had never had a friend like this before that I could be so open with without fearing the worst. I was glad to have a close girlfriend I could confide in and assist with her vision. I felt like I was contributing in many ways. She was so kind to me that I had no problem assisting her with whatever she needed me to do.

She was going to her hometown and invited me to go with her. I had never been to this area before and was excited to be traveling. I was more taken back that she wanted me to meet her family. That made me feel special and very close to her. I saw her in a new light. I had a best friend.

When we arrived, we went to her sister's house where we were staying. Her sister had a son that was not home at the time; we would meet later. After the introductions, we went to her mother's house and I met her. They all were very embracing and treated me as if they knew me forever. We chatted with her mom for a while and headed back to her sister's place. Once we got there, everyone was trying to figure out what we were going to do that evening. As they were coming up with ideas, her sister's son came in the room and said, "Hey everybody, what's going on?!" with a huge smile on his face. He was much younger than us, but looked like much fun. We were introduced and they continued to decide the activities for the night.

Her nephew said something about shooting pool and I immediately sprouted up. "I love to shoot pool", I shouted. He said, "Bet, let's go!" I looked at my girlfriend and her sister and asked if they were coming. I felt a bit uncomfortable going without them. They encouraged me to go and have fun, so I did. I had not been out and had fun in such a long time. We went to a club that had a pool table inside. I did not even pay attention to the dance floor, I only wanted to whoop him in a few games. We had a few drinks and chatted a bit. The place seemed to be full of a younger crowd that was very carefree. It was surprisingly fun.

After finishing up our games, we went outside and sat on the hood of his old pick-up truck. All of the action actually happened in the parking lot. He went inside his truck and sparked up a "phat blunt." I had a blank stare on my face as I slowly reached for it and lit it up. We sat in that parking lot for about two hours.

Once we returned to his mom's house we sat out back and smoked, drank, and talked some more. Everyone was sleep, so we did not want to wake them with laughing throughout the house. I asked the pondering question, "How old are you?" He said 23. Oh my . . .

I did not know why that mattered, but somehow I did not care. I had fun and I owned it. I started smoking again, and I owned that too. I felt I was doing very well, and still was. What was wrong with a little fun? Everything seemed to be going smoothly in my life. This added to it. I enjoyed him and he said he enjoyed me as well. He asked for a number where I could be reached. I told him to contact me through his aunt.

What was I starting?

I had been on the premises for about a month or so now and had been speaking to my girlfriend's nephew on the phone for a couple of weeks. He was wanting me to come and visit, but I was unsure about that although I enjoyed his conversation. He was noncontroversial and offered a sense of relief to my life. He was young and carefree and I envied that.

My girlfriend's personal life was not going so well. She lived with her man and they were having some issues. This added a negative vibe to what we were doing relating to the housing development. A lot of work still needed to be done and no funds were coming in. I remember telling her I could go to a club and get whatever we needed in about a week or two. She laughed and said, "Girrrr no!" That was the end of that idea. But it did not leave my mind.

Because of the toxic atmosphere happening around the complex, I opted to visit her nephew. There were buses that left our area and went to the casino where he lived. He would pick me up from there. It was perfect. I could get away, venture something new, and escape reality all for $10.00. I stayed a few days and returned. I could see that becoming a frequent thing, and it did.

There was no progress with her business and not much was being done any more. It seemed I was doing more odd work than necessary to earn my keep. It got to a point where I felt more like the help rather than a friend assisting a friend like it began. I am not sure if it was her personal life or the stress of getting this business up and going, but I was nobody's slave. I wanted to help as much as possible and kind of felt obligated because I was living there. The more time went by, the more I felt in the way. The line of communication became static.

I tried to understand what the problem was, but I was not the kind of person who asked questions. I let things fall where they may. I began to travel to see her nephew more often. I would rather be out of the way than in the way.

While visiting with her nephew, she made a call to him complaining about my whereabouts and what I was not doing around the premises. I could not understand the complaint being there was nothing to do. I cleaned the units, handled paperwork, answered phones until it rang no more, and was there for her personally. What else was I to do? I also have to admit, I felt a little bitter because of her being distant with me once she started encountering the problems with her man. We were like strangers walking the premises. She had everything in her unit. I had no TV, no radio, and no food. Traveling did not seem to be a problem to me because I would be one less bother.

My new young friend had moved into an apartment with one of his best friends which gave him a little more freedom. They had good jobs, ate well, and had much fun. This was so relaxing to me. I did not have to worry about anything, did nothing, and was stress free. We smoked, drank, and laughed every day. I stayed at the house while everyone went to work. I had not a care in the world. Wherever we would go he made me feel special. It was a small area, so everyone knew who I was with. That was a different feeling for me and I loved it.

His family was pretty spiritual. He had always talked about knowing he would be a preacher. We spoke about God here and there, but not too often. His mother was a very special woman along with his brother's wife. These were some strong women who took care of their families. Nobody is perfect, but I could see something wonderful in both of them. These two women had come to visit the transitional home premises one time to see what the talk was about concerning my girlfriend's new business venture. While there, they came to my unit and saw how I was living. I did not complain. I told them I was glad to have a place to stay and appreciated her having me. Later that same evening, my girlfriend went out leaving me with nothing to eat. To my surprise I saw lights pull up and the patter of feet coming up the steps to my door. It was these two women bringing me groceries! They said they did not know I was here like this and wanted to bring me some food for myself because she was not feeding me. All I could do was cry . . .

After hearing about the event with his mom and sister-in-law bringing me groceries in the middle of the night, he had no problem with me staying with him as long as I wanted. We appreciated each other at the time and lived in the moment. Because I did not complain about the conditions of my living situation, the depth of my frustration was not known. Yet, I was grateful for having a place and being a part of something wonderful that was developing. When that was not happening, the joy that was once shared was gone. I felt a little lost, but he came along. He offered wind to my sail.

I was not doing anything while there with her. What we started was not there anymore. I do not blame the relationship with him. Her business was not working out which I believe kind of pushed me toward him. I decided I was staying with him for a while until she decided what she wanted to do. I found a job at a local drive-through daiquiris spot. I made much money and had fun doing it. I was fitting in and did not feel in the way. I did not know how long this was going to last and really did not care. It was about right now. Starting over again . . . Then the unthinkable happened. Hurricane Katrina hit right outside the area where we were. Watching that on television was insane. And in a few days we had to evacuate, hurricane Rita was getting ready to hit our area. The family all met up and decided an evacuation plan. We were soon on the highway headed northeast.

The hurricane was not just in the area we were leaving, it traveled with us.

During this time, it was made very clear who was in charge, important, and relevant. Everyone had a room but us. I had some money and a check that could not be cashed. My friend did not have enough money to put a dent in anything. Because of our lack of, we stayed on the floor and ate leftovers. Honestly, because of the situation, I did not know what to think until we were told we did not mean much right now because we could not contribute.

I took some of the money I had and got us a room at a cheaper motel. The area we were in caught the outside breeze of the storm and had power outages scattered around that town. We were not far from his family, and had our own space and was comfortable in a bed. We were in walking distance to a little restaurant that was open and went there to collect ourselves. Shaking our heads, we could not wait to get back home.

We returned back to the hard hit of Rita. The city looked like a disaster zone. I had never seen anything like that in my life. Our mood fit the scenery when we heard we had to travel to his aunt's complex to stay while the city was being repaired. We gathered some of our things and headed out.

At least I was still protected despite the storm happening all around me.

It was disheartening having to return to her complex. After the treatment I received, I really did not feel welcomed. I chucked it up and did what I had to in order to get through this. Everyone was given a unit to stay in. He and I walked into ours and a toilet was in the middle of the floor. We looked at each other, laughed, and said, "Come on man!"

I told him things would be better once he received his check they were giving out for all of the hurricane survivors. I had an I.D from that city but chose not to apply for those funds. Something told me NO. So, I supported him and anticipated the outcome.

Once he received his check, it was as if what I did was forgotten. I did not expect a huge cut, but at least a portion of what I put out for us when no one else did. Another eye opener for me and I moved forward without a word. I felt as if I really could not say anything because I had no control. I did not have a place to stay, nor did I drive. I had a few dollars from the job I had and a check to cash. I just kept quiet and followed suit.

When we returned back to his city the apartment was tore up. There was a hole in his ceiling and through his bed where we slept. It was as if God said we were not going to be in that bed any longer. Our run was over. I knew it immediately. Not only had a hurricane hit the nearby areas, it also hit our relationship. I was seeing things come out of him that I could not continue to deal with. I had much fun with him and appreciated the shelter while going through the rift with his aunt, but when tragedy struck, I did not feel too secure. It was touch and go. Not that I should have had more than anybody else, it was just the fact that he was not able to take care of the situation as a man should be able to. When he received his money, he changed and acted as if I did not exist.

I had to think things over. I believe God allowed me to see just what I saw. I will always be taken care of, but not to my liking. Appreciate everything and anything all the time. Be thankful in all situations because it could be worse. Always do what you are able to do no matter what it is. It is not about the way something looks, it is knowing you have what you need. It is the wind beneath my wings that makes anything possible.

What I did know is God had me the entire time throughout this whole situation. I lent my services and had services rendered to me in my time of need. In the mist of transitioning myself, I ended up at a transitional housing program that was just starting out. It became clear that it needed much more assistance than I was offering. When you do not have the proper foundation, you are unable to build anything. The ground was shaky to begin with. I was able to learn a great deal about starting a non-profit and I am honored and feel privileged to have been able to be amongst those who were even in the position to think about starting a program. In the storm, I saw how family comes together to keep everyone safe the best way they know possible. Trying to sort out the specifics may be rough, but those who have will have. It allowed me to see exactly what I did not have. I know He had me when I did not.

Throughout it all, God kept me, and I got another chance . . . to spread my wings.

INSIGHT BEGINS
Chapter Twenty-Five

SCRIPTURE
Isaiah 66:2
".. Has not my hand made all these things, and so they
came into being?" declares the Lord. "These are the ones
I look on with favor:
Those who are humble and contrite in spirit," and who
tremble at my word."

After the hurricane things were very chaotic. I was left
homeless again because of the destruction done to my friend's
apartment. I was forced to retreat back to my girlfriend's until I
could conjure up something else. By this time, the building was
being used as a shelter for hurricane survivors who were out of a
place to stay. So it ended up being of assistance after all. She
could not house many tenants because of the work needed to be
done on the units, but it served its purpose for a few. That was a
positive thing to see out of all the negativity that was soaring.

In order for me to stay there, I was to clean the owner of the
apartment building's place of residence and help out around the
premises as needed. I felt so degraded but needed a place to
stay so I agreed to the terms. I settled back in feeling out of
place. My life now had no direction, and at times I felt it had no
meaning. How did I end up here after all I had overcome? I
could not understand but knew something had to change.

My girlfriend and I were not the best of buds as we were but
we were friendly. I believe she was doing all that she was able.
It is not like she was supposed to take care of me. I was just in
such a place of being lost that I wanted somebody to rescue me.

I would always try to make things work even though I could see the problem in it. I wanted better and could not find it. I said silent prayers to myself in a nonchalant way. My mind began to revert back to the club and the way I was. I could not help but to think it would really help me out right now.

I would take long walks to the downtown area. It had to be about 10 miles or so going and coming. I did not care about the distance or even where I was going, I only wanted to go. Nothing in particular was on my mind. I would look all around me as I walked. I could see possibilities everywhere and would wonder "how do I get that?" When I could not walk any further, I would turn around and return to where I came from.

I took these walks several times during the week, lost quite a bit of weight, and toned up very well.

During this time, I did much thinking about my life. I had all kinds of thoughts flowing through my mind. Decisions I had made, choices I thought were good, and the moves I made with my heart were all flooding my head. I did not worry about them being right or wrong. It was only the fact that I made them. I tried to figure out why.

Thinking back to my childhood, I began to feel the hurt and pain of yesteryear. Reliving the abuse, I became very angry. Why had this all happened to me? What did I do?

Then I began to feel remorse. I chose to be with a young man who was abusive and then have children with him. I made that choice and because of that, I had to deal with what I was dealt. I then thought of my children. Why was it my fault for him not allowing me to see them? Why am I to blame for everything? It appeared I was at fault because I was the one suffering at the moment. He went on with his life, took me to court for custody of my children, and then blamed me. I could not help but cry.

I was held accountable for everything regardless of the control I had or not. Because I was in what appeared to be hell, I was the culprit. So many things were entering and exiting my mind I became exhausted. I did not care anymore. I wondered briefly where God went. Did I do something else wrong and that is why I was suffering again?

Despite the uncertainty of my life at the moment, I continued to have a sense of will within me. I had to ride out this wave, but what a long one it was.

By this time there were four tenants in the apartment building. There was not too much for me to do anymore because one of the tenants was offered a job to work on the premises. It was more beneficial for her to receive than I. I would do odd, odd jobs. By this time, I really did not care. I needed to do something to make the days go by.

I did one of the tenant's hair, resurfaced a tub in one of the units, and continued to clean what was needed. I still had an uncashed check and a few dollars. I did not know how or when, but something would change very quickly.

I continued to be grateful for having a place to stay because it could be worse. Although this was a blessing, I could not help but to hate the conditions I was living under. It was not only the lack of, it was that I had no plan. I could not see how any of this was leading to somewhere. When I began assisting her, I could see an opportunity later down the line. Now, I did not see anything but despair. I seemed to be fading more and more.

I would look around and wonder how . . .

I became depressed in where I was. I continued to look around me and knew that this was not for me anymore. It did not feel right anymore. My attitude was slowly turning to frustration.

I had not been working with my friend any longer on the houses. I had not been getting paid and at that time was fine, but now felt that I should. I called him and demanded I get paid something for my services. I was tired of feeling like a step-child and wanted what was mine.

He was very disturbed that I would ask him in the manner that I did. I actually did not blame him, but I had turned all the way and needed to uphold this demeanor in order to carry out the mission I was on. I had to get out. I needed a change quick, fast, and in a hurry. I had it with this situation!

To top off my frustration, the owner of the apartment told me I had a few days to be out. I was not able to stay there any longer being that there was nothing for me to really do. I understood exactly what he meant, but dang . . . where was I going?

It seemed to line up with my plans of wanting to leave, so if I had second thoughts, this justified the first. I guess my heart and mind knew best.

After much harassment on my part, I received a check from the friend I used to do work with on the homes. I became a very aggressive, strong, and determined individual. I knew what I wanted and what I had to do to get it. I now had two checks and a little cash to work with to make something happen. My mind went to work.

I was going through my things and kept pulling out certain type of clothing. A little top here, a pretty colored blouse there, and some cute thongs. It was settled. I am going back to the club.

I went to cash my checks. On the way to the check cashing place I contemplated what I was getting ready to do. I could not see another way. I needed to leave immediately. I was not going back to my brother's place. Besides, he was moving again soon. So I needed to do something on my own. The only thing now was where I would work and how I would get there.

There was a new tenant that moved in and he had a car. I found my way . . .

I believe God allowed me to go through this hardship in order to build the boldness that came out in the end. There was lessons all the way through this experience, but staying strong and doing what is necessary rather than break down rings through the loudest.

I was not a very outgoing or outspoken individual. I would be quiet before I would complain about anything; unless I was drinking. For me to endure what I did took much strength that I know I did not have without God. The measure in how I was living was enough, but then to add the belittling work I had to do to earn my keep. Because of that, humble is in my vocab now. It did not matter what I thought of myself. It is where I was and what I had to do while I was there that mattered.

I did not complain, yet knew it was going to get better. I knew there was much in me to come out. "I am capable of too much" I kept telling myself. God put that in me a long time ago. Through each trial I went through I heard that over and over, louder and louder.

God showed me, again, to listen to my heart no matter what. I used to do that all the time, but felt I needed to do something different. He allowed me to see how pain comes in many ways. It may hurt sometimes, but it is necessary for the next episode.

Little by little I began to understand what drove me. I had not made an in depth conclusion, but I was on to something. Everything would work out as long as I followed my heart and not my feelings. As difficult as it was, it was possible. I had held my tongue that entire time. I did what I was asked to do no matter the task. I fell many times with smoking, drinking, and swearing but still had a heart full of love. I had a burning desire in my heart that was getting stronger and stronger.

I remembered how I used to make choices. I had to have a deep yearning in my heart that drove me. I was learning that it did not matter where I was or what I was doing as long as the pulling was in my heart. As soon as it stopped, something was about to change. I could always feel that something was alright or it was not.

God showed me how to look within and trust it. Insight began while the outside conditions were not so good.

AS IS
Chapter Twenty-Six

❧ ✠ SCRIPTURE ✠ ❧

Hebrews 11:1
Now faith is confidence in what we hope for and assurance about what we do not see.

Checks are cashed and a plan is set. Since I figured out what I wanted to do, I have felt 100% better about my situation. I was not excited about going back to the club, but I was excited about gaining some control (I thought I had) over my situation.

I continued looking through my things to see what I could wear. I had a lot of cutting and adjusting to do in order to get through a few nights of working. I set out to go to an adult store to purchase a pair of dance shoes. I planned to get the cheapest pair to get me by. I was not into what I would be doing, but knew I needed the gear. Being that I did this before, I knew the specifics of what was necessary and what was over glamorizing myself. The bare essentials would be fine . . . at least they would be for now.

I also had to speak with the new guy who moved in about driving me to the club. I knew off the bat that it would not be a problem. I saw him staring at me when he moved in. I was still going to offer him gas money although I know he would have done it for free. I did not want to take full advantage, but was going to use what I could to get what I needed at the time. I was not having sex with him! Definitely not. He would take the money or forget it.

There was one thing I had not figured out yet. What club was I going to dance at? I did not know this area, or any other for that matter, to know of any clubs. I instantly remembered the name of a club I saw in the phone book when it was mentioned once before about me doing what it took to make some money if I really wanted to.

I had to get there and at least see where it was and how long it took to get there. I needed to scope out the surrounding area for rooms. If I was going to be dancing on a regular for a while, I needed a place that was nearby and I could get to very easily from the club. I needed to do some investigating.

I called up a friend I met when I first got to town. I told him my plans and he was amazed but intrigued. So he came by with a disturbed look on his face a day before I had to be out and took me by the club. When I got in the car he said, "What in the world are you doing?" I told him I had to do what I had to do. We proceeded to the club. When we arrived he would not go in, so I went in alone. I took a deep breath, looked around, and went inside. It was a small setup with a cozy little feel; almost like a neighborhood spot. I asked for the manager and walked over to the bar. There were a few girls working and a few guys checking me out when I walked by.

He came over and said, "So you wanna work?" He was a short bald-headed guy with an Arabic accent. I smiled and said yes. I showed him my ID, he gave me a briefing of what is expected, and showed me to the dressing room. Everything was well with me. I let him know I would be back the following day. It was all set. I was working again.

When I got back to the car, my friend asked how it went. I let him know as he sped off down the road. It was pretty funny because he appeared to be sorry for me. I let him know I would be just fine, but he could come and be my bodyguard. He then asked me how much money I had. I thought that was an odd question to ask at this time. Instantly I could feel the change in the air and it did not feel good. I looked at him and said "not much, but I will." I did not say any more the entire way back.

I saw from him I had to get into another frame of mind. A man was going to see me differently no matter who I know I am. It was not about me anymore; it was what I was getting ready to be doing. He did not see me as the woman he met several months ago. He saw me as I was.

From that feeling I had in the car with my friend, I understood I had to go into another mode. I needed to put up my defenses and become withdrawn. I had to prepare mentally for what I was about to do. I was going into this solo. When I started dancing before I had someone there with me every day, all day. I had a sense of security from my man at that time. I was in a new place with people I did not know.

My mind also began to question what I was about to do. Did God show me all He did just so I would be right back in the club? What would everybody say about me now?

I did not have another way out that I could see. My brother was gone by this time, and I knew no one but my girlfriend and a few guys. As things stood, this was what I had to do. I had to be out sooner than later and had just enough money to get started at the club. I needed money now, which was the only way I knew, and felt strongly I was able to do it.

I just knew it would work out fine. I still did not know where I would stay. The last day had come and my first night was approaching. I was not too nervous and felt confident that all would turn out fine. I only knew it had to.

I knocked on the guy's door and let him know I was ready to go. The first thing he mentioned was gas, and I stuck $20 in his face and said let's go.

My first night at the club went very well. I already knew I would do well because I needed to. I did not even think about what I was doing. I enjoyed the freeness of it all once again. I did not feel stressed to make money or thought about where I was going to stay. I asked someone about a room and they gave me the name of a place right around the corner. The best thing is that it was in walking distance. I now had to find a way to get my things to the room.

After the club I began walking to room. I figured I would catch a cab and make a roundtrip. I made enough to pull it off. It would be costly but I would do what I had to do. As I was walking, many cars were honking and pulling over. I had my game face on and did not feel afraid in the least.

The strange thing was one small pickup truck slowed down, the window rolled down, and a voice said let me give you a ride. I cannot tell you why this voice sounded any different than the rest, but it did. I looked at him and got in. As my mind was saying "What in the &$%#, @%&$ are you doing girl?" I told him what I needed to do. He politely said, "Just show me where to go." We went to the motel so I could get my room and key and then headed back to the building to get my things.

I remember looking up at the sky saying thank you. It was all working out, as is, with no extra effort.

I had returned my keys to my girlfriend and gave her my thanks and appreciation. I believe she was a bit surprised, but knew I was more than capable. I did not look back once we pulled off.

So this stranger helped me carry my things into my room and stayed and chatted for a few minutes. He was very respectful but I knew he had to try his hand. Before his halo light dimmed, he offered me some money to help me out. I let him know immediately that I did not need that and that what he had done for me was more than enough. I was still kind of amazed that he drove me to the room, to get my things, and back to the room. These were not around the corner from each other. He insisted that I take the money and would not take no for an answer. I accepted with tears in my eyes. He gave me a hug and went on his way.

As I watched him pull off and drive away, I felt a huge sense of relief come over me. I was in my own domain with the ability to pay my own way by doing what I knew how to do effortlessly. I did not care what I had resorted back to. I appreciated it this time around. It was about independence and being able. I had been in the position of being taken care of and I was not comfortable at all.

Although I learned quite a bit, I was glad to be exactly where I was. A little cheap motel room was paradise to me as is.

I have every bit of confidence that God was with me the entire time throughout these events. The way everything played out was too perfect. Nothing flawed, went wrong, or faltered. I did not have a hint of hesitation in any move I made. Everything worked out as is.

During this time my faith truly grew. I did not have anyone to go through this with, so no one to give credit to. Because I was fearless, I know that was God. He enabled me to endure this time of being solo. I had no time to think about my circumstances, only to do something about them. I followed my gut and moved forward without knowing my next move. I knew it would work out.

It was as if He directed everyone to be exactly where they were just for me. Hmmm . . .

I realized God still had me even though I was headed in the direction of what is thought to be destruction. If it was not for me to be there, He would not have allowed it. He made sure I was taken care of while going down this road. He connected every dot. It was not by anything I conjured up because I did not know what to do. Once again it was on my heart strongly to go.

I had the bare essentials and was able as is. Only God can make that happen the way it did. I was safe and able as is.

BACK DOWN MEMORY LANE
Chapter Twenty-Seven

SCRIPTURE

Romans 8:5

Those who live according to the flesh have their minds set on what the flesh desires; but those who live in accordance with the Spirit have their minds set on what the Spirit desires.

Looking around me, I could not believe I was actually back in the club. I actually thought I was through with this life. As I sat at a table sipping on my drink I decided to get in the swing of things. I could not do this successfully thinking about God all the time. I got it in my heart and mind that I knew I had changed and I still was. I am just here briefly to get things in order. I did not put any pressure on myself by setting a time limit. I would let it ride out. I did not want to be walking around with anything on my shoulders. God was a part of my life now and that would not change, but I had to do what was necessary for me to pull this off.

Drinking and smoking was stirred up again in no time. It felt a bit different because my mind was clear at this time. I had not a care in the world. I was not thinking about anything or anybody. It was about me, making money, and having a place to stay.

The girls in the club were a little different from where I was before, but I never did concern myself with them anyway. I stayed pretty much to myself. When asked questions, I kept it brief and simple. I was not trying to get to know anybody and did not want anybody to know me. I was there for one reason.

It did not take long for me to gain clientele. I was always the first one there and one of the last to leave. I was on the grind. I enjoyed myself at the same time, but was still keeping it simple. Getting my own place became a focus. I was determined to move in an apartment that was right across the street from the club. Within a few weeks, I moved in a two-bedroom.

The guys were very persistent and paid a great deal of attention to the new girl; me. They were very curious and tried their best to get with me. I was not having it. I did not want to start out that way. I tried to keep it together, but I went against my rules. I went out with one of the guys I danced for. I figured it would be harmless. I went out with this guy for a short period of time due to another one that came along.

The DJ told me he had someone he wanted me to meet.

Once this man came to the club, we were introduced. He appeared to be very different to me immediately. He was very polite, but not in a fake way. When he looked at me, chills went through me. I spoke with him briefly and walked away. He never left my mind. Days after meeting, he tried to get me to leave out of the club one night by sticking his bank card in my bikini top and said he would pay for the rest of my night. I smiled, gave it right back to him, and said no. I could not believe it, but I did. I knew then I really liked him already.

I did not want to get caught up into anybody. I did not mind hanging out and having a good time, but did not want it to get serious. I wanted to keep my focus and not have my feelings belong to anyone but me.

I asked about water one day and he drove me to a nearby island. I could tell we were getting close to water by the change in the sky. Before I knew it, we rode up on the seawall where there was nothing but water. All I could do is smile and think about how he really listened to me when I told him about things I loved. I melted that day.

He had a decent job and treated me very well. I could talk to him about anything with no problem. He did not judge me and seemed to understand me. We both loved to love and enjoyed each other's company very much. I still was apprehensive.

I was unsure how to proceed with this relationship I was developing. I wanted love so bad, for so long and it appeared to be here. I know I had been in this place before and was hurt deeply. Although this felt very different than any other, I still resisted to open up all the way. He was not pushy and was not jealous at all. I continued to see other people as well as date him. I could not help to think of him.

Working at the club was coming along fine and I was making plenty of money. I had been in my apartment a couple of weeks when I received a call from my family stating my dad was bringing two of my sons to me. This was quite shocking and confusing, but exciting at the same time. It had been years since I had seen them. It would be wonderful to have them with me again. But the fact that my ex-husband had taken me to court for custody and child support did not sit well with me. Why in the world are you sending them to me when you have custody and I am supposed to be paying support? Not only that, why just two? I had three boys with him.

I began to feel the pressure. Where my life had become stress-free, it had just become tense. That part of my life was over as I knew it because of the circumstances. Now I am being faced with the same kind of challenges only years later. I was not going to turn down the opportunity to have my boys with me despite the ridiculous arrangement. I prepared for their arrival.

We, the new man, were talking on the phone and had been going out having a really good time. I was scared to let my guard down with him because of my past.

I knew I was going against my heart, but I could not help it. I went out of town with someone I knew from the club to dance at another club where he was from. I wanted to get away and see what it was like in his home state. I was about making money and that was an opportunity. It was not about the guy I was traveling with at all.

I received a call while I was there from my new friend. I let him know where I was and who I was with. I felt very comfortable telling him and did not feel I needed to lie about anything. He made me feel so good when he told me he would come and get me if I needed him to. He also made a statement that would change my feelings toward him a little further. He said, "I thought you were my girl?" I could not help but to smile big as I spoke with him outside of my hotel room while the guy I was with was sleeping. I immediately felt I wanted to leave. That day it was established; I was his.

As the days ran closer to the arrival of two of my sons (13 and 14), I began to get some things they would need. I had a two bedroom so one of those rooms was now theirs. I had a bathroom connected to my room so I still would have my privacy and they had their own. I purchased bunk-beds that I separated, a television, and a video game for their entertainment. I had gotten so used to being by myself, I did not have much in the house. I did not care about things. I only wanted my own space after being under someone else's roof for so long. I gathered the bare necessities and awaited their coming.

I looked forward to my new man meeting them as well. I had told him all about them and my situation. He was excited about meeting them because of my demeanor. I am sure it was a bit of curiosity. To see me in another light, mommy mode, would be different for him and me. I was letting him in.

I was overjoyed when my boys arrived. I could not get over how big they had gotten. They looked so much older that I realized how much time I had actually missed. It felt so weird to have something that belonged to me with me again. It was even stranger knowing I had to leave them and go to the club that night. I had to continue to work and I did not hide it from them.

They met my new man and he tried his best to make them feel welcomed. It seemed all they could do is think about their girlfriends they left back home. They interacted with him, but thought more of themselves. As long as they laughed and could talk, all was well. He shared some things with them and invited them to do the same at any time. I was glad they met.

I knew I had to enroll them into school, but they had to finish out the year they were in. Trying to do this was unreal. How am I supposed to enroll them into school with no paperwork on them? Their father did not send any kind of personal documents with them. I called and I tried over and over to get some cooperation from him and it was not happening. I could not believe it! What in the world did he expect me to do with them having no documents on them; not to mention he had custody of them as well? I was not able to do too much because I did not have the authority to do so. I took them to the school for enrollment and provided them with as much information as I could. They were said to take a test and they could begin promptly.

Summer was approaching and activities would be desired. All I could think of is how I was going to get them involved in anything without documents? Tension began to run high, but I was keeping it together. My new man was very helpful with keeping me calm. He would assure me I was doing all I could and that was good. It was not good enough for me though, and most of all them.

Without doubt, they both passed to the next grade. Because of one of them being withheld a year, they were in the same grade. Everything was well with that, but the concern was how to get them into high school. I still needed shot records, birth certificates, and the rest of their school transcripts in order to enroll them into another level of schooling. Again, I received no cooperation from the other side.

To my surprise, they were able to get themselves into a YMCA that was around the way. I had no clue where it even was. They had caught the bus, spoke to the person in charge, and received a youth card to enter the center. While I was very astonished at their abilities, it scared me as well. The independent factor was lovely, but they were in a new place. They were young men new to the area that no one knew. I knew how their tempers were when they were younger, so I know it had progressed just a tad. More was yet to be seen.

With strain on the school situation, there became an issue with them as well. As quickly as they were angels, they became aggressive, disrespectful, and disobedient. One would jump off the balcony and go where he pleased, and the other was screwing females he just met. I was not having it and approached the situation one day. Close to the birthday of the younger one, he became very rude and aggressive toward me. For a second I thought I was going to fight my child right in my living-room. As we were in the mist of the commotion, my new man called and could hear the strange tone in my voice. He asked to speak to my son immediately and informed him if he thought about putting his hands on me he had better think again because he would have to deal with him. I appreciated his protection over me, but believe me, I would have knocked my child out! I could not believe this boy bucked at me like he was going to do something. From that day forward, I did not trust either of them. How could this be?

After a few days of thinking about the entire situation concerning my boys, I decided to take them back home to their father. The way things were playing out, it was the only thing possible. There was no way I would have a child in my house that was willing to step to me. It was like dealing with his father all over again except this time it would not turn out with two people walking away. Lord knows I wanted them with me, but it did not work out in any way. I could not receive the help I needed as to enroll them into school. I could not do anything with them having no documents giving me consent or the authority to do so.

I told my new man about my plan and he agreed. We rented a car, told them to pack a bag, and we headed east. It was a short roundtrip. I dropped them off . . . literally, and returned home. I cried on the way back home because of the way it all turned out. From no cooperation from their father, their lack of respect, and my hurt feelings I just felt awful. I felt I did something wrong somewhere for this to happen like it did. The past ran through my mind over and over.

It all happened so fast. I was preparing for my boys to arrive, they were in my arms smiling, trying to situate them in school, becoming outrageous, and then bucking at me. I blamed myself.

This whole process was very challenging from dancing in the club again, opening up to a new man, and to having my sons come live with me after years of not seeing them. Although I wanted all of these things desperately, I could not do any in my own strength.

I always thought I was so tough until I realized God enables me to be for the immediate circumstance. The things I endured in the past helped build me and added an extra layer of durability to my life. I was only able to deal with the issues that arose because of the strength I received through God.

There were many options for me to choose from instead of returning to the club, but for me that is what I knew to do at that time. God allowed that to take place and successfully. He protected me the entire time and would not leave my side no matter what I chose to do. I followed my heart and God held my hand through it.

I should not have looked to my new man for any kind of strength and knew that God provided that for me. I did not think about God in every circumstance. I only would consider God when I felt I really needed him not understanding I always need him throughout everything I do. I definitely felt much protected when my new man stood up for me when my son stepped to me. I believe God used him in that way to let me know He had me, but I did not see God, I saw my man. I was wrong in that manner. God provides all protection, power, and strength that connects to me. I will never forget that and I will give credit where credit is due!

Knowing I do not have to fight my way through anything is a blessing. What God has for me is not difficult to handle. When confusion sets in, a way out will be made for me . . . in all things. I realized these events are connected by one thing. When dealing with today, I do not need to be afraid because of what happened in the past. God did not give me a spirit of fear. When that is felt something is wrong and it will be shown to me. I do not need to revisit those old roads. I learned to look forward despite the crash behind me. I am protected the whole way through the new avenues that are ahead of me no matter where they lead.

SURVIVING
Chapter Twenty-Eight

SCRIPTURE
Ezra 9:13

What has happened to us is a result of or evil deeds and our great guilt, and yet, our God, you have punished us less than our sins deserved and have given us a remnant like this.

Making the choice to take my boys back to their father after that whole ordeal drug up old feelings. Although everything was out of my hands, I still felt a sense of fault. Because I could not do anything to make things better, I had an overwhelming garment of failure on my shoulders I began to carry. On one side I could fully understand why I had to return them to their father, but on the other side I was angry that I had to encounter any of it. Why would my son's father send them to me and not provide me with any personal documents for them? What was he doing with them that would have them so disrespectful toward me? Just when I would answer a question, another would surface.

I had a battle going on inside of me. I could not grasp why I had to encounter that situation. With what I had learned while in jail, I knew everything happened for a reason. But what did I do to bring this on? Why did I deserve going through that? Better yet, why did my sons have to go through it? I felt like we were being teased. I wanted them and they wanted me. We were all suffering.

I had gotten past so much pain in my life to only have to go through more. This was not like the first 30 years of pain in my life, but it still hurt the same.

My new man was there for me as best he could be. He was with me during my crying evenings or drunken stupor. I do not know sometimes how I even walked around because I was so drunk. I still had my apartment but had really let it go. I never put any furniture in it besides in my son's room. I just did not care anymore. That place now reminded me of them.

He had a place out by the water where often we would escape. I believe he was dealing with a few things as well. He had children and was having a little difficulty with his ex-wife, so he could understand my hurt I am sure. I appreciated his compassion and willingness to stay by my side seeing how hurt I was. I am sure he saw more than I can give him credit for. He did not complain and embraced every feeling I had.

As much as he told me it was not my fault, I could not help to think it is all because of what I have done in one way or another. I was being punished for something.

I continued to work at the club and built up even more clientele. I began to drink more, but was still able to keep control of my emotions while there. I felt like I could snap at any minute. No one knew my troubles or anything about my life. They looked at me as someone who had it all together for the most part. I was holding on literally by a thread.

The thread I was holding on to was what I had learned previously while locked up. Deep down inside I knew everything would get better; just a matter of when. A still voice I would hear when I gazed off into my own world. I believed that to be myself and needed something to be more vocal. Hope stayed available.

I could not bear the pain of it all. I was so disappointed and discouraged to attempt anything else. It was as if my past came back to haunt me. I could not understand how I could want to do so well and not be able to do so. I was tired of trying and felt like giving up.

My attitude affected my relationship a bit. Because of my "I do not care attitude", I was a little on edge with him. I was not putting much thought into our relationship. I still wanted him, but put more emphasis on how I was feeling. Because I highlighted the problem, it became bigger than us.

I turned to the guys in the club. That was a way for me to disassociate myself from what was going on. My friend knew all about me and what was happening in my life. When I looked at him, I saw my issues. When I looked at the people in the club, I saw freedom. I did not want to go home. I started staying at the club until it closed to avoid my reality.

Not wanting to confront my emotions, I became resentful. My new man had lost his job and we were living off of what I made. He had little side gigs, but it did not bring in much. I did not want anything else on my shoulders because if something went wrong it would be my fault. I could take care of myself, but did not want to be responsible for someone else's well-being. I feared I could not do it.

There were a couple of times that I was deliberately trying to run him off to avoid him leaving me. I wanted to ditch him before he ditched me. I was acting horrible, being disrespectful to him with the guys in the club, and was thinking much of myself. I was not concerned with how he felt or what he needed. I loved him but it was overshadowed by my pain.

I began purchasing things without the thought of what he needed. Dealing with my pain, I was causing it somewhere else. I was cracking under the pressure I laid on myself.

My man would spend the night over a friend's house from time to time to make some money. I was definitely alright with that, but would miss him tremendously. That time allowed me to see how evil I had been to him.

Despite how I acted, I could see the strength in him as he continued to stay by my side. One night I disrespected him so bad he displayed his anger. I left him that night and stayed at a room. I was so angry with the way he reacted to me that I bypassed what I had done: I was having a drink with a patron in the club when he walked in to pick me up. I looked at him and continued as I was as if he was nobody. As I turned away from him, I resumed my conversation with the guy and we toasted glasses as we laughed. He was furious and told me to come on now!

As I calmed down in the room, I began to feel convicted. Little did I remember but God was still in me. I did not make that connection, but knew I had changed my mind completely about how I felt with what just transpired. I cried and prayed that God would bring him to me. He did not know where I was, but God did. If he came I knew God brought him.

I was going over and over in my mind about how I had been treating him. I knew I was wrong but could not understand how I could be so evil after knowing how it felt to be treated so badly by someone. Avoiding my pain was the only way I knew to hold on to myself. Now I was reaching for someone else.

As I was laying on the bed, I heard a horn blow several times. I jumped up immediately and opened the door to the room. I was way in the cut at the end of a brick wall, so I was unable to see. As I walked out I saw a little black sport's car parked sideways at the entrance area. I smiled so big and ran in the street waving my hands. He brought him to me!

As soon as he stepped out of the car, he looked at me with a sly grin on his face shaking his head. As he walked toward me, I could feel a new connection between us. We embraced without hesitation.

Even with my hasty decision, God worked it all out for me. I stayed in that room one night and did not have ID to get it. I had to ask the owner of the club to get it for me in his name. I did not tell my man where I was, but I guess from previous rooming, he knew I would be close to the club. The room was not out in the open where anyone could see me or even know I was there. God hid me away in the corner until I understood what I had done and felt the pain I caused another.

My man asked me if I was ready to go and we immediately packed up my things and left. We did not discuss what happened. I believe, just at that moment, we had a deeper understanding. God sent Him so there was nothing to say.

I never stayed at that motel down the street from the club again.

Because I believed my love came from a man, God kept him in my life so I would have something to hold on to. God is love and God is all things hoped for. I had a deep desire in my heart, not knowing where it stemmed from. Although it was really God, He strengthened my man to endure me because it is what I needed at the time. He needed it as well for his growth. Through my pain, insults, disrespect, neglect, drunken stupor, needless arguing, and his own troubles, God enabled him to stay with me. I saw something in him I had seen several times in my past . . . God.

He did not have a job and I felt a pressure that was not even there. I felt I failed in the past and would again. I was pushing away the real need in my life. Making money was not the issue. My feelings were. Since I had the thoughts I did, I would make very poor choices that could potentially hurt me in other ways unthought-of. I needed him more than he needed me. God, of course, knew this.

I always felt that I needed to look out for me in every situation because many in the past did not. I realized, I am not capable in the ways I thought I was. Once my protection was not there, I felt even more in danger than I actually was . . . God is my ultimate protection. I was holding on to hope and desired love. Through my man I was able to experience love time and time again. From the ache of my heart, I made painful choices that affected more than myself which allowed me to see I am loved throughout.

God strengthened a man for my benefit to put up with me even when I was flat-out wrong. I am sure it benefited him too, but I am seeing it from my view. I would have brought much harm to myself had I been single because of the way I was feeling. Because he was in my life, I was confined to him. He was my protection from others during my time of self-destruction. God knew I needed sheltering and used my man to do so.

While I was trying to survive, God was breathing life into me.

GETTING TIRED
Chapter Twenty-Nine

Isaiah 30:15
This is what the Sovereign Lord, the Holy One of Israel, says: "In repentance and rest is your salvation, in quietness and trust is your strength,"

The relationship with my man and I had become a much appreciated one after I came to grips with what was important. I faced another issue.

Confrontation began in the club with myself and the other dancers. I always sensed a tad bit of jealously, but never thought too much about it. I could care less what they thought. For some reason it was highlighted and was very noticeable. I had always made a good amount of money and never had an issue with anyone. Comments began to annoy me. Clients started informing me of things said about me and it actually bothered me.

I do not believe this started all of a sudden; it was nothing new. It had not made a difference to me what was said about me because of my focus, but lately my focus began to change. I wanted to rest. I did not want to have to make money anymore. I wanted to be able to choose what I wanted to do. I felt restricted to the club as if I had no other option. I looked at the other dancers in the club that were unlike myself which was just about all of them. I felt I was extremely different and had other possibilities. They had opportunity too, but seemed comfortable where they were and with what they were doing. My mind began to soar to new heights that I knew were obtainable.

I found myself sitting in a booth on more than one occasion talking to my client about God, careers, or his life. I was doing everything else except what I was supposed to be doing. So when it came to hearing what the other dancers were saying, I became annoyed because I really did not want to be there with them anyway.

It became uncomfortable for me to be in the club. Confusion and confrontation was everywhere. I could feel myself being pulled into the drama around me.

The unusual began to happen. I was being asked to have sex for money right in the club. There were many girls who did this on a regular and made it difficult for the ones who were not. Many of the patrons wanted me to flash my "goodies" to them. They used to be extremely turned on with the thought of me; now it was not enough. To top it off, one of the dancers rudely came into my booth while I was dancing for my client to look for something. I could not contain myself and lunged at her. The customer I was with restrained me and attempted to calm me down. He understood but whispered to me that it was not worth it and I was better than that.

There had been talk about how someone had sex with me. Many knew it was not true because of the many attempts by others. I did not bother defending the truth because it stood on its own.

On a weekly basis there was a fight of some sort in the club whether between the girls or the guys. It was not many new patrons, but many new girls. It seemed they were getting younger and younger which brought more ignorance, immaturity, and foolishness. Before long, the club turned into a totally different atmosphere from what it once was.

I began leaving the club earlier and earlier.

I mentioned my desire to leave the club to my man and he agreed. We just needed to wait until the right time to do it being he was seeking employment. He would be working soon so I began stacking the money I made for our move. We began looking at places out by the water so I could rest in peace. I loved the water and it seemed to be the perfect place to take a break and collect myself. I longed for the day.

Meanwhile, in the club there continued to be chaos. I would be brought in the middle of someone else's problem. I had to choose a side and then when I did not, both were upset with me. My customers began choosing the girls who "gave" more than I did. I did not mind that too much because I did not want to deal with the hot pursuit of something I would refuse to do. Because I refused, girls became angry and made up more lies. Some would ask what was being said. . . It was too much!

There were still a few good men in there that I could relate to and converse with. Yet, after a while they appeared tainted too. They would begin speaking about the situations and circumstances going on in the club and then would ask me for my input. If I did not want to indulge in that conversation, they did not want a dance.

I was coerced into activity I did not want to be a part of and it was getting more and more challenging to refuse because of the force of the suction of evil.

All of the strife within the club was bringing my spirit way down because I knew I wanted out but had to endure a bit longer. The closer it got the more difficult it became.

It got to a point where I just made what I felt was good enough and would leave. It became more and more apparent that these days were over. Seeing the new girls and the way the scene was changing was too obvious that my time was up. The excitement of being independent was long gone and I now wanted to rest. My mind felt exhausted and full. I needed time to process and sort things out without having to add anything else to it. Whenever I had eliminated one thing, another would surface. I was never able to really deal with any one issue fully and thoroughly.

I could feel the magnetic pull of the club as soon as I walked through the door and eventually would fall into their footsteps because of the overwhelming forces.

We had been riding through a familiar neighborhood out near the water since we decided to move and went ahead and filled out an application. The club soon become a piece of my history.

I was so blinded by everything I felt I had to do which in turn tired me out. Until I changed my thoughts about where I was and what I needed, I was not able to see. God put another desire in my heart and allowed me to see where I really was. How could I not see all of this in the beginning? It was all there when I arrived to the club; I only became tolerant and dismissed it so I could do what I came to do. God allowed me to experience all I did and gave me the strength to do it. It was only a matter of time until God would lead me to focus on the path I was actually on. When I stopped focusing on my independence and taking care of us, I could see where I had been all along. I thought I was tired emotionally. I became even more tired when I saw what I was actually up against.

My spirit would not allow me to endure the evils that lurked in the club once I knew better. I had to see I was capable and worth more before I could see less.

God allowed me to learn from the experience of working in this club. I believe it went beyond the club itself and was more centered on my thoughts of myself. What I felt I needed to do was understandable, but I thought less of myself. I grew very tired of trying to take care of myself. Within specific situations I was able to see I do not take care of anything. God has it all worked out even when I mess up.

God made it possible for me to get out of the club and move forward. I can rest peacefully knowing I do not have to do anything. God removed the pressure. I now had nothing to grow tired of.

LAID TO REST
Chapter Thirty

SCRIPTURE

Psalm 103:1-5

Praise the Lord, my soul; all my inmost being, praise his holy name. Praise the Lord, my soul, and forget not all His benefits - who forgives all your sins and heals all your diseases, who redeems your life from the pit and crowns you with love and compassion, who satisfies your desires with good things so that your youth is renewed like eagles.

It was a huge relief to not have to be concerned with anything except waking up. It felt very strange initially having nothing to do. I could exhale.

Living by the water that we once frequently visited was tranquil. We would come out this way when we wanted to escape our realities. Now I was able to live there. I could literally see the water in minutes from where we lived. I knew I would be able to get plenty of relaxation and begin to work on myself. I did not know what that would entail, but I felt it coming.

We would drive all over the island seeing everything there was to see. We both smoked, but that even seemed to be fading a bit. All of the debris appeared to be falling off of me. I knew I made the right move by leaving the club when I did. I was even more appreciative that my man was willing to take care of me now. He tucked me away in a beautiful place he knew I loved.

My man had a few friends that lived on the island. I had met them some time ago. Whenever we came that way, we would visit them. They were very welcoming to me and very easy to get along with. We had cooked out together, talked, laughed, and shared stories. I felt very comfortable with them. Once I quit dancing and began to relax, I soon felt a bit shy around them. I had removed my exterior and was revealing what was underneath.

Being with my man was very similar. He met me when I was very guarded and always on the defense. I was protecting myself from all that came my way and that was around me. Because of this, my true self stayed in a shell. By not having all the chaos in my life, I was coming out of that shell and it felt a little strange.

I found myself wanting to be underneath him all the time. I was so used to having a shield around me. I let go of mine but still needed that safety net and he was it.

We were over our friend's house one day and the lady of the house wanted to speak with me by myself. We had grown closer and she felt comfortable talking with me. I have to admit, I enjoyed speaking with her as well. It was almost like a counseling session. She really valued my opinions and that meant a lot. Although this was liked on both sides, I felt myself coming out which made me apprehensive. It was not new for me to give my thoughts, but it was new for me to give them and be so relaxed and unblocked. I was so free to say what I knew was really honest and without tension and stress on myself. It is one thing to give your thoughts; but when you are strained by so much on your own mind, you can easily add some of that into your advice. My mind was free of drama and I could offer my whole self to help someone else.

Layers of me were falling off.

There were many times that I would be home by myself. It gave me much time to think; sometimes too much. At times I felt very confused. I know I wanted something knew, but would keep thinking about where I was. Maybe I should go back? Then I would think about all of the drama that came with it.

I would go on walks and look at the scenery all around me. I began to appreciate all that I had at the moment. I tried to focus on all the positive things. I was tired of the negative things in my life having control. I was out of the club, had a man who cared about me and treated me well, and I was by the water relaxing with no worries . . . except the ones I kept bringing up.

I had nothing else to do but think. One day, I pulled out my Bible.

I read the Bible every day for a few weeks. It was as if I were in my own world. I became very curious all of a sudden. Whenever I would put it down, I would yearn to know more. Because my man was often gone, I was able to read all the time. But when he returned, I would stop.

I started to see him a little different. I grew to appreciate him even more, yet saw what was not right at the same time. I was not judging him. I only saw the love I had for him. I began to do the same for myself.

Whenever he came home, we would smoke and get a little something to drink. Because of the time in between, it did not take much for me to be high. At first I would want to resist, but the longer I indulged, the more I wanted it.

I did not read my Bible again for a while.

Since leaving the club, we had moved several times on the island due to finances. Even with all of that, I did not have a problem with it. I just rolled with it. As long as we were together I did not worry myself about details. Things were not perfect, but my mind was. He was there for me and me for him. That was all that mattered. I was comfortable with whatever happened, however it happened, whenever it happened. I had begun to surrender all. My resistance was fading and was clearly recognized.

We had moved into another apartment on the island, it was very nice and had an excellent view of the houses behind us. Living on the top floor was symbolic to the way I had begun to feel. I was on a high that no one could bring me down from. The only down side from these heights was my man worked in the city which meant days of being away. We did not have furniture yet or a television. During this time, I walked a lot. I also picked up my Bible again. I read faithfully every day.

Those few days for him being away turned into weeks. I stayed in that apartment waiting for him to return to get me through the electricity being shut off and an eviction notice. I was unable to take a shower or eat anything. I had no money and there was nothing in the house. I was in the apartment with a lock around the doorknob. I was able to leave out the house only if I stuffed something in between the door so it would not shut. I would only leave out to get some air and then I would return.

The rental office staff came to the door one day and needed to know the specifics of his return and about the payment of rent. I walked to the front office with them so that I could call him and let him know the happenings at the moment. To my surprise, I was very confident and stood up for him. Once he was on the phone, I could not help but smile as they spoke with him and questioned him. A sense of peace came over me and I knew it would all be alright. I spoke with him on speaker and he asked if I was ok. I replied yes, and he told me he loved me. I smiled and said the same. He informed them that he would be back by the eviction day.

As they walked me back to the apartment to let me in, they mentioned that I was a very good friend to be waiting for him in these conditions. I stated that I was fine and that God knew I was here. I smiled as I walked on and said I would be fine!

He was there to pick me up just as he said. I was very nervous that morning thinking he would not show up but that was the enemy bringing doubt into my mind. I knew in my heart he would be there. God showed me so much about myself while left there in that apartment by myself in that condition. I could handle more than I realized. A lot of old thoughts were thrown away.

I became accepting to others and the way they were. I had a sideways judgment before and would think negatively inside. I let that go, and patiently tried to understand what was beneath the surface. I could see me in them one way or another. I appreciated what was in front of me instead of longing for what was not there. I still wanted, but was not upset because I did not have it . . . yet.

Within this period, God was allowing change in my life. Removing those things of the past and letting me realize there is more to me. It is amazing when things are eliminated from your life what you are able to recognize. It may not be understood, but I acknowledged it was happening. Because of this, I had much hope and knew more possibilities were available to me. I did not need to know the specifics. I only was excited to begin to feel there was hope. I was reaching. I was not sure for what, but it did not matter. I had something else to grab hold of. God was uncovering a part of me I did not know existed. Old ways were laid to rest.

CANNOT SIT STILL
Chapter Thirty-One

❦ SCRIPTURE ❧
Psalm 127:2
In vain you rise early and stay up late, toiling for food to eat—for He grants sleep to those He loves.

After being out of the club for a while and much time to myself, I was beginning to get restless. I did not want anything in particular. I did not know what would satisfy me. I could not think of what to do, say, or eat. I needed something, but had no clue.

We had moved closer to his job which was lovely. I could see him more and was not so alone all the time. After that long solitary confinement at the previous apartment, it was nice to be around him again. I would assist him in getting ready in the mornings and anticipated his arrival in the evening. I enjoyed cooking for him and tending to him in every way.

While he worked, I had the desire to draw. I used to draw a lot when I was younger and was very good at it. I drew while I was locked up also. That talent had increased from what I remembered and I wanted to see what else I was able to do. I began to draw people out of the magazines I had. I had never drawn portraits before, but craved to do so. I began to draw face after face. I amazed myself with the skills I was using. I do not know how I knew what to do, but I did. Whatever I saw on that page is what I put on the paper. I was writing more as well. I used to write a lot, but when I allowed everything else to cloud my mind I stopped. I was now free to do so.

From the improvement in my abilities, I was able to see how I was blocking my creativity. I was becoming free.

As I was seeing capabilities in me displayed on paper, I began to wonder. Out of all my talents, which of them was I supposed to be using for good? I was able to do so many things. Creative in so many ways, can pick up any and everything after it is shown to me, and willing to do all. What is it I am supposed to do?

I was drawing one time in the McDonald's. My picture was spread all over the table as I went from picture to picture. Many people walked by and complimented me on my ability. One older man told me that the police department needed someone like me to be a sketch artist and I should check it out. Another man wanted me to draw a portrait of him and his wife. I remember thinking, "Is this what I am supposed to do . . . draw?"

I was invited with my man one day to join him with a few of his co-workers for dinner at a nearby restaurant. I was excited to be around some of his friends. When we first got there I felt pretty comfortable. It was refreshing to be among some professional people rather than a rambunctious group. The conversation was business at first and then each of them spoke about their personal lives a bit concerning different matters. We all laughed and were enjoying ourselves. Then all of a sudden I felt very anxious and out of place. I began to look at everyone as if they were so far above me. I did not belong with this group because I did not have a job nor did I have any type of direction. I got very stiff and quiet. I could feel a shift in the room and I was left out.

After that dinner, I knew I needed more. I had this feeling before, but it was more intense this time. There was something for me, but I did not know what.

I did not feel completely worthy of my man anymore. Here he was moving on in his career and I was doing nothing. I used to take care of us and provide. I felt needed and useful then; now I was useless. I felt he did not want me as he used to. He now was around professional women and I was less attractive to him because of.

Although I was seeing great things come out of me and others could see it too, I did not believe it was good enough. I looked at others and doubted myself. I wanted what I thought they had.

I was withdrawn from my relationship because of what I thought I lacked. I turned away from him because of what I thought he did not want any more. When he came home late or went back out after work to make his side money, I began to doubt where he was because of my insecurities.

I could not sleep and would walk at night. It did not matter what time it was. I needed to get out of the house instead of waiting for him to get home. I started thinking about being left in the other apartment and got a little angry. I had been through so much and I did not end up anywhere. I could not figure out what all of this was about. I did not have an appetite. It was no need to cook being that I had no one to cook for. What little I had to do was no longer and I began to feel lost.

I would wait up for him at times knowing exactly what I wanted to say as soon as he came through the door, but once he arrived that nerve was gone and I felt angry again. A few nights I would sleep on the couch. I knew I was wrong but I could not help it. My heart was confused.

No matter how crazy my behavior, he would always give in. I know it bothered him and was reason why he stayed gone sometimes, but he always turned back to me. He was faithful in that way. Deep down I did not feel like he was cheating on me. Because of the way I felt about myself I put those ill thoughts in my head about him not wanting me anymore. He never gave me any reason to believe those things in the first place.

He would embrace me as if nothing ever happened. He would tell me to just relax. Why couldn't I be content? I had gotten through all the recent tough times with no problem and now I was struggling again. The difference this time was I was struggling with myself and projecting it elsewhere.

My man came to me one day and said that we have a choice. Although he was working and able to pay the bills, put food in the house, and able to buy what was needed, we had a decision to make. I never would have dreamed this in a million years.

Instead of living in our apartment we would pack up our things, put them in storage, and live out of our car. No bills, no responsibility, and no concern other than what we wanted to do. We both looked at each other and decided that was what we were going to do. He made sure I was sure and we packed everything up.

I do not know where that thought came from within him, but it surfaced. Faced with the thought was not baffling at all. I was rather excited and felt it would be adventurous. Once again a change was occurring and I was alright with it. I did not understand it, but was very willing.

We chose to live out of our car while living in a perfectly, convenient, affordable apartment.

I had no clue what was to come. I had no clue why I chose to live this way. I was beginning to give up all the things I thought to be precious and needed. I was more interested in being free; whatever that meant. Not being confined to anything or having to comply with anything. We made all the choices; which were very simple and plain. It was not about what we had or could get, it was just existing moment to moment. What I thought was important, was not anymore.

We did not know what we were going to do day to day. We did not complain about anything and were ready for everything. We never stayed in the same spot and continued to be on the move. Not quite searching for anything, yet looking for everything.

This was the beginning of freeing experiences in my life.

I believe from the beginning of our move, God allowed me to see something new developing in me. In seeing my talents, it was not about what I was able to do, it was who was giving me the ability. I am sure I could have taken that talent and used it for good anywhere, but that was not the plan.

Being around a professional group of people allowed me to see what I wanted. Becoming angry and doubtful sparked a desire in me that was not there previously. I saw me in them. Not necessarily wanting their position, but wanting to be a part of one common goal.

Pulling away from my man was me not wanting to confront the issue of feeling worthless. God put a compassionate man in my life, who although had his own issues, was able to cater to mine. God separated us purposely in order for me to see my mistakes and pull my desires to the surface.

Choosing to live in our car I believe was led by God as well. There was a lesson to be learned that I was not aware of yet. Because of the peace we had while making the choice, I know God was with us. There were no doubts or concerns about who, what, when, where, or how. We had a confident guided desire to not sit still.

ON TO SOMETHING
Chapter Thirty-Two

❧ SCRIPTURE ❧

Galatians 2:20

I have been crucified with Christ and I no longer live, but Christ lives in me. The life I now live in the body, I live by the faith in the Son of God, who loved me and gave himself for me.

This was something exciting and very strange that we had chosen to do. Why in the world would we want to live out of our car? We were wanting to be departed from the responsibilities of life and do as we saw fit. Live off the land so to speak. We had some money to work with and did not concern ourselves about what we would do when it ran out. We lived in the right now.

We would go over friend's houses and converse with them. It always would be at a time when they were eating or getting ready to eat. He and I would laugh and say, "We are right on time!" We did not try and work it out that way; it just happened to be.

All of our things were in nearby storage so when we needed to change our clothes we did. We would go in a fast food restaurant or gas station to brush our teeth. And when we really needed to do more, we rented a room. Otherwise, we would sleep in the car in a low-key area. Lean back, roll up the windows, and call it a night.

Everything was working out just fine. I do not believe anyone knew we were actually homeless. We moved around the same, looked the same, and behaved the same.

It really became a freeing experience living out of our car. We never talked about the crazy adventure we were on. We would only look at each other and smile. It did not matter what we did throughout the day; anything was fine.

We were able to smoke our "Mary Jane" and grab a drink here and there. Budgeting was not a problem. We would buy something off of someone's dollar menu or go into the local "Wally World" and get something that would last us during the day. Being by the beach made this venture a bit pleasing. Sitting and walking by the water by day and having sex in the lifeguard stands by night. We were living vicariously through every mood that hit us.

From time to time we would drive back to the city. It took up too much gas to go often. But to show our face and mingle, we made an appearance every now and again. We would find a spot and bunk out there. He sold DVDs as a hustle so we always had a little cash coming from somewhere everywhere we went. Some days were slower than others, but it came. We sometimes had to sit in one spot for a few hours to make some money. We always made it worth our time.

We did not complain and went with how the wind blew.

On some days we would park the car and get out and walk around. There is a diverse group of individuals down by the beach. There are those who drive up in their fancy fresh waxed cars. Then you have those families who came to spend the day by the water. I saw couples hand and hand walking slowly together laughing. Several people were getting their workout in and jogging along the seawall. Some were walking their dogs, playing with their dogs, or just sitting with their dogs. But what captured me the most, was those who looked homeless.

On occasion, there would be a man or a woman near the beach that was twisting up palms into a variety of attractive shapes. They were not dressed very well and sometimes had an odor. They were always pleasant and kept a smile on their faces. We would always try and give them something just because. It was interesting to look at them and watch them shape that palm leaf into a mystery twined shape. Each time I saw them before I would think, 'Wow, it is some talented homeless people out here trying to make a buck. It must be hard for them.'

I soon realized that I was in their world now. I may not be dressed the way they were, look the way they looked, or have what they have. Although it was a choice, I was homeless too trying to make a buck. Once I put myself in a category with those homeless individuals on the beach, I saw things a little differently. Even though I was basically on the street like they were, this was not me.

Yes, we could wash up, could get money by hustling, and ate daily. But all in all, this was not our life. I do not know how or why they were there, but I am unsure if they would choose to be there. I was able to identify with them on a level I could have never done before. When I hear someone talking about surviving on the streets, I partly understand. Because we were still able to have made a little difference.

We were sleep in the car one evening parked right by the water. I was in the driver's seat. Sound asleep, I was awakened by him tapping me on my arm saying, "DRIVE, DRIVE!" A man with a gun tapped on his window, showed him the gun, and said to go. I did not know what was going on until we got on another street. Once he told me I still could not believe it. We looped around back to that same area and just that quick the police had him surrounded while putting him in cuffs. I do not know where the police came from. We did not hear any sirens.

I am sure it was a worse experience for my man because he saw that gun tapping on the window right by his face.

I have a new found respect for those who are on the streets. It is not just a freeing experience to live out of your car. It is at times degrading, uncomfortable, dangerous, fearful, trying, discouraging, and not for everyone. It became real very quick.

The fright of the man with the gun terrorized our thoughts; we were pretty shaken up. We rehearsed the scenario over and over in our heads with all the what if's.

The same way we did not know why those individuals were homeless, was the same as not knowing what drove that man to be on the path he was on. What I did realize was: the same way we were saved by him letting us go, his life was saved by the police catching him and putting him away. Even if it was momentarily, he was off the streets.

But God . . .

It was realized that being that free is not for us. I believe God allowed the both of us to witness the troubles that lie with these troubled individuals. I do not believe that experience was about us at all. At any moment we could obtain whatever we wanted because we had the means, but we chose to take the simple route over and over again. It was put on our heart to do so.

It was a very humbling circumstance to endure daily the lack of bare necessities for life. It was not just about being comfortable because we could be comfortable anywhere. It was the mindset while doing so. We had faith every day and did not put anything in the way. Our minds were free from harm and did not draw upon any. God allowed us to lower ourselves to a place we never been and probably would have never chosen without His lead.

I no longer feel like things are what life is about, because I did without. I lived without any of the perks and still had a marvelous time. It was a very different way of living not having the comforts of a home and its luxuries. They are not necessary, they are convenient. I had lusted after the things in life forgetting about life itself.

I like nice things and all the comforts that are available to us, but I know that if it was gone tomorrow I could survive and not faint. God supplies my every need. The things we needed were provided for us. It may not have been the "normal", but nevertheless, it was there and we looked good doing it.

It was not a smart thing for us to sleep in such open areas of the night. Evil lurks in the darkness. We did not give any thought to anything negative. We always said it would be fine. Because of our willingness to sleep in the mist of darkness, God thrived on our faith. All of our know-hows fell by the wayside and we stepped out on faith.

Choosing to be homeless was interesting. Everything that was learned was a lesson well learned. God was increasing my faith. Giving up the things of this world concerning comfort and opting for "living off the land." After this situation, my entire perspective on life changed which threw me for a loop. What I thought, was not at all. I looked at people differently. I could not look down on them being I was where they were. Choice or not, I was there right beside them for the same reason.

We did not directly pray to God and ask for His protection, but it spoke from our hearts. We were not depending on ourselves because we had nothing. We held on to a hope. Hoping and believing everything would go as we needed it to.

God worked it out every day. He provided just enough and we did not complain. It was difficult, but God got us through it.

We are all the same. One choice away from being in someone else' shoes is always lurking. I thought we were on to one thing when we began this adventure, but we ended up on to something else.

SEEING MYSELF
Chapter Thirty-Three

SCRIPTURE

Proverbs 4:26
Give careful thought to the paths for your feet and be
steadfast in all your ways.

Because of our wake-up call from the guy with the gun, we decided to make some money and change the situation. It was not safe on the streets as we were attempting to live.

Things got a little frustrating after that situation. I do not know if it was a conscious effort or not, but I was now scared of the choice we made. How could I be so foolish? This was my thought for a few weeks.

He found a job in a local grocery store. We knew it was a last resort, but he opted to do it any way. It took up time and provided some funds for us. It was going to serve its purpose. While he worked, I would keep the car and ride around. Most of the time I would find somewhere to park and sit in that spot for a while trying to waste the day away until he got off. This was very boring and gave me too much time alone. All I could think is it is back to the same thing again.

I figured I needed to find something to do with myself too. I thought about what our plans were to be. What was our next move? We did not have any real sense of direction. We were just living. Now that he was working again, I was left with myself. For me, that was not too much.

Looking out on the water as I sit awaiting my man's departure time from work, I reminisced over the past years. What did it all mean? I could not help but to continue to think about what I was doing, or not doing. This routine continued for a couple of weeks.

I grew tired of sitting by the water and began driving around the island. It was pretty wet outside one day I was riding around. I had a lot on my mind but was trying to brush it off. I had decided to go to a clothing store and browse for a while to waste time. While turning at a light heading through an underpass the car continued turning and crashed into the guardrail. I did not know what happened. I sat for a minute, straightened the car out and continued driving. As I pulled off I could hear a double thump as one of the tires spun. "OH NO!" I yelled.

I pulled into a nearby parking lot to look at the damage. The tire was bent. All I could think about was telling him. He was going to be upset. This was all we needed. We already had nothing and now the car is messed up too. I dreaded driving to his job, but I did.

"Come outside" I said as I saw him down one of the isles. He saw the alarmed looked on my face and asked, "What?"

As soon as he saw it, he lifted up one of the shopping carts and slammed it down. I felt horrible. All I could think about is how I was feeling when I turned that corner. The car was out of control the same way my life was.

He did not say another word to me for a while.

I was already feeling alone and worthless with no direction. Now he was by my side and not speaking to me. I felt even worse. And on top of all that, I lost my ID and SS card!

I could not help but to turn this back to him and blame him for our entire situation. I faulted him for allowing us to be out here like this. I resented him. We both made the decision to make this move, but now that everything was wrong, it was on him. I knew I was wrong in so many ways, but I felt bad enough for other reasons. I could not bear it all.

We were riding one day and I just flipped. I know I was fed up with the emptiness I was feeling. Nothing was going right, we had nothing, and we were headed nowhere. I cannot even remember what was said, but it was enough for me to tell him to stop the car and let me out.

He let me out on a corner of a street and I walked toward the shelter on the same corner. I stood there for a minute and looked around. What am I doing? I was losing it! I wanted him to come back so bad. But he did not. I walked back to our storage area and hung out there in case he came. He did not.

I went to one of his friend's house and stayed with them a few days. It was a young couple who rented a room out of a rooming house. I slept on the floor right beside their bed. This was not going to work for long, but I had nowhere else to go. He would call them to check on me, but did not speak with me.

I had started a job at the same store he worked at but a different location. I only had it long enough to get a check and then I quit. I was giving up on everything. I had already lost everything.

I walked over another one of his friend's house and saw the car. It had been fixed and the hood was warm. They claimed he was not in the house. I busted in the front door and went all through the house looking for him. "Where is he?" I yelled.

I went outside and headed straight for the car. I thought to myself, "If I set off the alarm, he will come out." I kicked the car over and over. The alarm was turned off but I do not know from where. I repeated kicking the car several more times until I tired myself out. I cursed everyone out and then left. After that incident, the young couple I was staying with said I had to leave.

I was having a breakdown.

Somehow he found me and told me to get in the car. He took me to a nearby spot and told me he was done. I felt my world crumble just like my mind was doing. My whole life was crashing before my eyes. What started out so lovely and freeing became a nightmare.

I pleaded with him for the longest not to give up on me. He refused. I admitted to acting crazier than crazy and that I needed him. He exhaled several times and said "ok." He shook his head, I sighed and cried, and we drove off to the city.

I believe God was beginning to bring me to the end of myself. I was searching for something and still did not know what it was. I was reaching everywhere but to Him. I had given up everything, lost just about everything, and almost destroyed our car. Through it all, He allowed my man to once again endure my tantrum.

Outside of seeing life in a different way, I was seeing myself at my worst. But God . . .

CROSSROADS
Chapter Thirty-Four

SCRIPTURE

Psalms 133:1
How good and pleasant it is when God's people live together in unity.

When we left the island, he mentioned that he would try and find daily work. I was unsure what that meant. It ended up being a place where you sign up to work daily and receive a check for the days of work you do. They would go to factories or warehouses and do packaging, machinery, or forklift type of work. I felt very out of place when I was there because of the people that were there. It was a lot of Mexicans and lower class African Americans. It was another humbling situation. I might have looked at them sideways before, but now was holding a conversation with them about how this daily work would pay off.

It is amazing how I thought one way about a specific kind of person because of the way they looked, dressed, or carried themselves. After sleeping in our car and now at this place, I looked at everyone the same. We all have the same common goal. It really does not matter what we look like trying to get it.

I had a temporary ID that I was able to use for a short period of time. We had a chance to go together to the same place. It was not that bad. I had to separate boxes and hangers, organize shirts, and price merchandise. It actually was very simple work. It was just very boring. I see why this kind of work is not popular, but it paid pretty well. I had a different respect for factories, plants, and warehouse workers.

There was a park right across the street from this daily work office that we would go sit in. There were a variety of people in the park playing with their children, jogging, or walking their dogs. We would sit at a bench and watch the scenery. One day we got a little frisky while I had on a skirt and had sex right there in broad daylight. I had lost all sense of decency; but it was thrilling.

We would buy beer and sit in that parking lot for hours wasting time until the next run to a job site. He would work more than I would. It helped us with money, but was getting very tiresome living this way. To keep us sane, we would stay high one way or another . . . drinking or smoking.

Being in the streets still had my mind thinking in survival mode. Inside I did not feel that way. I knew I was more than this although I was very willing to do it. I seemed to be getting pulled into another way of living. I started thinking I may as well go back to the club. Pawn shops, daily work, drinking, smoking, and sexing in public was becoming the norm.

I really have a different respect for people of all walks of life. Throughout my club experiences and now being closer to the streets there is a closeness I never thought I would feel. Not that I am from the "hills" or anything, but I was not in situations where I dealt with this group of individuals or this way of life. I realized I am just like them. I had hurts and pains that led me to make choices that put me in compromising situations more times than one. Because of the choices, I was surrounded by individuals I would have never chosen. When making the choice, I was not thinking about my whereabouts and who would be there. I was concerned with how I would feel at that moment.

Having been around such a diverse crowd opened me up as an individual as well as my perspective. I was able to see more than one view from the same circumstance. I thought back on how I used to think . . . which way now?

After working for a bit at the daily work place, we went over to his best friend's house to stay for a few days until our next move. I used to dance with the best friend's girl and the best friend was the deejay who introduced me to my man. This seemed to be a perfect plan when we arrived because of the closeness I thought we all shared. We all smoked, drank, and loved music. We would laugh, talk, and shoot pool in the garage the majority of time.

One evening we all were sitting around talking and the club had come up in conversation. I mentioned to my fellow dancer that I thought about returning. We went into her closet and she pulled out some shoes she still had because she no longer danced. The guys had all gone into another room so that left her and I. I had asked her, hypothetically, if we were to break up would I be able to stay at her house.

This question came up because I was noticing how they all knew each other for years. Other friends would come over that I knew, but they all had one common bond. My man. I felt at times like the odd ball. I had no family in this city, no money, and nothing to claim but him and that barely felt like mine. I was hanging on for dear life literally. The idea of the club came up because I knew I could make some money and get a room and gain some independence and control again. I did not believe I fit in any more once we were there for a while, so I asked if I would be able to stay.

She said, "Yeah, girl! Of course you could." I smiled and said "ok, I was just wondering."

This chick went and told his best friend some other story and they all come back to me saying, "You can't stay here if you and he broke up. He would be here, not you." I thought to myself "yawl act like I said we were breaking up. I just asked a question to see where I stood with yawl." My man now comes over to me and asks what this is about. I told him and he got offended. "What in the world did I say wrong? Everybody here is friends and family. I felt like the outsider although I am here, so I just asked a question," I said to him. He did not like that or the fact that I was thinking about the club again. I could understand the club, but because of the circumstances it was an option for me at this point. I was not going to stay in their house much longer; especially since they said I could not stay there.

He and I kept going back and forth. All of a sudden I was dialing my father's number. My dad drove from San Antonio to pick me up. He was there in several hours. I walked to a nearby gas station with what I had on my back, my phone and charger in a book bag, and waited on the curb until he got there.

I believe this situation was pretty easy to see. God allowed me to lose everything and be separated among the friends in order for me to move on to the next phase of my life. I had already gained the understanding and reality of living on the streets and in a car. I changed my perception of people altogether. I no longer had judgment on individuals no matter what their situation. I had been in several levels of living within a short period of time and could relate with anyone in the same position no matter what gender, age, or race.

This was not the first time I had lost my belongings or left them somewhere. I was more concerned about getting around some people who knew me and would help me. I know in the past I did not receive the assistance I needed, but many years had gone by. The circumstance of my life seem to point back home and that is where I was headed.

I got in my father's car with my backpack and phone. I had called my now ex on the phone before leaving and cried to him because of the separation I knew we would now have forever. That part of my life was over and I knew it.

I understand that this experience was not about me. God allowed me to see others just where they were by allowing me to be there as well. It was always known that I could change my situation at any time. These individuals were not that fortunate. I had a preconceived notion about individuals that had less than. I always thought they did not try or did not care. I came to know that they had emotional, mental, and financial issues just as anyone else because of events happening in their lives. I had issues from my past. I did not receive the help that I needed when I asked for it. I made choices that put me in the situation I was in. I had to do what I needed to do to survive. The club might offer a little more than what they were doing, but they did not like what they were doing either.

We all have many similarities no matter how different we may look or seem. We were all on the same path coming from different places. We all have to make choices in order to change the situation we are in. God wanted me to see how all of our roads cross.

REGROUP
Chapter Thirty-Five

❧ SCRIPTURE ❧

James 4:2
You desire but do not have, so you kill. You covet but you cannot get what you want, so you quarrel and fight. You do not have because you do not ask God.

The ride to my dad's house was long and quiet. I could not believe I had left my man and situation like I did. I knew I was fed up, but wow! I did not even take a change of clothes.

I told my dad the story and he just listened. My dad is a really good listener, but he will get his five cents in there. He always has something miraculous to say, but I was really in the dumps. I did not necessarily want the relationship to end, but because of the circumstances I did not see a choice. We could no longer take care of one another in a healthy way.

I have not reached out and asked anyone for help since asking my mother when I left my ex-husband. I felt so rejected then that I dared not to ask anyone anything again. God knew that too; hints why He used my brother. In this situation I really had to. I was getting ready to be on the streets the way they were talking.

I was not going to stay at my dads' for long. He was going to fly me home to my mother. I had not seen her in a while and still had much attitude toward her from the past. I had a few days to get myself together mentally before returning home after almost ten years.

I did not talk too much while at my dad's house. I mostly cried. I felt a little like a failure having to return home. I did believe I did well for a single woman with no assistance from anyone. I do have to give my brother his credit! He provided the foundation in each city.

I reflected on everything that has happened from the time I left home years ago up to this point this point. I was not eating much, but smoked plenty of cigarettes. I was wearing a size 7/8 at this time weighing about 130. I was the same size I was in high school and this was 18 years later. I was thinking, this is how I was when I left home in my senior year of high school except I am not pregnant. Broke with nothing and no clue what I am doing.

I needed help. It was time I went home and mended everything from the past. It was time.

Although I was going to my mother's house, I did not feel comfortable because of our relationship. I dreaded arriving there.

I could not stop thinking about who I just left. We had shared so much so fast and it was over already. I had moved on plenty of times before, but I was getting tired of this. I really had a love for him. Our situation got really out of hand. We were led in that direction but it still did not feel good. I was losing a good friend. He stuck by me in the roughest of times. We actually slept on the streets together. He definitely would not be forgotten.

One thing I was upset about leaving was my Bible, writings, and drawings. I could not believe I left those. I was in such a hurry to not even consider bringing them. If there was a time I needed my Bible, it was now. I was thinking about God. He was there when no one was. He made everything happen for me when I desperately needed it.

I wanted to hook back up with God.

I cried for what was behind me and what was ahead. I appreciated those who were there for me when I needed them and remembered those I assisted in their time. I recapped the negatives that sent me through a loop. I anticipated what was to come. I believe the future will be just as tough as the past. I still had to get through both.

After pondering over the circumstances I once was in and where I am going to be, I realized it all is necessary. Things were falling apart where I was and it was apparent I needed to go. The only other way to go was further down. Going to my mother's house is necessary for me to deal with our relationship. I did not know how or when, but I knew it would take place. I would see my children and I am sure I would see their father. All of my pains would have to resurface in order for them to heal.

One thing I did notice is I carried them everywhere I went and it affected all my relationships; friends and personal. I had to rid of these demons and begin a life without lugging my baggage around. I needed to do this once and for all and this was the opportunity.

God worked it all out for the good. I saw and experienced what I needed to carry back with me. I gained strength, a new sense of self, and much understanding. God put me in a better position to accept the scars I have.

Because these steps are ordered by the Lord, I knew it will all work out one way or another. It may not be easy or be pleasing, but it will be better than it was. The fact that I am even able to have the opportunity says enough. It presented itself because God opened that door. It was not time before even though I wanted it to be.

I always wanted things when I wanted it, but God says He puts it in order. He leads me the way I should go. When it is time for me to gather my things and go, I will do so not because I always want to, but because everything is grouped that way. There is only one way to go and He is the leader.

Instead of grouping together with others to figure something out that ultimately will fail anyway, I'll regroup with God.

BACK HOME
Chapter Thirty-six

1 John 3:2
*Dear friends, now we are children of God, and what we
will be has not yet been made known. But we know that
when Christ appears, we shall be like Him, for we shall see
Him as He is.*

I could feel the anxiety building up as I waited for my mother to pick me up from the airport. When she pulled up I was excited to see her, but knew this was going to be tough.

I loved my mother but was very angry with her for things of the past that had never been discussed. Whenever I would bring them up, she would hang up the phone or avoid the topic altogether. This would anger me even more because it left me feeling she did not care about my feelings.

Here I am, your grown daughter, telling you I am hurting because of some things that occurred when I was a child that you took part in. How could you not want to help me? I wanted nurturing, compassion, explanations, thoughts, hugs, empathy, acknowledgment, and understanding. I did not feel validated. I needed my mother and she was not there for me.

When I looked at her I would see the mother who was there taking care of me. Paying bills, cooking, buying me clothes, and all the other things to maintain a household with children is what I saw when I looked at her. I also would see someone I wish she was. I wanted to look at her and see all the good times, but I could not. I could only see what she did not do. I would instantly get sad.

I could not stand to hear her speak about anybody else because I could hear the concern in her tone which reminded me of what she did not have for me. I would look at her with such disappointment in my heart and wonder why she did not have that for me.

As I gave her a hug I could feel the tears welling up because I always thought of that very hug throughout the years over and over again. I had been yearning for that embrace for a very long time.

It was a quiet ride to the house. I stared out of the window looking at the scenery. I visited home from time to time, but to know I am here to stay made everything look very familiar. We pulled up to the apartment and I let out a big sigh. Here we go!

I did not have much with me so it was pretty easy to unpack and settle in. I took some time to make my room mine and soaked in the fact that I am here with my mother. She got me acquainted with everything in the house and let me be.

We sat with each other talking about the area and what was going on with different people. As I sat there, I could feel myself tensing up. I was very uncomfortable. I had so much built up inside. I knew it would be released very soon. I tried to stay calm and continued to show respect. I contained myself for the time being.

I stayed in my room at lot of the time with my door closed. I did not want to be bothered because I could feel the rage inside. Being around her was bringing up so much hurt. If I was to be around her, I knew she could sense something or maybe even feel the hatred I had toward her.

After a while I know she could feel the resentment coming from me because I was basically ignoring her. She stayed in her room and me in mine.

I was thinking about my children a lot. I wanted to see them now that I was home. They were much older and could make the decision to see me if they wanted. No one could stop them from doing so like it was done in the past. When I thought of them, I got upset even more. I blamed my mother for me being apart from them because she did not help me when I left my ex-husband. I asked to stay with her with my kids and she told me no. I had to take them back to him which is why he raised them. He took me to court when I had nothing. I always figured if I had her help, I would have been able to raise my children.

I would think about how they felt all these years and that would bring up how I felt as a child. Having to live in a home with an abusive parent who favored someone else over you. I also wondered about the anger they would have toward me because I was not there with them. I imagined all the lies told to them so they would hate me and blame me for everything. The more I thought, the angrier I felt. The angrier I got, the more I resented my mother.

I avoided her as much as possible.

My mother was going out for the day and asked me to go. I, of course, said "No." I remember her coming in my room saying, "You are going to go. Get up and get ready." I did not even look at her because I knew I was not going anywhere. I continued to lay in the bed. She returned to my room and sat on my bed. I stared at the wall wondering what she was sitting next to me for.

My mother let out a big sigh and said, "I am sorry Kris! I am sorry, okay?" I looked at her with such disappointment. Is that the kind of apology I am supposed to receive after all that has happened?

She left out of the room and asked me to get dressed again. I laid there for a moment. As I gazed at the ceiling, immediately a thought came to me: At least she apologized. You never got that. She must be feeling something. It is a start.

I cried and then got dressed.

I know God brought me home to mend issues of the past. I knew it would be difficult and had avoided it for years. I was so hurt for so long I did not know how to deal with it anymore. To be confronted with the individual who hurt me so much was tough. I could feel the rage in me and the need of an embrace full of love at the same time.

God allowed me to see the wrong I was doing by holding all that anger and then showed me the act of forgiving right in the mist of it. Although it would take some time for me to fully grasp the concept of forgiving, it was a start.

We were both in a new place.

It was very difficult for me to forgive my mother because I did not agree with the way she apologized. I felt I deserved a long drawn out explanation and lots of hugs and kisses. What God showed me was I needed to except it just as it came. It is not about how I want to receive it. It is that I received it.

There was definitely much more we had to work through. I still needed answers and wanted to hear specific things come from her mouth. For the time being I was comforted with her ability to acknowledge an apology was even needed. She let go of her grip, so I had to let go of mine. Although we are headed in very different directions, we both are headed back home.

CONFRONTING ISSUES
Chapter Thirty-seven

Proverbs 15:13
A happy heart makes the face cheerful, but heartache crushes the spirit.

I was able to drop some of my animosity toward my mother because of her apology to me. I did not agree with the way she did it, nevertheless, it was done. I appreciated the fact that she brought herself to say something to try and reconcile our differences and to decrease the static in the house. It was not totally removed, but it was easier to maneuver.

We talked a little more, but I still held a grudge toward her because it was so much that was not discussed. It was difficult for me to hold on to things and not be able to talk about it. She is the kind of person when she does not want to discuss it, she won't. No matter how much you stress to her you want to, she won't. I never thought that was fair but what could I do. I could not make her talk. That is what made me so frustrated with her. I felt she did not care about my feelings enough to try and ease some of my pain. How could my own mother not care about how I was hurting?

I also knew that I was back in the area where I would see my boys eventually. I would have to see their father as well. I did not know what I would say, how I would feel, or what I would do. I had a sore spot in my heart from him too. To look back over everything that has transpired in my life, he was a huge part of my pain.

I was in a huge sulking quicksand hole. It was pulling me in slowly. All I could think of at this point was what was wrong, who had done it, and how in the world could I overcome it.

Because of the agony I was facing, I went to stay with my younger sister and her boyfriend at that time who lived not too far from my mother. She and I were not super close, but we were cool enough to co-exist.

My sister made room for me by putting me with her youngest daughter. It was alright, but not exactly what I expected. What could I say? I was glad I was able to get out of my mother's house.

It was a bit uncomfortable for me because I really just wanted to be alone. Because of her two daughters and boyfriend, there really was not room for that. Thank God it was warm outside. I was able to take long walks or go and sit by the lake. That was refreshing, but not exactly what I needed or wanted. I struggled for days trying to figure out what I was going to do. After speaking to my sister, we came up with the idea of me trying to get a job at the local Dollar Store. I thought that would be something to keep me busy. It was not the best, but it was something more than what I was doing. I went and applied and was waiting for a response.

I could not believe the response that came back from the manager of the store. They said that I was not applicable because of my background. I did not know if it was the employment history, my debt, or the jail time. I was deflated. I did not know what to do. How in the world could I be turned down for a position at the Dollar Store? I was through.

My sister had a bar in her living room. Her boyfriend sold "Mary Jane." I began drinking and smoking.

Going back to old habits took the edge off, but did not curb my emotions as it used to. It is almost as if it made it worse. I was more conscience of what was wrong in my life.

I did a lot of crying and a lot of thinking while having time to be alone. My thoughts did not come up with a resolution, but things were coming to the surface. I was able to see things just for what they were. I had to face these things whether I liked it or not. This was my life now; messed up and lost.

I became very agitated and wanted to be alone more than usual. Everything got on my nerves. It was as if all things were magnified times ten. My eyes were opening right before me. This was something I had never experienced, so I was unsure what this all meant.

My sister's boyfriend had always seemed "shaky" to me. For the simple fact that he sold drugs and kept them in a house with his immediate family. I knew from past experiences that this kind of person was a liar and could not fully be trusted. This was confirmed for me one day when he made a comment about me stripping. He crossed the line and I was no longer comfortable around him. I did not tell my sister about that conversation because she was too wrapped up in her little world she would not have wanted to believe the truth. Everything was well because they broke up later anyway. I needed to say nothing. That issue confronted itself.

I needed to do something else, go somewhere else, or try something else. I did not know what to do at this point.

One day my mother called and said she was on her way to the house. It was a bit surprising, but kind of wanted by this time. It would be good to see her because of the way I had been feeling. I was looking forward to her being there.

When she pulled up, I was looking outside so I stepped out of the door. When I went outside, I saw two other people in the car. I was unsure who they were until they opened the door and stuck their head out. OH MY PRECIOUS GOD!!!!! It was two of my boys . . . one being my youngest.

She said she was driving along a nearby road and saw them walking and told them to get in the car and brought them to me. I was so excited I did not know what to do. I kept staring, kissing, and hugging them. I could not believe I was looking at them. I had been thinking about them, but did not know when I would get the chance to see them again. They spent the day with me.

Seeing them made me want to change everything in my life. I did not want a drink or to smoke anymore. A couple of days later I called my mother to come and get me from my sister's house. It was time to get things in order.

It was beginning to be obvious to me that time spent alone was actually time with God. He is able to slow me down whenever necessary to allow me to hear Him. Whether I realized at the moment it was Him really did not matter. That fact was I heard the messages coming in clearly. When things were being highlighted and magnified, that was for my benefit. It had always been there, but was now for me to see so that I was able to move forward without looking back.

I had realized I needed to face my troubles and not continue to run from them or hide behind drugs and alcohol. These things always resurfaced when I was faced with the opposition. I knew I had to gain strength in that area. God was working on me and I was happy about that. We would work out the kinks later. The important thing was I was confronting what was needed.

God continues to show me that the grass is not greener somewhere else. Problems will arise everywhere no matter what. I thought going to my sister's house would be better than where I was. It was actually worse. It was necessary for me to go there. God wanted me to see that her household was not as grand as she made it out to be. There were more things going on there than met the eye and it allowed me to put a scope on myself.

I ended up running right back to where I was supposed to be all along; with my mother. My troubles began to look resolvable. Looking at someone else's issues sometimes makes it easier confronting your own.

SEEING THE LIGHT
Chapter Thirty-Eight

SCRIPTURE

Philippians 4:11
*I am not saying this because I am in need, for I have
learned to be content whatever the circumstances.*

Being back home with my mother was not too bad. I began seeing her as I wished her to be. I did not know if that was good or bad, but I was glad to be there with her. I wanted her for a long time and here she was. I figured I just needed to enjoy what I could and throw the rest away. It was not easy putting the past hurts behind me that I figured she caused, but I put up a huge effort. I tried to look toward the future and keep it moving. I had a new start, so I attempted to give us a new start as well. I wanted better, so I saw better for the time being.

We were able to get along for the most part. We conversed more, and laughed a little. Since I was not working or involved in anything I had a lot of free time on my hands. I was very bored at times and forced to confront myself on many levels. My mom was gone the majority of the day, so I had a lot of me time. I spent a lot of time on the computer playing games and engaging on social networks. I was not very familiar with the concept of them but found it time consuming. I met many people online, but was not very interested in them. Chatting from time to time was fine, but for the most part I was not fascinated.

When my mom came home from work, she would get on her computer as well. Thank God she had two computers because one of us would be out of luck. While home, she was on the computer just as much as I. We would laugh and talk about things we saw on the sites. For the time being, it was nice just being in the same room even if not saying a word. Silence was good for us too.

It became very boring being in the house with no one to really connect with. Although I became a person to keep company, I never really had that close friend. I did not have anyone I could talk to about what I felt inside. There was so much emotion flowing through me and I was unable to direct it.

I had many talents I thought about using, but was unsure what exactly to do with them. The things I did in the past just did not seem to fit the present time. I enjoyed each talent greatly, but wasn't in touch with them for some reason.

I thought about people that I had met up until this point. Reconnecting was always an option to me. It was difficult to let go of the past because the past was so familiar. I did not know anyone, had nowhere to go, and not too much to do. I sought people out but was unable to get in touch with anyone.

A lot of thinking, quiet time, and playing on the computer became my routine. I felt as if I was falling into a hole . . . a deep one.

Being alone gave me much time to think about my situation. My life became my focus.

Where had it gone? What was it for? Why did I do the things I did? Why did certain things happen to me? What was next for me? What am I able to do? How will I make it alone? Will I ever find anyone else? Will I ever stop hurting? Am I strong enough to move forward? Am I loved? Why am I alone? Why am I so unwanted? How come nothing works out for me?

Am I loved?

With doing so much wondering about myself, to my surprise I would see a light at the end of the elongated tunnel I was in that would pull me back to life.

My mother began taking me to a church she had been attending. She was not a "church" woman per say, but did go in and out here and there as far as I knew. As a child she did not attend church with me and my brothers. I did not grow up with her talking about the Bible or God. If you were to ask me if my mother believed in God I would have told you no because she never spoke of Him or ever gave any inkling that she knew anything about His presence. It was very interesting when she asked me to go.

I had been pretty upset with God. I was baptized as a child believing that if I did so, He would save me from the pain I was enduring. I thought about Him from time to time but felt He did not like me very much, let alone LOVE me. I acknowledged Him much more than I used to, which was due to reading while my ex was at work.

After the second time there, I felt something in the pit of my stomach. I heard someone speaking in my head. It was a very faint voice, but very present nonetheless. I became engulfed with every word that came out of the pastor's mouth. I loved music so hearing the choir was a treat, but these songs made my bones vibrate. The words resonated in my mind so deeply it was as if I were saying them myself.

In a very short period I had a yearning but did not know what it was. It felt like something was dying to get out of me. I began to feel hope.

I developed a feeling that there was something in this world just for me despite my circumstance. It felt as if I had come to a place where possibility was on the horizon. I still was not sure where I was headed or how it would transpire, but I knew something was happening. I had a huge fear. I was now scared of the unknown, but at least I was not as deep in my hole. A peak of light was coming through.

I did not expect anything to happen while attending church with my mother especially after a couple of Sundays. The people were very welcoming and it appeared to be very pleasant. But for me, I wasn't interested in anyone. For the first time, I was interested in something other than myself. Something was shining and I could not see where it was coming from. I needed to find that.

It is amazing how God will allow you to be in situations and you really have no choice but to turn to Him. Even when you are not expecting to feel a thing. All He needs is a willing heart. I was yearning on the inside for something so much more than I knew. I never called His name with my mouth. I did not think God cared about your mouth because we say all kinds of things and feel something completely different. Because of the pain I was harboring, I would not admit out loud that I needed.

It was as if daybreak had come and I could see the way to go. I still did not know where I was going, but I was headed in the direction of the light.

BORN AGAIN
Chapter Thirty—Nine

SCRIPTURE

Romans 12:2

*Do not conform to the pattern of this world, but be
transformed by the renewing of your mind. Then you will
be able to test and approve what God's will is— his good,
pleasing and perfect will.*

Since I stepped foot into this church, I have been feeling a tug from somewhere beyond my knowledge. My heart felt like it knew it from a far place from long ago and was yearning to reconnect.

I knew once my worries became distant thoughts, a strong desire for better would rush in from afar.

I looked forward to going to church, but at the same time, it was a scary thing because it was something new. These were waters I swam before yet never went in the deep end.

It was always a pleasure starting over in a new place. There was always the excitement of the unknown. This time the unknown was appearing to be a much more serious place that really gives you what you ask for. I always hoped for so much more and so much better. I saw opportunity in front of me, but was unsure if I was really ready.

It was said that you could be made all over again. I could be brand new. The past could be behind me and I would have a new start. Isn't that what I had been doing? I had always expected something more and different every time I moved on. Why was this time different?

I was afraid of change. This was a different kind of change. I began to think I was not good enough for this. Then I started doubting that God would even accept me after all I had done. I figured He wasn't there before, why would He be there for me now? No matter what would pop in my head, the desire to know was still toying with me. The conversation in my head would linger on but my heart knew something different.

We went to church for the third time. People within the church became more familiar with me which made me feel a part of a little family. I liked it and then I did not. Everyone I ever became attached to was no longer in my life, so I did not want to go through that with these folks. It was nice to be received, but I was still focused on the words that came out of the pastor's mouth. I wondered what he would say this time, as we waited for service to begin.

On this particular Sunday, the choir sang extremely touching songs that were bringing tears to my eyes. If I did not know any better, I would have thought they were singing directly to me. I would look at my mom and grab her arm like someone was trying to get me. I felt so helpless and weak. I kept taking deep breaths and adjusting myself in my seat. I became very uncomfortable, yet intrigued at the same time.

I had never felt the way I did sitting in church that Sunday. I had so many mixed emotions. It was like a spotlight was on me the entire time. I know everyone was not looking at me, but it honestly felt like it. I knew no one, yet felt like the center of attention. I did not want to get up and leave although it would have relieved me of my jitters.

As I sat there, I held on to my mother like a little girl. I felt like a baby holding on for dear life. For the first time in years, I did not want to let her go, but something else greater pulling me.

As the service continued, I grew more and more afraid. I knew something was happening but was unsure what it was. I had that feeling like something was about to happen to me. It was very overwhelming. My hands were sweating and my eyes kept watering. I did not have anything specifically on my mind that would bring me to tears.

As the speaker of this day spoke, again, I could feel every word as if they were my own. No one knew me, so I can't say somebody told her. I was more in awe than anything. It was so powerful the way these things were occurring.

I remember being baptized as child, never had these feelings before. I was being drawn in by an unknown force I could not shake. I could not control my emotions. Something else was taking control over me.

Everyone was at the alter for prayer. After it was over, the woman who delivered the message that morning was receiving a message from God to tell one of the members of the church. As everyone was walking back to their seat is when she began pointing someone out. I turned to look up and she was pointing at me. I looked behind me as if someone else was there. She began to speak to me. I was in total shock. First, I could not believe she pointed me out. Second, I could not believe God was talking to me through her. Everything she said was right on point. What was even more convincing is that no one here knew me or my story to tell her. I knew it was true. She said that God was telling me to let it go. "Let it all go", she said. I stood there with my mouth open.

When they opened the doors of the church inviting individuals to join, I walked up immediately. With tears in my eyes, I accepted God into my life for the second time. I was saved for sure this time. I just knew it.

Of course there is not any quick change within an individual as soon as they are saved . . . except just that, you are saved! I knew no matter what I had done in my past, I had been forgiven and now will have eternal life because I confessed with my mouth that Jesus died for my sins and had risen after the third day. I am not doomed to hell when He returns, I will go to heaven and be with God one day. Most of all I knew things would be better. I still did not know how or even when. I was just excited I not only had a fresh start, I had a hand to grab hold to beyond any other for the rest of my life.

I knew I had a lot to learn and understand. The fact remained that I was brand new and did not have to be tormented with wrongs. I went in filthy dirty and came out white as snow. A fresh start, a new walk, and clean slate.

God knows exactly when He wants to change our lives around. Being put into a situation that will leave me yearning for Him and only Him. He can touch your heart like nothing else known to man. He will enlighten your spirit unlike any pleasure you've ever experienced. You will melt at His every Word because you know it to be truer than your truth. He will take you to a place that you cannot help to seek it out further. You know that you were already here by way of your mother, but God takes you through a new canal that births you all over again!

NEW DIRECTION
Chapter Forty

James 1:25

But whatever looks intently into the perfect law that gives freedom, and continues in it—not forgetting what they have heard, but doing it—they will be blessed in what they do.

After giving myself to Christ and accepting Him into my life, I felt brand new. It is not something that can really be explained. It is a definite knowing deep down in your spirit that something is different and more is to come.

I was to be baptized very soon. I had been baptized as a child, but this had a different meaning to me this time. I knew I was changing my ways and a new me was to develop. I was looking forward to what was to surface and who I would become. Again, I know I still had a lot to learn and it would not happen overnight. But because I was willing, I felt very positive.

Right before time for baptism I informed several people that were close to me at the time. It hurt a little bit, but I was informed that no one would be able to witness my ceremony of freedom.

The day came and I was excited and nervous at the same time. It felt like I was coming to an initiation. I could feel the newness of it all. I was about to enter a place I had never been before. My mind was changing, my actions were becoming unfamiliar, and my words were exploring themselves. Everything was new.

As I was sitting on the first pew along with the others to be baptized, an overwhelming feeling of removal came over me. As we were told to kneel down in front of our seats, I began to cry uncontrollably. I did not know why and I could not stop it. We were told to get up and proceed to the baptismal pool. On the way there, I saw the pastor as we walked by his office. He looked at me as I wept and made a wow-like face and said, "He is blessing you right now!" I cried all the way until I was dipped backwards into the water.

I was not aware of how new and life-changing things would be. The old self had been washed away and I was a new creature in Christ!

My thoughts were not set on the past anymore. I looked for better things to transpire. It was not an immediate process, but I knew it was coming. That was the important thing. My thoughts had to be on something other than what it was on. As long as I saw more than what was, I was alright. I began to have this mind set. It made my life a little easier to deal with.

I began to read and write more. So many new ideas, concepts, and ways of being were coming to my mind that I had to write them down. It was non-stop. I was being filled with so much knowledge and wisdom. It was amazing how much was being deposited into me. Because of the freeness I felt, I was able to concentrate on so much more. I could also see so much more. Knowing something is coming is wonderful, but at the same time it can become frustrating. Because I knew something was coming forth, I wanted to know what it was. And more importantly, when?

When I was not writing or reading, I was watching television or on the computer. At one time I was able to watch or get involved in just about anything. Certain programs on TV and specific things on the internet began to bother me. The content was just too explicit for my ears or eyes. Things that used to make me laugh just was not funny any longer. Cursing even left a piercing sound in my ears. It was very strange. Things were changing right before my eyes.

I continued to attend church. My mother was going out of town a lot at this time so I needed transportation to and from church. This was not a problem. The question was asked one day in church if someone could assist me and there were many volunteers.

There was a woman who began to be a spiritual sister to me. One day after a prayer at the altar, she informed me that God wanted her to tell me to read and watch as many spiritual programs as possible. This was very interesting being that my behavior patterns had changed drastically in that direction. From that day on, she became my friend. Any and everything she could assist me with, she did. She had given me clothes when I did not have many. She gave me spiritual books to read when I had none. She invited me along with her on a woman's retreat the church was having when I did not have any money. She became my friend when I did not have one.

I did not know how to act with her. She was a very real individual and had no cut cards. Although she went to church, she would continue to be herself which was very straight forward, despite the God within. She made me laugh, yet made me think as well. She was very educated and loved the Lord. I began to appreciate her in many ways. I never had a friend like this. She was helping me in a positive, godly way. This was new to me, but very good for me. She influenced me to be better. She turned me more toward the Lord.

I had never been to a woman's retreat before. It felt like I was a part of something meaningful. I was still in awe at the way this came to be. I was asked by my new friend I barely knew to join her because she did not want to share a room with anyone else. I was feeling privileged to be asked and to be a part of this event.

There were two classes that were being held; one for married women and one for single women. Although I was separated from my husband, I was not divorced yet. Because of this I chose to attend the married class.

The way the class began is not the way it finished. The women started off talking about their marriages and how long marriages were. When it came to me the whole direction of the discussion changed. I explained my situation:

"Well, I am married but have been separated for over 10 years. He was abusive to me and I left after the last episode. Because I am unsure about the terms of divorce according to the Bible, I have not filed. I no longer believe I can file. I read that he has to give me a divorce." I was quickly interrupted by a minister who proceeded to tell me, "according to Matthew 19:8 and what it says about a heart being hardened, you are able to divorce him." I was immediately relieved and realized this was my reason for being here. After that, the women began to speak about the troubles instead of the "perfect" happenings in their marriage. Many questions and comments began to flow because of what I had revealed. The whole direction of the class changed. I was so glad I accepted the offer to go on this trip.

I was asked to sing a song that following evening. I did not know many spiritual songs, but had one that had been in my heart for a while . . . What God has for me; it is for me.

I was enjoying going to church and all the changes that were occurring within me. To help the days go by and not become so frustrated with things not happening as fast as I wanted them to, I was hooked on an internet game. It took up a lot of time and I was able to listen and comprehend my thoughts. I was learning a new way of being and had to accept it all. I wanted more and craved for it daily, but tried to remain patient. I did not know how to move forward, but was waiting on the Lord.

One day as I was sitting at my computer my brother called me. He asked if I wanted to do volunteer work at his office. "YES!" I responded very quickly. He told me the place and time and said he'd see me then. I was so excited. I was so glad to be a part of something. At that time, he was a national coordinator for HIV and AIDS so I knew I was a part of something great. I was looking forward to this opportunity.

After being there several weeks helping pack boxes for trips, putting together information for rallies, and making phone calls to affiliated persons, my brother had another opportunity for me. He knows my story and knew I would love to work with women in similar situations. He also knew someone who worked at a woman's organization and told me to go and see her about volunteering there as well.

It was amazing. When I was locked up several years ago, I had written out an outline for a transitional home for women. This organization represented everything I wrote about. They worked with women who were formally incarcerated and who needed assistance in reentering society. They assisted with obtaining ID card, birth certificate, medical records, educational and career training, and housing. There was also a HIV and AIDS testing area and a clothing boutique for those who needed clothing. I knew this was the place for me.

I began volunteering there and was headed in a new direction.

God allowed me to be alone for a while and collect all that came to me. Knowledge, understanding, and most of all a new attitude. Because I was able to focus differently, I was able to see what was in front of me instead of behind me. I was always facing backwards and to the side of me. Being exposed to new people, places, and things allowed me to desire what I saw or became a part of.

God knows exactly what He deposited inside of me long ago. He knows exactly who to bring into my life at the proper time to get me to see the view I need to see.

My new friend was a real individual; like me. Intelligent like me and had a very giving heart. I saw me in her. I saw the possibilities within myself through the relationship I had with her. When I did not have, she gave me just what I needed. I needed to know what to focus on. God used her to help me see.

My brother has been a guide for me in many ways and God used him again. Volunteering at his job was a way for me to give of myself for others, be a part of something bigger than myself, and for me to see that I was able and willing to do so much more with my life. There is so much out here that I can participate in and use what God has blessed me with.

I looked at everything completely different. I used to look down and now I was looking up.

Now that I was in a place of helping others, I was also able to see me. I could see a different interpretation of who I was. Among many things I was a very giving, helpful, loving, caring, curious, intriguing, inspiring, encouraging, motivating, and yearning individual. In helping others, they were indeed helping me. And while others helped me, I could see what I wanted to do for others.

God gave me purpose a long time ago. I was still on the path to find it, but at least now I am headed in the right direction. I know I had the leading of the Lord. I knew I was moving forward with the right attitude. I had something else to grasp and knew it was within my reach. I was pointed in a new direction with many options.

PROMOTED AGAIN
Chapter Forty-One

SCRIPTURE

Romans 8:5
*Those who live according to the flesh have their minds set
on what the flesh desires; but those who live in accordance
with the Spirit have their minds set on what the Spirit
desires.*

I was enjoying volunteering in the clothing boutique at the woman's organization my brother led me to. I received much fulfillment in knowing that my participation was assisting someone in what they needed. My job was to keep the clothing neat. Being my creative self and needing things to be in order and decency, I rearranged the entire room. I separated the clothing by size, color, and item. It took me no time at all and I enjoyed every moment of it. I was able to use my creative side which gave me satisfaction.

Not long after beginning this volunteer duty, I was being directed somewhere else. The woman I spoke with initially to get this opportunity was trying to get me a paying position. I told her I appreciated that, but I was happy to be part of what they were doing. She called down to the transitional facility they had right down the street and spoke to the Director.

A few days later I was to meet with this person and see about volunteering at the transitional house. It was so close to what I had written about while being in jail I did not know what to think. I had not seen the place yet, but knew it would be very similar. I had seen and learned so much by working in the boutique. I had no clue what I was in store for at the transitional.

Sitting in the front of the main office, I was waiting to meet the director of the transitional facility. I could feel this was another opportunity for me. I had a sense I was being guided along. Amazingly I wasn't too nervous, just anxious. As I looked up, I saw this woman walking down the hall. She walked right up to me and said with her deep voice, "You waiting for me?"

I looked up and said, "I believe so." She was a tall, red-boned woman, braids going to the back, wearing men's clothing, and walked with a slight pimp. I was told to come with her. We proceeded to her car and drove down the street. The transitional facility was not far from the main office which was pleasantly surprising. We walked inside and she showed me around. It was a three level townhouse that held four women at a time. She explained the mission and began telling me about the facility.

She was unsure what she needed me to do, so she found something simple like organizing some papers. I was ecstatic about being there. Life had jumped off the pages and manifested. I had written about a place like this when I was locked up. To be in a facility that resembled that was amazing to me. I was happy to be a part of anything that had to do with assisting women to reestablish themselves. Because of my past, I could relate to them. Although their situations are very different from mine, still I could relate.

I finished up my duty for the day and was told to return the next day at a specific time.

I was overjoyed about having something to do and that I really wanted to be a part of. While I was locked up, I wrote a two-page outline for a transitional home after conversing and observing the women I was confined with. I did not know why or really where that thought came from because it was rather random. To now be volunteering in the same kind of place I had written about was so unreal to me. I was up for whatever would come of it.

I returned the next day as asked and she had more miscellaneous stuff for me to do. I really did not mind because of where I was. Continuing to file papers, clean up, and listen to her conduct her business was alright with me.

As time went by, I would meet more of the staff members. There were different shifts; morning, evening, and over-night. I began to see the duties of the staff and longed to be one of them. Resident Monitor was the position that oversaw the women who lived in the home. Some of their duties were to see them off in the morning, make sure they took their medication(s), and observe them in the evenings until bedtime. It appeared very easy to me, yet I was still satisfied with being a volunteer.

The Director would have me ride along with her to different places throughout the day. We would eat lunch, drop off information at fellow organizations, or seek out other facilities in the area. It seemed that she was running out of things for me to do within a day, but would always find something. I appreciated it and always looked forward to the next day.

Spending so much time with the Director allowed us to get to know each other better. It was pretty obvious from the time I met her that she was gay, but that did not bother me at all. By this time in my life I was not offended or had any judgment toward anyone for their personal decisions. She was very fun to be around and I began to respect her a lot because of her position. She had an extremely strong personality, was aggressive, and very forward. These qualities caught my curiosity because they were characteristics I wanted to possess. She also had a story that illuminated her position at the facility. She came from a rough background and had done some time in prison. Once released, she went through a program that helped her out tremendously. That very program gave her an opportunity to be employed. She now ran their facility.

I figured I could learn a lot from her. Being able to participate in whatever was needed at the facility and as her right hand allowed me to pick up much more about this organization and what it had to offer. I was absorbing so much and had made a new friend.

She asked me if I was interested in a position. It was an on-call position, but would pay well. I accepted immediately. I volunteered for a few more weeks before beginning the job. Whenever someone was unable to cover their shift, I was to come in for them. I did this several times before becoming a part-time employee. I took my position very serious and wanted to learn so much more. I was going beyond the call of duty while covering my shift. Refolding linen, organizing shelves, and coming in early was no problem for me.

Before too long I was asked to be a full-time employee. Resident Monitor was now my position. In a few months I moved up from volunteer to a full-time resident monitor. Not long from given that position, I was offered to be a Resident Monitor Coordinator. I knew the director had some say in that, but I did not mind. I felt I worked for it. I was her right-hand along with doing my duties.

I was working so much until I was unable to attend church more regularly. I talked to my pastor about it and he stated that I wanted a job and now God has blessed me with one.

Knowing I did not have an education to hold this position, I knew it was the favor of God. Although I was not in church, I felt a bit of fulfillment. I tried to remain who I was becoming in Christ, but really did not know if I was doing it correctly or not. All I knew was opportunities kept coming and I was accepting them.

My co-workers talked about me behind my back due to my constant promotions. I did not pursue them and their accusations and felt no way toward what they were saying. I enjoyed what I was doing, enjoyed the company I was around, and looked forward to more. I finally felt needed. I was doing something worthwhile and it was making a difference. I do not know how I got here, but was going to cherish and enjoy every bit of the experience.

The Director and I became very close. We knew each other's families and would spend time outside of work together. I believe this made others a bit jealous and felt this is how I obtained my promotions. When in the facility, I did exactly what I was told and some. I loved my work and was very interested in what I was doing. This organization was for a good cause; assisting women who were incarcerated and in need. I could relate to these women and was glad to be a part of their journey. I knew I worked hard and did not pay attention to what others were saying.

During my progression in the organization, we went through a major change at the head of the organization. Our Executive Director was replaced with another woman who was drastically different. She was making many changes that we all did not understand, yet abided by. She came down from the main office to look over files, the facility, and our work. One day she wanted to have a meeting with the Director and asked me to leave the office. While I sat in the living area, I wondered what was transpiring. Being changes was occurring, would I be one?

After a brief meeting, the Director came out and said she wanted to speak with me. With my stomach in my throat, I proceeded into the office where she sat behind the desk. Looking me in my eyes, she asked, "How do you like working here?" I answered quickly saying, "I love being a part of something so wonderful. Whatever I am able to do, I am willing." She informed me that the Director had a lot on her and needed some relief. She wanted her to go out into the field more and not be so tied down to the facility. Someone needed to take up the slack. She then said, "I am promoting you to Case Manager."

I was so amazed to be in the position I was in. I had never done this kind of work before, but felt I was very capable. Even more so, God knew I was.

I took this position just as serious as I did when I was volunteering. So much was coming my way and I really did not do anything to deserve it. I did what I was told and what I felt in my heart. This was a new opportunity for me to show abilities I did not know I possessed. God was using me in a mighty way and I was very appreciative. I had no clue where this would take me and really did not care. I was glad to have the chance to assist these women as well as my boss in whatever way needed.

I must admit, it felt good being lifted up and not even knowing it was coming.

Thinking back on how this began, I only wanted to be a part of an organization who assisted women in need. I knew what it felt like to not have, be pushed away, and feel unwanted. We all need assistance at one time or another for many different reasons. No one is better than the other regardless of what their position. We are put in a place where we are always able to learn from one another. Growth can come from and through anywhere.

God began showing me how my life could be used to help others. Allowing me to be a part of something wonderful was just the eye opener. I also learned that doing the best I could with an open heart would take me to places I never knew were possible without my doing. I did not set out to try and get higher positions, it was given to me. I could feel myself being carried from one point to another.

God does the promoting and we do nothing to deserve it. Because my God is great and lives within, I knew I was destined for great things. My knowledge and understanding escalated as well as my position. It wasn't so much the position that was so boundless, it was knowing I could at any time be promoted again!

SETTLED IN
Chapter Forty-Two

SCRIPTURE

Ephesians 4:31-32
Get rid of all bitterness, rage and anger, brawling and slander, along with every form of malice. Be kind and compassionate to one another, forgiving each other, just as Christ God forgave you.

Being promoted came with more responsibility that I was ready for. I almost felt like I needed to prove things to myself rather than to others. Because of my promotion, my co-workers continued to have a negative attitude toward me. I still did not allow that to phase me, nor did I let it affect what I needed to do. I did all that I was told and fulfilled the obligations that were set before me. I was settling into my skin.

There was an opportunity for me to take classes that would improve my skills and comprehension of the women's circumstances. Being certified in areas would also provide me with the creditability from those who would come to verify those working at the facility. Looking up classes was a bit challenging because of the education that was needed in order to enroll. I did not have my high school diploma and began to see the hindrance it could cause.

It was suggested that the Director and myself take a Domestic Violence course. This was an opportunity I was excited about as well as a bit apprehensive. I had dealt with domestic violence as a child and within my marriage, so I was very familiar with how it can affect someone. I was now afraid of what this course would bring up within myself. Because it was to better myself for these women, I opened myself up to the idea and looked forward to it. This opportunity would benefit many other than personally.

Beginning this course was a bit challenging, but I was able to look past my own issues and dive into the issue at hand. There was a lot to cover that I was not even aware of. There was so much in determining the circumstances between two or more people within this type of situation. Emotions run high at the time of the violence, but the specifics have to be determined and a conclusion needs to be set forth. A lot of these facts were sparking more and more of my interest because of my personal situations.

Others within this class were from other organizations that assisted women in need. It was intriguing to see all the avenues that were available for those who needed these services. Conversing and sharing stories of how this class would help them professionally gave me more insight on what I was doing there. I felt privileged to be amongst these women. They held some of the same positions that I was familiar with and some I did not. They all had an education beyond myself where I knew I could learn a thing or two from. They have been holding positions within this field of Social Services for years beyond my few months. Because of this, I was feeling like a sponge.

I always thought because of my past I would owe someone something because of the choices I made. I allowed my feelings to dictate my actions at times that were not so great. Being in this class gave me an open heart; more open than before. It was not about me anymore; it was about anyone else.

I believe by this time I was getting comfortable with my new position and duties. I was enjoying the closer interaction with the women who resided in the facility. I felt a deeper sense of respect coming from a few individuals. It made me wonder at times, was the respect for the title I held or me as for the person I was?

My co-workers were still a bit stand-offish but I did not mind. I wasn't there to make friends, although I did want individuals to like me. I began to feel like an outcast and figured it would allow me to concentrate on what I needed to do instead of getting caught up in gossip and mess around the workplace.

I felt a lot of favor coming my way from the Director of the facility. Our friendship grew as we continued to venture out together in and out of work. She was still inspiring to me and offered me something new. I had never dealt with an individual such as herself and was very intrigued. I also felt that she took the place of a lot that was missing in my life. She was a strong woman who was very dominant and treated me like a man would. What else did I need?

As the Domestic Violence class went further into our lessons, the topics began to cover very "close to home" issues. I began feeling a bit uncomfortable while conversing and participating in the discussions held. I knew at this point that this class was doing something for me personally although it was for the women I desired to assist. The positive attitude I had initially began to lesson and I didn't have the enthusiasm to go to class.

Something was happening that made me uncomfortable. It was for my good, but hesitation was setting in.

I was becoming very discouraged. Within the Domestic Violence course many issues were coming up that allowed my mind to travel back to my circumstance. I became less active in the class and did a lot of listening. Because of how I was feeling in my class, I was a little less attentive in the facility as well. I continued to monitor the ladies, but may have showed them less attention than usual. I am certain they could see a slight change within me.

I wasn't sure how to translate what I was learning in class to my life now. I was allowing myself to sit in confusion which stunted my progress and performance. I thought of not attending any more classes. I missed a couple, but did not quit.

Sitting in class one day we were going over telling family, notifying police, and exit plans for the domestic violence survivor. While listening to these procedures I began to think of my situations and what I did not do. It began to make me very upset. I ended up leaving out of the class briefly to smoke a cigarette. The Director of our facility came down and asked me was I alright, and I proceeded to tell her: "I am feeling a bit upset. I never did any of these things. Had I done it, the outcome of my situation may had been different. I would not have been separated from my children and angry for years making crazy choices." After my last word to her I immediately felt a relief.

Once I was able to acknowledge my pain and confess it to someone, it occurred to me . . . Because of what I went through and my mistakes on how I handled my situation, I was equipped to assist anyone in these situations much better. I could inform them of what not to do and why. I had a story that would encourage the individual to do what is necessary because of the hardships that may come if you did not.

I went through my circumstances for others to be directed elsewhere.

Gaining understanding was a tremendous help for me in my Domestic Violence course. I was continuing to fall in the bondage I used to be in by being submissive to my feelings from the past. It was alright for me to acknowledge the hurt I felt at that time in order to relate to someone's situation, but I did not need to let it detour my purpose at the moment.

Becoming a certified Domestic Violence facilitator was for the sole purpose of me assisting others in a situation I had been through. I was allowing the enemy to bring me down because of mistakes I made at that time. What I came to realize once I acknowledged my pain and confessed it to another is that I went through my circumstance just like Jesus went through His for us. Now, I am nowhere comparing myself nor my situation to what Jesus went through. I am merely stating that we go through for a purpose just as Jesus went through for a purpose.

It was very comforting knowing I am able to help someone that much more because of what I went through. It makes helping someone that much more purposeful. Understanding brings about motivation and I am settled in that.

From being in this Domestic Violence class, I learned that it truly was not about my encounter with DV. It hurt me to my core to have to relive those events and feelings. What God showed me was I went through that experience to direct others away from it. Because of the familiarity, I was taking the course very personally and lost sight of why I was there.

God showed me that this is possible in many areas of my life. I lose sight of what I am really doing because of my feelings. It is understandable that this class would drag up old feelings, but I needed to understand why and what the purpose was. It was for me to feel what I felt so I could let it go. I am no good to anyone else if I am focused on myself.

God allowed me to see I had to get comfortable with where I had been and what I had gone through to get to where I am now. It is a difficult process but very rewarding to others. I was being renewed and settling in to realization and understanding. I was settling into myself.

ALL GROWN UP
Chapter Forty-Three

2 Peter 3:18

But grow in the grace and knowledge of our Lord and Savior Jesus Christ. To Him be the glory both now and forever! Amen.

Analyzing where I am in my life right now, I am in a very different space than I have ever been in my life. To be a part of this organization, personally makes me feel so blessed. I knew as a child I was capable of many things. I saw myself very different than others and was set apart. I did not choose this; it is how things panned out. I always allowed my situation to dictate what I thought I was able to do. My self-esteem was very low, felt I would not be a part of anything, yet wanted just the opposite.

Because of my past, I figured I would not be able to accomplish dreams and goals I had. I had not finished school, didn't have much job training, and didn't have a circle of friends. I always felt so alone and defeated.

To look around at my surroundings at this time gave me a sense of hope. I knew there was something greater than me. I did not totally understand it, but I was aware of it. Nothing that was happening was done in my strength or know how. Everything happened as if it were laid out for me. Each step connected to the next and I had no clue where that was leading. I only went with what was given to me. I was directed and I followed.

I had always felt young at heart, therefor probably acted a bit immature for my age. I still was holding on to the fairy tales of life and having a difficult time facing my reality. Having a full-time position at an organization known throughout the District was a huge uplift to my ego. I was more appreciative than anything to be able to belong to something so fulfilling and to be able to use my life experiences that I thought were so horrible for the good of others.

I finally held my head high. Not because of how I dressed, the amount of money I had, or the people I knew. I held my head high because of what I was recognizing deep within that had been growing in me all along.

I began to see myself very differently. I am around so many individuals who are able to teach me things I did not know. It did not all fall under God's Word, yet I was able to see right from wrong through their actions because of what I did know about God's Word. It was difficult at times to differentiate what was proper and not because of the business aspect of why certain things took place. The world became my teaching ground in a way I never looked at it.

I was not a mature Christian, but I knew a lot. Understanding came through events that took place, things I did or said, or how others behaved in specific situations. It was as if God was allowing me to put His Word into action through my daily life. I no longer wanted to do things that did not matter pertaining to my job. I could see the need for so much.

Observing the way others handled issues of the world became my way of seeing myself. I either wanted to do things the same or not. I found myself set apart from their thinking. They thought in a business way, and I thought in God's way. I was slowly learning that the world was not performing acts of God, they were performing acts of self for themselves.

I felt a greater responsibility was on me. It was my duty to use what was given to me to help change the lives of others for the better despite where I was or what others were doing. I had been provided with a platform to perform God's task and not the tasks that were set before me by my employer. I knew I still had to follow their protocol, but implement my talents and gifts to better the program. I could see where my input mattered.

Not only was I growing in my position and as a person, I was growing spiritually.

There were many aspects of this job that I loved. What they stood for, how they assisted women in need, and how they came together to help a cause. There were also things I did not like about it. There were many individuals who used their "title" to identify who they were as a person. I understood the knowledge that came with training and education, but I could not see how that would dictate their character when assisting others. It was as if they through their weight around instead of really trying to find solutions to the issues.

Following guidelines are understood, yet when someone's life is on the line I believe there are grey areas that do not fall under these man made guidelines. If the resources are there and the capabilities fall under what is possible, then it should be done. But because of business and meeting quotas, the heart of the matter went out the window. Because of that, some women were left standing as when they came.

So many resources were available to these women, yet the setup of the programming was not connected to them. We had the chances to affect these lives in a tremendous way. There were ways to get funds that would enable many possibilities. I saw where funds were misappropriated that could have gone to something meaningful. But who was I but a "newbie" feeling I could save everyone. I knew more could be done and wanted to do so. I sometimes felt I was in a losing battle, yet knew the war was not over.

Talking about doing and actually doing became very visible to me. It seemed very simple to me, but I was always told it is much more to it. If this is so, why not do that much more? My compassion for others and creative thinking was growing.

I did not want to become one of them, yet found it difficult to stand alone. There were some of my co-workers who felt as I did, but overlooked their heart's cry. To have something so powerful and effective seemed to be a waste when it wasn't used properly.

Although all was not proper, the base of it all was situated. I was aware of how to have increase and not use it wisely. Just because it is there does not mean it should be used however we see fit. It should have been used the best way for the program. Lasting decisions should have been made versus short term choices that looked good for appearances.

I began having a negative attitude about how these businesses were ran. I believed it started from the top. We could only do what we were allowed to do. If you did not play along, you could possibly lose your job because you are not following the program and your performance would go down.

How could we have so much, yet do so little? My patience and tolerance was growing stronger.

Sitting in a meeting, I glanced around the room looking at all my co-workers and realized they were just as lost as these women we attempt to assist every day. Yes, they had a wonderful position, made a few bucks, and had an education, but inside they were very sad.

I realized, if you have to strive so hard to uphold a title that was given to you by a boss, you really do not know who you are in the first place. I began to understand how they talk with their education and not with their hearts because in all actuality they both come down to the same thing. The right thing to do will work out regardless of what guidelines are or protocol is. The focus is too much on what does not matter, when it should be on what does.

I began to forget about titles, education, degrees, business, and anything else that would hinder me from focusing on these ladies. I almost got caught up in this made up world of tradition and laws, when I knew in my heart that this world should be based on helping one another up to see their way to Christ.

If it did not have a purpose, I did not want to be a part of it. I stayed to myself and did not socialize within the workplace. I might have looked like an outcast, but I felt like a winner. Despite what was around me I kept my heart open to the matters that were in front of me. I realized there are no grey areas in God's Word despite what could or could not be done within an organization.

I was growing away from nonsense.

Able to look past the imperfections of this line of work, and the character of many allowed me to keep the pure view I had initially. Briefly, I allowed myself to doubt what I was a part of and why I was placed here. It did not matter what wasn't right. All that mattered is what was.

I thanked God for me learning this lesson. It is very easy to be discouraged because of what we are surrounded by. What God allowed me to see is it does not dictate what my role in the situation is. God directs my steps, not anyone else. For me to get caught up in the faults, it does not permit me to recognize the beauty in a situation. God works it all out for the good no matter what is happening.

This lesson learned could be used anywhere I was. I could feel a growth spirt every time I thought about it. It was lovely to take a trying situation that could have had a negative effect on my attitude and actions and see it turn into something wonderful and extremely helpful. When I spoke about adversity, I was able to use this teaching and speak with authority because I knew it well.

Immaturity sticks their mouth out and gets upset with anything that is not as we know it. Even though something may be against what is "right", I realized that God can take anything and turn it around. I have seen it too many times. In knowing this, I have to continue speaking His goodness. As long as I stick to what my heart feels and knows, I would be just fine. It did not matter if I was standing alone; ultimately I would not be.

I was growing right before my eyes.

I was able to see the realities in everything around me. Instead of allowing me to detour my passion and be lead in the opposite direction, I was able to gain understanding through it all.

It doesn't matter what is seen. What matters is what is not seen. God allowed me to go through these emotional changes in order for me to recognize His truth. I had come to a place in my life where things really started to matter. Everything touched my heart in a way it never did. To be taken advantage of or seeing lack where it was possible to give really angered me. This gave me confirmation that there was a greater purpose for my life. Not that I did not know that, but to have a personal experience with revelation makes it that much clearer.

I was able to circulate through the workplace with my eyes and ears open in a new way. I appreciated everything no matter the situation. I knew it was for me in some way to help me get to the next level in my life as well as assist others in a greater way. I was finally feeling a part of this world. I had meaning in a way I had not known.

Growing does not come with age, it comes with understanding. If you have no understanding, you are not able to grow. I was growing up and had much more to come. It was good for me to see myself this way. It enabled me to expect more. Growth spirts were on the way!

EXPERIENCE
Chapter Forty-Four

1 Thessalonians 5:18
Give thanks in all circumstances; for this is God's will for
you in Christ Jesus.

I have been through many experiences: Sexually abused, physically abused, teenage mother, dropped out of high school, abortion, separation, drugs and alcohol abuse, and sexual immorality. There are a few more far and in between, yet these are the ones that stand out the most. They were not easy to go through, nor were they easy to get past. It took a great deal of time to heal from some and some wounds were still being healed.

Moving through my life I have appreciated a lot. I cannot say much for the bad times, nothing good anyway, but know that I have learned a great deal from them. I had always thought that someone hated me tremendously for me to go through so much until my life did a 360*. There were more good times now and I could look back and be thankful I was not where I used to be. Although it was rough, I knew there was much more ahead of me than behind.

Being thankful for all I had was easy. The difficult part was being thankful for all I had been through. To view all that was presently taking place in my life became pretty easy to be thankful for my past. Those experiences brought me to where I am and allows me to handle what was to come. Had I not been there, I would not be able to assist others, have compassion for others, relate to others, or even love others. My involvement with my past has lead me to places I only dreamed of. It was not the highest I could go, but it sure reached new heights.

I was ready to experience more.

Having had much experience in many areas, I figured I would not be shaken in any kind of way to steer me off the course I was on. I have been through abuse, so not concerned with a rowdy person . . . I had something for that. I had been with plenty of men that I was not concerned with sex or a relationship with one. My children and I had come to a point in our relationship where I was forgiven, for now, for the pain of my absence in their lives. I did not have any anger on the surface that would rupture, nor any hurt that I could feel at this time. I believed I was at a place of contentment.

I had a new job, had reached a promotion frequently, and had gained much self-confidence. I was becoming very familiar with my daily tasks and was meeting many individuals who had an effect on me. It was a very spongy time for me. I soaked up everything I was around that meant the least bit of anything. I was so intrigued by everything. I was wide open to new possibilities and endeavors.

Not really focusing on the relationship the Director and I had formed, I began to notice a difference. I became very close to her in ways I did not plan. She seemed to fit every avenue of my life that was not whole. Although my mom and I were sociable, we were not 100%. My sister had a major problem with me and I did not know why; which was nothing new. I and my brothers were fine but just not as close as I would have liked to be. They were very busy with their careers and I understood that, but nevertheless I missed them. My oldest brother was the one who recommended this place to me, so of course I kept him in my heart. And, I did not have a best friend. She seemed to fit in every void I had and it was very comforting to have someone around for every aspect of my life.

One day she kissed me on my lips and I did not turn away. This was an experience I never had!

This kiss that took place was very odd let alone different. I could not understand how I allowed a woman to touch me inappropriately. I had always had an issue with individuals who were gay, lesbian, or homosexual. They could do whatever they felt, but I did not want any part of that choice. Now here I was permitting this very act I am against to happen to me. I went with it.

Honestly, as odd as it was, it empowered me in a way. It was like it provided me with a strength that had not been touched. I did not care what anyone thought, believed, or felt. When she and I were together, there was not a sense of embarrassment or fear. I knew we got stares, but I did not care. For about the third time in my life I was truly living in the moment.

I did not admit to many people what this relationship was or stood for. I did not even know myself. I knew I was not gay nor did I have an interest in women sexually or physically. It was all emotional for me. I wasn't certain what I was experiencing.

I almost felt as if I were making an indirect statement to her; "I will take a stand with you." I ultimately knew it was about me. What was I doing? Why was I intrigued with this person? Why did I not care about being seen with her? Why did my morals and beliefs go out of the window? Was I really gay? What was my real thrill? These questions along with many others continued to run through my head repeatedly. Yet it did not stop me from being with her. I felt we were more of good friends than in a relationship. I could not fully grasp the concept that I really wanted this life, but I could not understand why I allowed myself to be in it at the time either.

Because of the relationship, I had it easier at work. I still performed my duties but would be able to have a lot of lead way. I definitely can say I used it to its advantage, but still appreciated my job very much and cared a great deal about what it stood for.

She and I became closer emotionally in many ways. She met my family and became more aware of things I shared with her about my past. She even met my sons and became a help to them when needed. In every area of my life at that time she filled the voids. It became clear to me after a while why I took to this relationship. She possessed many things I was desiring at that time and the company also felt good for a change. I could be me with no problem, got just about anything I wanted, loved my job, and had special privileges. If I wanted to go somewhere; we went. She took me out to eat, took me shopping, listened to me, encouraged me, assisted me with personal issues, and so much more.

Although this seemed very fulfilling, I knew this was a sinful experience.

After a period of time of holding the position of Case Manager, I was asked to work at the main office of this organization by the Executive Director. I was given the title Programs Assistant. But before being asked if I wanted to come work in the main office I was asked about my relationship with the Director. As shocked as I was, I denied everything. I stated that we were very good friends who spent a great deal of time together, but were not in a relationship. By listening to her speak, I could tell that there had been much talk about the Director and me. I honestly did not care, nor was I going to confess to a relationship that I knew was not favorable or understood by my heart. I cared about her, but not enough to claim we were together.

I felt in my heart that we were very good friends. I knew I was not gay, was not attracted to her in that way, and was only enjoying the benefits that came with this experience. I did not believe I was telling a bold-faced lie, but actually I was. Because of my job, I was not willing to put minor details on the table to satisfy the ED's curiosity. I also did not want the Director to lose her job. I was told I would not be the one in trouble because she was my superior. I could not see telling on anyone in this circumstance. It had to work itself out.

I never believed I was wrong in this situation. If I had it to do again, I still would not tell the unnecessary details of our relationship. We had a friendship with many benefits on both ends. We got out of it what we wanted at that time. Because we were not in a committed, fully fledged relationship, I was not admitting to what was asked.

I honestly thought about her and the damage it could do in the long-run. Ultimately, she later was let go but under different circumstances. It ended up being difficult any way for her. I never will know what the outcome would have been if we told the truth. It was too complicated for me to confess; especially knowing I did not really want her like that.

Satisfying ourselves ended up being a difficult experience and I believe lying about it had its consequences later. I lost sight of the beautiful experience I was originally given. I was just promoted but felt untrustworthy. This had to change.

Although the experience with the Director was wrong in many ways, it allowed me to understand things in a different light. I had a certain attitude toward gays, lesbians, homosexuals, bi-sexual, and transgender at one time. I knew this choice was totally against God's Word and there is no right in it whatsoever, but because of my choice, I was able to build a sense of compassion for them. I could never understand what they were going through, but I could understand their desire to want just like anyone else.

She provided so much for me; so I thought. I know that God uses people no matter who they are. We are to learn throughout all situations and circumstances. I had my selfish reasons for partaking in this kind of relationship, yet learned a great deal from it. It wasn't so much about it being a woman I was involved with or that she was my boss. It was developing feelings for someone I never would have before. I never thought I would ever be close in an intimate way with a woman. I never had a best friend, so this wasn't something I was used to. It was nice having a person around that could satisfy me in multiple ways.

Ultimately, I know God was showing me to love everyone despite faults or things that look wrong to the world. He is the ultimate judge and will dictate what can and cannot be. He allowed me to go through this for His purposes. I could have been directed out of it. It was my choice, but He allowed it to be. It was a negative situation used for the good.

Something amazing came out of it. My heart grew larger and fonder of those I would have never had contact with because of the relationship with her. I met so many individuals of many walks of life. I learned about myself and what I was capable of. I saw that I could bypass boundaries beyond my thoughts. No, it was and is not right or okay to go against God's Word. I am merely stating many things are possible and have many outlets.

I had come to a new place in my life where I was more confident, direct, and outgoing. She offered me a way out of my center and I accepted.

What I know now is God offers that and so much more. I actually had it before she came along, but she was used so I could experience the possible.

From this relationship, I learned how to open my heart to the taboos of life. Without her, I would not know the side of life I embarked in. I was able to see individuals and not their labels.

God allowed me to be in this relationship. No, He does not condone anything I was doing, yet knew I would get something out of it. My heart was opened personally after being hardened for so long. What better way to open my heart than to use something so farfetched, that anything else would seem so simple. I was so closed to the idea of intimacy or even emotional ties with anyone. God allowed this amazing woman of courage, strength, endurance, selflessness, kindhearted, and I could go on . . . to come into my life and give me another view.

In the end, this allowed me to experience God's love. A saved individual's sins are forgiven. If the same act is repeated, then we choose our own desires over what He commands. I knew this relationship was wrong for so many reasons, yet to experience God's love for individuals, I would do it again. Everything works for the good of those who love the Lord.

REALIZATION
Chapter Forty-five

✕ SCRIPTURE ✕

1 John 2:27

As for you, the anointing you received from Him remains
in you, and you do not need anyone to teach you. But as
His anointing teaches you about all things and as that
anointing is real, not counterfeit – just as it has taught you,
remain in Him.

I was appreciative once again for being promoted to a higher position. I was now Programs Assistant and working at the main office. I missed the transitional home because I knew everyone, knew my position well, and I was very comfortable. I now had to get familiar with my new position and the people within this office.

It was a different atmosphere where I was now. Everyone had college degrees and held their positons for a while. If they did not work here long, they had been in this line of work for several years. That made me want to do well and at the same time made me a little nervous.

I realized I was in another chapter of my life and many changes were to come.

Being in this office made me look at myself differently; once again. I would question my being there. I did not have what they had. I had never done this type of work. I really did not even know what my position actually meant. Why was I put in this place?

Sitting in meetings were interesting. Initially I was lost. I did not know what they were talking about. I did not know the programs and events they were discussing. I felt so out of place until I just really sat back and listened instead of judging myself. Once I took myself out of the equation I could see clearer.

I was put with two women on a particular project. It was called RDP, Re-Entry Demonstration Project. They seemed to be best buds in this office. I kind of felt out of place with them as well. I was not a part of any conversations, did not have a daily task, and had to sit in an office with them. I was not liking this new position.

I was the newbie and realized that quickly.

Because I did not know exactly what to do within this new position, it made me feel incompetent. How could I perform well if I had nothing to do? The two women I was working with would provide odd tasks for me to do just to pass the time. I began to resent them and carry a bit of an attitude around them. I would think you would want to make your new co-worker feel good about being in the office, let alone working directly with you.

They did a lot of talking about people that I found very disrespectful and rude. I was not liking my surroundings at all.

I spent a lot of time floating around the office and found myself in the intake office quite often. The lady that worked in there was very sweet and helpful to all who came through this office. She was the first person seen past the receptionist. She was the one who spoke to you to see exactly what services you needed and where to direct you within the office. I liked her position and what it stood for immediately. In between appointments I went into her office and sat down. She looked at me with a smile and said to close the door. She began talking to me in a way that made me feel so much better.

After our conversation, I had a little more direction than I had before. She knew a little about me and I knew a little about her.

I went back to my office with those two women and began doing my own thing. In between what they needed me to do, I worked on another project I was told was needed.

I did not need to condemn others nor bring up their name. It appeared it was already known and others in the office were hoping I was alright in there with them. I realized I was not the only one feeling the way I was and also realized we did basically what was necessary to run this office. I needed not to concern myself with these women.

Having a little direction made me feel a great deal better until I was in these two women's presence again. It was as if they did not want me to interfere in their work. This job is supposed to be about each person coming together and assisting the needs of others. It appeared they were only concerned with their own needs.

I began taking on finding housing for the ladies who needed somewhere to live. This had not been done in a while, obviously, because the notebook was way out of date. The resources for finding housing was very old and would not help me one bit. I had to start a new book with new resources to benefit this quest.

Because these women did not have much for me to do, I spent a lot of time on this project. They would travel in and out of town to the prisons along the east coast. During this time, I would assist with the folders they would take with them. Whenever doing a task for them, I did it to the best of my ability.

Personally, I felt as if these women thought I was incapable of doing any "real" work. What I began to realize is I was capable of more than I realized. My project was coming along just fine.

One day I came into the office dreading to see these two women in our little area. My face was long and I did not look approachable at all. As I walked into the office they were conversing about something and all of the sudden . . . utter silence. I made the statement, "Don't let me stop you." One of them looked at me and said that my aura was bringing them down. If I felt a particular kind of way that I should leave. So I did.

As I was on my way home I felt defeated. I felt I had allowed them to get the best of me even after I had attached myself with a project. I had a direction so why was I letting these two women upset me so much?

I decided from that point on that I was there for a reason and it does not matter what anyone thinks about it. It would be better if everyone liked me, but they did not have to. There actually was not a reason they should not. No one knew me nor knew anything about me except the lady in the intake office. She was the one who gave me hope. Something happened in that room behind those closed doors. I opened up to her and I listened.

God had already prepared me for this position and place in my life. I did not need anyone's approval. I also did not need to carry anger around as if it were hindering me from something. It then becomes me who is the problem and not anyone else.

I realized I was my problem and not anyone else. I am equipped for everything God allows in my life. For those things I am not, He is equipping me at that time.

I had a sense of relief. It has nothing to do with what others think about me; it is about what I know God has placed inside me. It is not about what others are able to do; it is about what God blessed me to do. There is always a plan and a purpose for me wherever I go. Even if I make a wrong choice, a lesson will be brought out of it for my good.

In the end I came out victorious because I sought after what I needed to and did not waste time on the foolishness. I realized I just need to stay focused on my task at hand and not those who are against me. That would be handled in time.

I realized I am able to cope with all things no matter who I am around or what I am faced with. God has equipped me to do so. I needed not to focus on what individuals think or how they act toward me. I should always, to the best of my ability, keep my focus and carry out God's will at that time in my life.

God will allow me to be in situations that challenge me and enable me to be better. Strength is gained through each trial. It is not for me to give up. It is for me to bypass the unnecessary and to know the difference.

Being able to realize in the mist of the situation that this is for you no matter how difficult. Press past it and use the tools that were provided for you through all the circumstances you have been through in life. The tools are there, we have to realize and utilize them!

CAPABILITIES
Chapter Forty-six

SCRIPTURE

Philippians 4:13
I can do all this through him who gives me strength.

After being in the office for a while, I got the hang of things. I headed the Housing Program, still a part of the Re-Entry Demonstration Project. There was still a bit of turbulence between the three of us, but I let it ride because of what I was focusing on. I was now able to channel my desire to assist these women into finding the appropriate resident placement for them temporarily or permanently. This made me feel needed.

I also became a part of the intake process. After the nice lady and I talked behind closed doors, she was aware of things I was able to discuss with these ladies. If they had any kind of abuse issue, she sent them to me and I would provide them with the appropriate resources that could assist them further. It felt regenerating to be able to use my past to assist another woman. I never knew this day would come where I was able to sit and listen to another woman's story and in turn share mine and it was beneficial to her.

It came to be that it wasn't about my abilities in a specific area of study, years in a position, or who I knew. It was all about my expertise in my life. I was fully capable of telling someone about my story to encourage them or inspire them to know all could and would be alright.

I was enjoying being able to use my issues to assist others. It did not feel like work any longer. I remember hearing once that you should find something you enjoy doing and get paid for it. I began to feel as though this was it. It took no effort and felt so fulfilling.

There were times when the stories I heard went beyond anything I even experienced. It became difficult to console these women, let alone direct them to the proper place. I wanted to guarantee that where I would send them would be as passionate about their feelings as I was; and I knew I could not do that. I felt so sorry for these women and wanted to provide the world for them. I could see myself all over again. I knew their pain. Although our stories were different, the hurt and pain remains the same.

One thing I did notice is that they had faith in God. It was not "proper" to speak about religion in the office, but behind a closed door I would do so. I did not need to say much. As soon as I mentioned Him, their face expression changed even if for a moment. I knew there was hope and prayed they knew the same.

I would find myself going the extra mile to assist someone. I would go beyond the services we were supposed to be providing. There was one young lady who was trying to get in touch with her son. She mentioned she wanted to use a popular social network to reach out to him. I took her in an office and began the process of connecting for her using this social network. A few weeks later she let me know that he responded and they were going to meet up after not speaking for years. I was so excited for her. Although she had so many other issues, I felt special to be a part of that reunion that was going to take place all because of helping her a little further.

I was capable of assisting her a little more than expected, so why not?

As time went on, I became familiar with the women that were coming to get assistance from the organization. I did not know everyone's name, but knew their faces and situation. I had housed a few women and was able to direct a few to counseling. I wanted to do so much more, but was happy with what I had accomplished.

I was a part of the RDP team, head of Housing, assisted with intake, and did a little help in the clothing room. My hands were full and I loved it. I felt I was helping tremendously with what I could do in each area.

The E. D. called me into her office to inform me that I would now be going along with the two women I was working with to the prison in Philadelphia. It was interesting how this came about and even more interesting what was said to me. We had a meeting including all of four persons. The E. D. was introducing a new program she wanted to try out. After going through the details of the program, she said I was going to manage it. I needed to come up with a game plan of how to get this up and running. To my amazement I smiled and was stopped dead in my enlarging dimples when one of the women said, "Are you sure you can handle that Kristine with all you are doing?" I looked at her with a "no she did not" kind of look on my face. The E. D. continued speaking and I interjected and said, "Wait, excuse me but I need to go back to what she just said. I can handle it and everything else just fine thank you!" Everyone looked at me strangely and smiled. I was so tired of their sideways remarks and putting me down as if I was incompetent.

I walked a bit taller after being told I am about to create and manage my very own program. I had never done this before and did not know where to begin. Was I being tested or just given the opportunity to see what I was made of? Either or it was my time to show how capable I am of running a program and managing everything else I was doing.

It seemed as if there were many who wanted to see me fail. Any question I had about anything was as if no one knew a thing. I understood from the beginning it was going to be all me. To my surprise I was paired with an intern who was going to do the logistics of the program. That was a bit of a relief and a blessing at the same time. I now had someone who I could bounce ideas off of and have another point of view. I created and she wrote the vision out in proper form.

I did some research on programs to get a concept of how one came together. There had to be a purpose and what it stood for. I was told by the E. D. that I would need to know this program like the back of my hand. I began to understand the idea, but still did not connect totally with it.

I could start to feel my creative juices flowing after a while. I then had to come up with a name. I liked puzzles so I thought an acronym would be fun. I had the word and only needed to come up with the words that described it to a tee. It wasn't long before it was written in stone. It was announced at the next meeting and I got a unanimous handclap. It felt great!

Working with this young lady taught me quite a bit. I would always think something was so difficult because I never done it before. Putting this program together allowed me to see that it is not as difficult as you may think. As long as it is taken piece by piece and section by section, it is pretty simple. Like anything else, when you look at it in its entirety it seems overwhelming. Yet when taking each task one by one, it appears acceptable.

I was being taught along the way yet teaching her at the same time. She got to understand the inside of the program while she brought it to life on paper. We accomplished a lot together without knowing much of anything. We were guided by what we were already gifted with and were able to teach, correct, and direct each other to a completed program.

Although I had never been in this position before, I began to understand that I can do anything I set my mind to. Situations within the office was very trying and had me on the way out of the door, but God! He touched my heart and allowed me to have another perspective. It was all about what I was looking at.

Individuals will always attempt to trip you up, persuade doubt in your mind, or tell you that you are unable to do something. As long as I am able to hold on to truth, know in my heart that God placed me in a position I had nothing to do with whatsoever, and has a plan for my life, I will be just fine.

I almost allowed others to dictate what I am capable of. They have no clue. I have no clue until God reveals it to me. Each time a new task is placed in front of me I have the opportunity to see just what I am made of and what I am able to accomplish.

No one can stop the capabilities God has enabled me with!

SELF-WORTH
Chapter Forty-seven

Proverbs 28:6
Better the poor whose walk is blameless than rich whose ways are perverse.

I had been at the main office for quite some time now. I was comfortable with my position and was doing pretty well. I began to pay attention to detail around the office. Although the concentration was not on me, I still felt highlighted. By seeing what was happening around me, I could see me more. Changes were happening underneath the surface and was very apparent to me. Individuals that had been there before me were leaving or being fired.

I distanced myself from the two women I shared the office with only to move in with women who came in while I was leaving. I was enthused about this arrangement, because I had no negative vibes and could remain silent with no problem. I could work at my own pace and had no concerns or worries of others over my shoulder.

The E. D. told me I was not engaging in conversation with my co-workers. Personally I did not feel the need to chit chat about pointless things that I actually had no care about. She felt I was secluding myself and showed no team effort. Heading my own programs and assisting with others kept me pretty busy. Whether or not there were positive outcomes often, the work was put in. I felt I was doing my job and put a lot of energy and determination into what I was doing. Unless I needed another's input, there was no need for conversing.

It went from what I am unable to do to I am not into everyone in the office. I thought we were here to assist the women that came into this establishment for our services. I wondered why that could not be seen. It was as if what I was doing was going unappreciated.

They were focused on me and I was focused on what they were supposed to be doing. Who was this all for?

I found that I was having to stand up for myself more often. I did not really say anything to anyone who was trying to put me down or make snide comments. I figured it was better to let that individual look simple on their own rather than have a debate. I soon learned it wasn't about trying to win anything, it was merely stating the truth and it would win on its own.

We went to visit the Philadelphia prison as we usually do periodically, but this time I was a bit under the weather. By the time we got to our hotel, my voice was fading. It did this quite often when the climate changed. I was due to speak to the women about the program but knew I would not be able to speak loud enough where they could hear me. One of the women decided she would speak for me and if I needed to say something I could tell her in her ear and she would relay it to them.

All things went very well. She did the majority of the speaking, yet I was so excited once she began talking about it, I started to speak anyway. Overall, it was a success and many signed up.

Because of how I was feeling, I left to go home early. We receive monies for the trip from the job for our travel and expenses. I was not given any monies upon my leaving, so I used the money I had and would get it when they returned. One of the ladies had given me cab fare, yet I gave her back the change. This meant I would receive what was already owed plus the amount I returned to her.

When they returned to the office I awaited the distribution of funds. She proceeded to give me the monies and I politely told her she owed me more. As always, she was loud, wrong, and trying to dispute her logic. I allowed her to finish and then went back through the entire scenario again. I was not loud, but was very direct and spoke in an authoritative tone. Once she added it up in her head, she realized she was wrong and gave me the rest of my money. How could you argue with the truth? It didn't matter about what she thought, what mattered is what was.

Some of the others in the office could hear the conversation, yet could say nothing. She tried to make me look bad when all the time she was on the underside of that coin. I suppose she had to finish it off by telling our boss that I did not do the speaking during the presentation of the program. It really did not bother me. It finished off well and was very effective.

Once I thought about it later, it wasn't about my voice doing it, it was what it stood for. Because of that, I stood for something as well.

I was enjoying the peace within my little space within my office, but when I walked out into the space where everyone else gathered, it felt tainted. I could feel the change in the atmosphere.

There was more talk about each other in the office than it was about the welfare of our clients. So much focus was on what someone thought about another, and there was no truth to it. I did not like this and did not associate with it. I never was one to sit around and talk about people unless it was to assist them with something. This was not the case and wanted no part of it.

I was able to see what it was like here at the main office. It was funny because initially I was so excited about working with such professional, educated individuals that could teach me so much. It turned out to be teaching me more of what not to do.

This was causing a bit of separation in the office when we all should have been coming together for a common cause.

I continued to assist the other programs and enjoyed doing so. I was now assisting with HIV services and picking up donations. Regardless of what was happening around me, God still was using me.

The difference in the office began to affect my work ethic. I remained concerned about our ladies and assisting them as much as possible, but it was a team effort. If I had a problem with someone, I sure did not want to communicate with them about anything. It made it difficult to take care of the needs for an individual because of the attitude behind my co-workers.

It was to the point where they would talk about the clients. How can you call these women names or give your opinion about them? We are not to judge, but to look at their circumstance for what it is and do the best we can to find a solution to their issue(s).

It was amazing. I was in a position to assist others and worked with those that were to do the same. It is to be thought that we were similar creatures. I began to feel more like those who came in for assistance than the ones helping. I wanted assistance as well in how to cope with this corrupt group of individuals portraying a human services support system. Their behavior really had an effect on me.

I did not want my emotions to change the way I cared about these women. They were worth all the effort, regardless of what people said about them.

Although I felt so good about working for this organization, I began to doubt myself. I put out so much effort to meet the needs of these women. It seemed that it came to a point where nothing was amounting to anything. No housing available, disinterested in programing, unavailable funds, not meeting qualifications, and so much more was surfacing that made things more difficult. Why was I here?

My boss called me in her office and said to me, "I am trying to see where you fit." I am thinking to myself, "What?!?"

With so much going to the left, I wondered was this that one thing that was right. Was this my exit? In the past, when my time was up everything seemed to change for the worse. It felt like that time. She proceeded to tell me that there had been a cut in funding and hours had to be cut. Because I was one of the last hired, I was the first to be cut. I went from full-time to part time in a split second.

Immediately I felt anger and then hurt. My eyes watered and then suddenly I felt a burst of strength build up inside me. I felt like everything was just fine. I could see how things were changing, so maybe this was God's way of moving me out before the stuff really hit the fan.

I politely replied to her, "Okay, no problem." Honestly, I still felt just a bit saddened because of what this place once stood for. It felt extremely pleasing to be a part of something so giving and caring toward those in need.

I made a phone call my friend who directed the transitional home and filled her in on the news. I was now in a similar position as she. I could feel her pain, yet could provide her with some inspiration at the same time. She had been let go a few months before. We made a difference when it counted. God used us in a mighty way regardless of what the establishment was turning out to be. No need to be upset.

I knew this season was just about over. I enjoyed making a nice salary, all the lessons learned, watching myself grow, meeting new people, assisting women in need, watching faces light up, providing hope, and all the other positive things I encountered while being a part of this organization. I know I was moving to part-time, but I knew soon it would be over. It had never been about the money, yet I would not work for basically nothing doing almost everything.

God offered me the opportunity to grow in so many ways. I was allowed to see past myself and indulge in other's lives in ways I would have never before. Those who worked with me, those who utilized our services, those we were affiliated with, those who made donations, those who partnered with us, and those who took the least bit of interest in what we had to offer taught me a great deal.

I knew the women who needed assistance felt a particular kind of way about coming into our facility. It takes a lot of guts to set your pride aside and ask for help or admit you have a problem and need assistance in a certain area. I began to feel them even more once I was demoted to less hours. It did not make me less of a person because I was not able to do what I wanted. It did not change who I was because I did not reach the heights I thought I would within this organization.

I offered much to everyone I came into contact with while upholding my position. I may have lost hours, money, and even promotions, but I will never lose my value.

There were no hard feelings toward anyone at the organization. I was happier with the opportunity to experience something new. I started off volunteering and moved up six positions in two years. I could not be anything but thankful. God allowed me to see the abilities He placed within me. I was also able to see how much I cared for others and how much we were alike.

I also saw what I did not want to be. I had always wanted to work in an office downtown and was given that. It was more of a status thing in my mind that became something so much realer than that.

There are many educated persons out here that feel they are above and beyond everyone else because of a degree, yet they are only educated in a specific area of study. A degree does not enable you to identify with individuals on a compassionate level. It does not give you the right to demean people because you feel you are in a powerful position. Education does not provide an individual with the compassion necessary to assist those who are in need of services.

Traits needed to successfully interact with individuals when providing services come with experience. Personal experience will enable you to associate an individual and offer a token of love with whatever you are giving. You will not put the person down because they have traveled a different road than you when you have experience. You will not look at them any different than yourself because you know you have had difficulties in your life as well.

God allowed me to see the good, bad, and ugly within human services. People can be cruel. Just because you are a part of the flock does not mean you have to fly with them. Continue to fly as you have been taught. It is very easy to follow the crowd. But if that crowd isn't headed in the right direction, look for the light. God always offers a way out. It may look as if you are alone, but it is actually a blessing in disguise.

So many changes happened to that organization after I quit a few weeks later. It lost more funding, moved into a smaller building, misappropriation of funds, changed Executive Directors again, and lost more employees. It was obvious things were turning for the worst and it was proven. Vengeance is the Lords.

God will close a door so that a better one will open. God knows we are worth so much more than what people say because of His purposes. The lovely part is when we know our self-worth.

IT IS POSSIBLE
Chapter Forty-eight

Ephesians 6:10 -12

Finally, be strong in the Lord and his mighty power. Put on the full armor of God, so that you can take your stand against the devil's schemes. For our struggle is not against flesh and blood, but against the rulers, against the authorities, against the powers of this dark world and against the spiritual forces of evil in the heavenly realms.

I have always known I was able; able to do anything I wanted to do. The question is, "Was it the correct thing to do?" It may seem right at the time because of the emotions involved, the circumstances, or the options available. This was my confusion for a long time. Because it is possible, is it right?

Often times my decisions got myself into a lot of trouble, yet that trouble did not seem too bad to me at the time. It may not have been for everyone, but seemed perfectly fine for me and my situation. Choices are often made based on our personal experiences. Because we know something to be true either through ourselves or someone else, it appears to be the way to go. Until we take that route and see we should have went another way, we do not see the wrong in it.

I had pretty much done a lot of what I wanted to do. Some good, some bad. No matter my choices, I am glad I made them all. It allowed me to experience so much. I loved and lost time and time again. I tried new things all the time; some hurtful and some not. I met some interesting individuals who have helped me and meant me harm. Because of them, I have learned so much about myself. I have traveled to places where I probably should have never been and other places that showed me something beautiful. I have experimented with my body by adding things to it, exposing it, and removing things from it. I have helped many people as well as hurt them. I was able to learn a great deal throughout all my experiences.

Although all my choices were not the best, I still had opportunity. Possibility still awaited me.

I can say I tried a lot of things. They may not have all worked out, nevertheless, the attempt was a learning experience. Some things taught me to leave it alone, about myself, and about others. Other things gave me experience, deeper understanding, and the ability to press on.

I have met many people along my path. I was among individuals I thought I would never come into contact with. I thought we had nothing in common and had no use for each other's company. Although I did not always participate in what was around me, I had an inside peek at the activities that were in front of me. I did learn that when I continue to subject myself to a certain crowd, I am more than likely prone to indulge in whatever is before me. I was fortunate enough to stick to some of my beliefs and not fall for everything.

It was difficult at times to read individuals. They would come off one way and end up another. I used to believe if someone was nice to you it was because they were really interested in helping you. I now believe I need to be cautious. There are many individuals who are very nosy and only want to know your personal business to spread lies on top of what they think they know. Jealousy runs deep and spreads mighty wide throughout those I have met. I never felt I had so much for someone to envy.

What I came to realize is it isn't so much what they can see, it is what they cannot see. They did know that it was possible for me to obtain whatever I wanted, but why not themselves?

It is amazing how a desire would be in my heart without it ever being a thought. I later realized that God would plant it there to point me in the right direction.

When I am up to no good, it usually is something very selfish. I am satisfying a craving or curiosity. It did not involve helping anyone nor did it help me in the end.

I had all kinds of desires, but not all of them were good. I could tell the difference between something I wanted to do from something I needed to do. I would think about what I wanted to do for a while. What I needed to do would either be done or put off, yet knowing it would get done one day. It does not take much thought when it is destined for you to do something. God had already situated it for me. I had nothing to plan or figure out.

It was always possible for me to get into some kind of trouble. It was also possible for me to do what was in my heart . . . I just did not do it.

I used to believe I was not able to accomplish much because of the hurt I allowed to weigh me down. I knew I was talented and gifted in many areas, but could not get past the pain I felt. Because of the pain, I would give up on what I knew I should do. I would choose to do something that satisfied me momentarily. This would go on and on until I felt a little better. When the pain returned I would repeat this same pattern. It was almost like I was not worthy of anything better. Why had these things happened to me in the first place?

There was always a burning desire inside for something more fulfilling. I somehow knew it was possible.

When presented with an opportunity to better myself I learned to accept the changes and take advantage of a situation instead of turning away from it. I realized it was the unfamiliarity that scared me so much and I did not want to fail at it. So much in my past had gone wrong; I did not want to add to it by messing it up. I would look at this as a time for growth and a much needed change in my life. I did not want to be afraid of doing well. My past was not going to hold me anymore; I hoped.

With a new outlook on choices, I was able to look at the positive in my actions and determine whether I should or should not be a part of it. I prayed I could keep this attitude and remain on the straight and narrow. I was at least glad to have gained this knowledge. Whenever I felt in a jam, I had this moment to look back on. This feeling of hope would never fade. It would only enhance my moving forward.

What I also realized is no matter what I did in the past, all my desires were still possible.

With the position I held at the organization, it allowed me to see I was capable of a lot more than I thought.

I used to have a pretty big attitude and would not let anything slide. I found that I was able to deal with a lot without raising hell about it. I must admit, if it was excessive, I would make it a point to bring it to the appropriate party's attention.

I had been through a lot in the past. Rape at a young age left me very curious still. Abuse in the home left me questioning my self-worth. Becoming a mother in my teen years had me feeling resentful because of the turnout. Abuse in my marriage had me searching for my value. Separating from my children left me lost. Dancing for years gave me a sense of power, yet taught me how to wear a mask. Embarking in drugs and alcohol allowed me to see how much pain I was really in when it did not cover the pain any more. All these things were in my past but played a huge part in my present.

God allowed me to see that no matter where I have been or what I have been through, it won't break me unless I allow it to. It isn't about the things that happened to me, it is why it happened. It was never about me. It is about the possibilities they bring to others.

God plants desires in our hearts that never go anywhere. They are the things that we are designed to do. Although we may make some choices that seem to take us off track, they really allow us to be on track. Making a mistake allows us to understand the better choices in our lives. Gaining understanding is sometimes dealing with the unfortunate circumstances and situations. How else would I have known how bad I wanted something unless I knew what it was like to not have it? He allowed me to make my choice in what I felt I needed at the time. I eventually would tire of what I was doing and choose to go in the proper direction for my life.

God never allowed more than I could handle although it sure felt like it. He allowed me to see possibility is always there when He is a part of your life. Of course an individual can get to certain heights without Him, but it will not last successfully. God used my situations to show me that He has always made it possible for me. This is how I was able to move forward. Because I ignored it does not mean it was not there for me. I am able to think back to all the times He was standing right there for me and I rejected Him.

I do not have to be remorseful about what I have done or what did not happen. I only need to know that with God all is still possible!

TIRED OF BEING TIRED
Chapter Forty-nine

SCRIPTURE

Matthew 11:28-30

"Come to me, all you who are weary and burdened, and I will give you rest. Take my yoke upon you and learn from me, for I am gentle and humble in heart, and you will find rest for your souls. For my yoke is easy and my burden is light."

After my hours were cut back, I continued to work for several weeks. I believed that displayed my loyalty and dedication. It would allow everyone to see I really cared about these women and it was not about the money.

It seemed things became even more difficult than before. I could feel a shift in the atmosphere. More were laid off and fired. Attitudes were becoming worse around the office that made it pretty trying to concentrate on my duties.

I found myself on personal calls looking for a way out. Speaking with ex-boyfriends to see what they were up to and maybe I could visit . . . and possibly stay would provide me with some direction.

The women we assisted were noticing changes taking place in the office. They were used to dealing with a specific person only to find that they were gone. Working on projects or a situation for months only to find themselves right back in the same place if not worse. They now had to find another individual they could trust which would be difficult. Depending on people is difficult enough. They opened themselves up to someone only to not have them anymore. To be let down and have to move forward with a stranger would be tiresome.

I found myself wanting to move on because I was tired of the mess that was going on.

As I looked around, I saw the purpose of this establishment but could not see the passion any more. I felt it inside, yet did not see it around me. It helps to have unity among those with the same purpose to successfully fulfill a need.

I had not placed a woman in housing in over a month, facilities were requiring absurd qualifications, some women were not following through on their end, we had no employment manager any more, and it was talk of misappropriation of funds. To me it looked like all hands were pointing towards the exit.

My heart was holding on while my mind was growing more tired. It still was not time yet, but I knew it was coming.

It was not easy staying somewhere you knew you were leaving, yet also wanted to stay. I loved what we stood for, but that had changed. Because of the firing of different people, positons were left open with no one to cover the responsibility. The women were at one time promised the best care and service. Now it was make do with what is available. It just did not seem fair.

I often wondered what the boss lady thought of this. She was the new Executive Director coming in to better the place, so to speak, and it has gone downhill. Since her taking over, funding was lost, the transitional house was closed, many were fired and others quit, we moved to another location losing many women, and passion for what we were doing seemed to diminish.

The office may have been open, but we were just existing. The people we were supposed to be assisting were getting the worst hit. I know they were tired.

I had to come to the realization that things were changing and I could not control it. Although I loved what I was doing and have ever since I began volunteering, this run was just about over. I was unsure what I would do next. I continued to make calls to an ex, but it just did not seem right in the long run. I called old friends to see what they were up to in hopes that I would go visit and maybe begin a new start.

I continued to contemplate what I should do. I was not liking where I was at or how I was now feeling. I dreaded coming to work every day. I came in late and left early. Something had to change or make me change.

One morning I was in my office and the E. D. called me into her office. I was unsure what this was about, but it could not have been worse than anything already was.

I walked in, shut the door, and sat down. She looked at me with this smug look on her face and said, "I do not see the use for you anymore. I do not see what you do that adds to this organization." I just looked at her and felt she was exactly right. That was my call to exit. I had been waiting for the right time to go and that confirmed it. I don't know if she could sense it or if God just used her to send me on my way. He knew that would definitely do it.

I called in the next day and turned in my resignation. She asked me to bring my key and door pass to the office, sent out an email stating my resignation, and that was it. I did not even clean out my desk. I just left as if I never was there.

I felt a bit of sorrow because I did enjoy where I was and what it all stood for, but my time was up from being tired.

It was a relief to not have to be in a place that appeared to be deteriorating. I know that my time was up and a new season was beginning. I had learned so much while working at this organization. It was still amazing to me how I came to be in a place that I wrote about once before. I cherished every moment and lesson I encountered.

I did, however, feel a bit lost because I was unsure what I would do now. When I began volunteering, I could see me being a part of this organization for a while. I guess a while was the three years I grew, was promoted, and blessed to be a part of many programs. I believe God allowed my vision to come to pass to establish more faith within. I got a bit comfortable all the while needing, shaping, and molding. This opportunity allowed me to see the possibilities that God has for me. He showed me my dream was true yet I still had a lot to learn.

Although there were some trying situations while employed there, I was able to learn from them. Even though I did not understand everything immediately, He would bring it to my remembrance when need be and I would realize the strength that lies within. When I grow weak, God is there to lift me to new heights beyond what I can imagine.

I did not know where I was headed, but did know I did not have to be tired any more.

I thank God for the direction He continued to point me in. It was always something new and exciting. I knew I was being carried because I did not dictate my course any more. I used to make decisions off of my emotions. I have to admit; I still do at times. But the difference is I recognize it now. I have an understanding that when I am tired, I do not have to figure things out myself. God will always make a way. All I have to do is wait on it. I was very impatient before and would want things to happen immediately. Again, I still do, yet know the difference. I do not have to know the next move. I no longer am tired of being tired. I can rest assured knowing God will give me rest.

NEW LIFE
Chapter Fifty

❧❳SCRIPTURE❲❧

1 Corinthians 5:17
Therefore, if anyone is in Christ, the new creation has come: The old has gone, the new is here.

Laying on my mom's couch I cried and cried. It seemed as if what I had hoped for fell through and I was unsure the direction I was heading. I was tired of feeling defeated and felt I was at another low. I was alright with quitting my job because of the way things were turning out. I knew a change was needed, but had no clue what I would do now.

I had made plans to move in with my "girlfriend." We would be roomies. We were such good friends and knew each other so well, we figured it would work. Until another blowout surfaced between the two of us, I thought I had it all figured out. I believe this needed to happen to detour me from making the wrong move.

Because of my plan not working out with living with her, I was lost. I was supposed to be past all this stuff. It seemed I would have learned something but fell right back into the same train of thought. I would think to myself, "What kind of growth is this?" As soon as I thought I knew, I knew nothing at all. I continued to cry on my mom's couch.

My mom had retired recently and was planning to move down south. I was so happy for her and wished her all the best. As she was planning her future elsewhere, I was wondering where else could I go. She saw me on the couch crying and just looked at me as if she knew my pain. I looked back at her with the lost baby face. Then she said, "You could come with me."

I knew it was genuine and the direction I was supposed to go in because I did not ask. She knew I was trying to work something out before she left to go out of town. Although she did not like my plan to move with my friend, she allowed me to try and find my way. Knowing it fell through, she embraced me with an invite. I love my mommy.

She offered me a new start.

I was so excited about knowing where I was going to be. My mom and I had begun to become close again, so this would provoke a closer relationship. I had no clue exactly where down south we were moving. I did not know anyone. I had no clue what I would do, and I actually did not care. I was only concentrating on moving past all I had been through and starting over again.

I suddenly felt lighter and refreshed only from knowing I had somewhere to go. It was amazing to me that I was so comfortable about moving to a place I had never been. Although I have moved before to unfamiliar places, this seemed very different. Before, I had a different attitude with a different agenda. I was always running from something bringing my troubles with me. This time, I was tired of carrying baggage I did not need. I was leaving the old behind and only traveling with what I needed for my future. If I had no use for it, I was not bringing it along. It was time to rid of the unnecessary personal belongings.

I was shedding the old allowing the new to come through.

We were due to travel south to check out the new house. I brought along some clothes to put in my new closet and mark my spot. The adjustment had begun.

On the way down south I began to wonder: "What am I going to do in the country?" "I will miss all my friends." "I do not like starting over again." "What does this house look like?" "Will my mom and I get along like we used to?" "Is this the right move for me?" "Will I meet a man down here?" "I do not want to be alone." All these thoughts began to bombard my mind until I told myself to chill!

It was evening when we arrived to the new house. My mom was to receive a key the following morning. We peeked inside the house to get a sneak view. It was beautiful. The neighborhood was lovely and very quiet. It was a very, very small town with a lot of crop fields. I was not used to this, but began to feel a sense of serenity. It was calming to my spirit immediately.

The next day we stepped inside. It felt even better than I imagined when looking in from the outside the night before. It was very spacious and country like. It was going to be my mom and myself until otherwise directed. I felt safe and encouraged.

Why did I have doubts in the first place? I knew this was where I was supposed to be because of the way it presented itself to me. I was given a fresh start in a new place and I needed to fully embrace it. I was glad I traveled to view the house with my mom. I could finally see some light shining in my direction. The way was already laid for me; I only needed to follow. I was ready.

I placed my clothes in my closet right away. I had claimed my room and all that was to come. I was ready for the move. I could not wait to get back to the old house so I could pack.

As I packed the rest of my things, I could not help to think about all I was leaving behind. I have started over more than five times. Each time I thought I had reached much further than the last, but still had a way to go. I had a little animosity in my heart for those who have hurt me in my past. I was not as angry as I once was, but still held a grudge. I tried to tell myself it did not matter anymore. No matter how many times I had to begin again, I had an opportunity to do it again and now do it even bigger.

While packing, I decided to pack up all those negative feelings. This baggage would not be going with me.

Before my mom and I left the house down south, I told her to leave her Bible open on the mantle. Allowing God's Words to fill the room is exactly what I needed. My heart began to open up to the new direction I was headed.

When we arrived out our new house to stay, I was so excited about the newness of it all. My mom had to go back to the old house to settle loose ends which left me at the new house alone. I unpacked everything in my room and put it all in its place. I also unpacked the majority of the living room and the kitchen and put everything in its place. Arranging the front room, putting away dishes, and sorting out other things within the house is where my attention was. While doing this, I felt right at home and looked forward to the rearranging that was going to take place in my life.

God had sorted things out for me once again. Just when I did not know where I would be He provided more than shelter for me. I still did not know what I would do here in this new place, yet I knew it would be a start to something great. Because I had no ties with anyone or anything, I was able to begin fresh. Everything about this particular move was new. The house, the city, the people, and most of all my outlook.

Suddenly, I felt very sorry for anything I had done in the past that was harmful to me or anyone else on any level. It was as if I gained a new found understanding about the chances that are given. And not even so much chances, but new opportunities to take what was learned from the past and add to my life now to make a difference in the future. I was so grateful to all those who crossed my path so far. I had a lot to bring with me that will enhance who I am becoming.

I got down on my knees every day, asked for forgiveness, and gave thanks to God and asked for direction.

I am so thankful that God continues to allow me to grow. I have moved several times throughout my life and was able to start over time and time again. It makes a huge difference when you come to specific points in your life and begin to realize the seriousness of why you are here in this life. I had not figured it out yet, but I was well on my way. Because my eyes were open and I was open to receive all that came my way that was positive, I was entering a new life.

A new way of thinking, behaving, reacting, progressing, loving, searching, relating, worshiping, praying, and a new way of believing are some of the things I was about to encounter. All of the past was behind me. My mind was clear and free of all that was holding me down. I finally felt ready. Ready for a new life!

Who knew that what was ahead of me would change my life in ways I never could have dreamed of.

HE CALLED ME
Chapter Fifty-one

✖SCRIPTURE✖

2 Timothy 1:8-9

*So do not be ashamed of the testimony about our Lord or
me his prisoner. Rather, join with me in suffering for the
gospel, by the power of God. He has saved us and called
us to a holy life—not because of anything we have done
but because of his own purpose and grace. This grace was
given us in Christ Jesus before the beginning of time, but it
has now been revealed through the appearing of our
Savior, Christ Jesus, who has destroyed death and has
brought life and immortality to light through the gospel.
And of this gospel I was appointed a herald and an apostle
and a teacher. That is why I am suffering as I am. Yet this
is no cause for shame, because I know whom I have
believed, and am convinced that he is able to guard what I
have entrusted to him until that day. What you heard from
me, keep as the pattern of sound teaching, with faith and
love in Christ Jesus. Guard the good deposit that was
entrusted to you—guard it with the help of the Holy Spirit
who lives in us.*

With many things that are new, there is an excitement. The
ability to start fresh and begin again brings thrill because of the
clean slate that is presented to you.

When I first moved down south, I was very excited and
looked forward to what was to come. It did not take long before
I became bored and wondered what I was going to do. My mom
and I rode all over the area to acquaint ourselves with our
surroundings only to find there was not much here. I began to
miss my friends from back home and began to make some calls.

For a brief period, I got very creative. I was making things and putting together scrapbooks that were really amazing. I thought for a minute, maybe my artistic side is showing itself and I am supposed to do something with it. That did not last too long. I began reading my Bible and working out daily. This put my mind at ease for the time being and kept me pretty busy.

When my mom would frequent this area before moving here, there was a church she would attend. I ended up joining the church although feeling very strange about belonging to a church other than my former church. It felt like I was cheating. I wasn't comfortable with the church itself, but yearned to grow closer to the Lord.

I had kept in contact with my "girlfriend" from back home. She wanted me to visit from time to time, so I accepted. It felt good initially to be able to regularly travel back and forth. It was like I had the best of both worlds. So, whenever I felt like getting away from the boredom I was experiencing, I was able to take a train ride back to my hometown all expenses paid. When I first began to visit it was nice being back home. Seeing old faces and doing things I used to do. After a while, I became bored with it. The same behavioral patterns were occurring and I felt like I was on a merry-go-round. My life was changing and I could tell. The things that used to interest me were no longer pleasing to me. Each time I made this trip I would wonder why I was going.

Each time I would return home I would dive right into my Bible. My mom and I attended just about every church service. This was very good for me because my spirit was being filled. The closer I got to God, the freer I felt. I had a bit of a battle still going on concerning what I wanted to do. I began battling more with what my life meant. What was I here for? Why had I been through so much? What was I supposed to do with it all? I began to search.

I had not obtained my GED yet and had gotten some information about an adult education class that was right down the street from me. I enrolled immediately. I was a bit nervous being I had not been in school for over 20 years. Apparently I did pretty well on my pretests because I was put into the "A" classroom. This was the top GED class. This made me feel very good and as if I was headed somewhere. I was not exactly sure where. Within a couple of months, I obtained my GED. It was a very gratifying moment. I thought about this day for a long time and it finally presented itself. My dad flew in to see me walk across the stage. What a proud moment for me!

I thought about putting my hair skills back in action, so I went to a Cosmetology school to enroll. It seemed to be a smooth process until the school rep said she did not hear anything back about my financial aid after several weeks of waiting. That appeared very strange to me, but I just moved on to another school. It was the same issue. It was something about not receiving a specific type of information needed. I could not understand and began to get frustrated. Something else was blocking this.

I began writing up proposals to different programs that had been in my head for years. So many ideas were running through my head I did not know what to do with them. I was at the computer for hours every day. Logos, mission statements, business names, and concepts were running through my mind nonstop.

On one of my trips to visit my friend, I met with my former pastor. It was interesting because I began to feel different around him. I could feel things I did not before. It was as if my senses increased tremendously. I did not know what to say because I was not certain of what was happening. Even more interesting, he knew something was happening with me because he asked me if I felt like I needed to be alone. I told him yes I did. He offered the next time I came to visit to get me a room. Now, because this was my pastor, I thought nothing negative from anything we would discuss. I knew I was searching for God and did not see anything other than God in him. But, this time was very different.

We would always talk over a meal. While on one of my visits, we went to eat and he made a statement to me that I could get a drink if I wanted one. It was funny because I was thinking of getting one, but changed my mind. I did not feel it was appropriate to drink in front of my pastor. Not only that, I really wasn't wanting one. I was feeling a high I had not felt before and wanted it to continue. So after our meal, we took a walk outside. We took a few steps and then he guided me in another direction. We headed toward a building and then stood near the wall. We were still in plain view of others but off to the side. It felt very, very strange to stop where we did but again, I did not think too much of it. He leaned toward me and gave me a hug. While releasing from the hug, there was a slight pause as our cheeks crossed one another. Immediately, I felt uncomfortable and pulled away and chuckled. He asked what was wrong and I replied, "Nothing at all." He suggested that we leave and I agreed. I did not say anything the whole ride back to my friend's house.

What I took from that situation is I was developing some keen senses. I did not know what it ultimately meant, but it was more beneath the surface. I did not want to judge or determine anything about it. It felt more to me like discerning spirits than recognizing a man coming on to me. As time went by, I was being ministered to through my spirit what was happening. I was still a bit confused.

After returning back home, I had begun a fast. I was not eating anything and was drinking only water with cayenne pepper and lemon mixed in it. I had read that it was good for my skin and health since I was not eating any foods at all. From all the Bible reading I was doing, I did not have an appetite for food. I only wanted to read God's Word. I did not come out of my room unless I had to use the restroom or go for my morning walk. There was no watching television except for spiritual programs and the radio had to be gospel. My ears began to be sensitive to anything other than God's Word.

It was funny because I could see that I was changing, but could not stay stuck on a thought. Whenever my mind would wander, the thoughts would immediately go away and scriptures would pop in my mind. It was like my spirit would not allow anything negative to form in my mind. I felt a sense of great power and awareness that I had never felt before. I continued to read and meditate on God's Word.

My friend back home had wanted me to come visit again. By this time, I was feeling apprehensive because of the changes that were occurring within me. She and I used to be in an intimate relationship and I knew she still had feelings for me. I was in another state of mind and believed I was in that relationship because of the issues that were in my life. I spoke with her on the phone about how I was feeling and broke down in tears as I explained to her that I did not want to disappoint God by being with her. I could not continue our relationship like it was. I had already come to terms with my feeling toward her. She knew I was not interested in women the way she was. I loved her as a friend, yet had gotten over my personal issues that lead me to her in the first place. In no way did I want to hurt her feelings, yet I knew I had to do what I felt in my heart.

I accepted the invitation once more and decided we would talk once I arrived about where I was in my life. As I prepared for my trip, I felt very confident in all I was doing. I knew what I stood for and believed it would be received with open arms. I shared this with my mom and she was a bit leery because she was unsure how my friend would accept it. My mom gave me a gift to give to my friend. It was a little odd, but was a very nice gesture.

As I arranged my things to leave, I decided I would speak with my former pastor again and ask him about different things I was going through. Maybe, just maybe, he could shine some light on what was occurring in my life. And as that last evening before leaving came to a close, I had a sudden feeling to wash my feet and I did. I definitely wanted to talk with my pastor.

The morning of my departure I woke up feeling so refreshed and geared to go. As I got out of the bed, I began to feel something overpower my body. The best way to describe it is like a trance. I felt compelled to go to my mom's room and speak with her. I had no idea what I was going to say. It was just a prompting telling me to go to her. I got to her room and just stood there in utter amazement. She looked at me with a puzzled look on her face. I walked over to her and began speaking. When I first started talking it was like I was just babbling and then all of a sudden, words just began to spill out. It seemed like I was outside of myself watching. I did not fill like I had control. As I was talking, I was tapping her on her leg, as if to say I am not speaking right now. I remember going back to my room and returning only to say more. This time I said something about her childhood. It was like conformation that God was speaking because there is no way I could know this. I saw a tear fall from her eye. When I finished, I raised my hands, shrugged my shoulders, and left out. Exhaustion came over me when I returned to my room. I sat on my bed briefly and then got ready to head for the train station.

When I arrived to the station, the conductor of the train met us in the waiting area. He had a bag of chicken and sides to eat during the trip. We became friends during my frequent travels. It was interesting how it began: I was standing in line to board the train with a frustrated look on my face. He walked by and asked me, "What's wrong"? I replied, "Nothing." Once on the train, he walked by again and asked again. I stated I wanted a window seat. He walked away and returned telling me to follow him. He took me to the business section of the train and seated me by the window. Feeling pampered I said, "Thank you so much." He nodded and walked away. From that point on, he always took care of me when I traveled. He even began paying for my ticket.

I introduced him to my mother and she told him that I needed to eat so thanks for the chicken. I was thinking to myself, "I am fasting." He assured her that he would take care of me and said his good-byes to her. Shortly after, I stood in line to be seated. I kissed my mom bye and told her I loved her. It felt as if I would never see her again.

I boarded the train and took my seat. After we traveled for a while I began reading my Bible. He, the conductor, checked on me a few times to see if I was alright. The next time he came, he took his shoes off outside of where I was seated and then sat in the seat next to me. At this time, I was looking out of the window crying. He held my hand and asked, "Is God dealing with you"? I quickly shook my head yes. He rubbed my hand and told me it would be fine. As my tears lessened he got up, put his shoes on, and walked away. Just as before, when I began to think about what was occurring the thought diminished.

Later in the trip, I received a call from my girlfriend. She was sounding a bit disturbed. I walked to the restroom so I could speak with her freely. She stated that something weird was going on at her house. She received knocks at her door, yet when she would open it no one would be there. She was speaking in a very angry tone that I was not comfortable with. I told her in an authoritative tone, "I would not be coming to your house this evening and will see you tomorrow. I cannot be subjected to any foolish and inappropriate behavior." She said alright and I hung up the phone. On the way back to my seat, I began to ponder on her negative vibe, but again the thought vanished from my mind.

I had no clue where I was going to stay for the evening, but felt I would be okay. On one of the trains' stops we had a brief break before pushing off again. I got off and sat at a bench on the platform. The conductor walked over to me and began conversing. He said that I looked startled. I told him I had just gotten off the phone with my girlfriend. He asked were we in a relationship. I said, "NO!" He said alright and walked away. Immediately I felt as if I was keeping something from him. Once we boarded the train and I sat down I knew I needed to speak with him again. When he walked by I told him to have a seat beside me. I quickly told him that I had to confess something to him. I explained that I was not totally honest with him about the relationship between my girlfriend and me. I let him know we used to be in a relationship, but were no longer. He smiled and stated that it was okay. I was overcome with relief. By this point, I began to realize clearer that God was with me.

Right before reaching my destination, I let the conductor know what had happened with my girlfriend on the phone and told him I needed somewhere to stay for tonight. He stated that I could stay with him in his room. He had a layover within the same area I was getting off. It was nearby, a downtown upscale area, and had two large beds. I agreed and waited for him in a designated area once we reached our destination. I continued to feel confident and secure with all that was going on.

Once arriving to the room, I put my bags down and took a seat on the bed. He indicated I needed to be alone at this time. I did not quite know what he was talking about, but said okay. He was going to hang out with a co-worker at a nearby bar and would be back later. I appreciated the courtesy and thanked him. He left and I sat on the bed. About 15 minutes went by and I began feeling very uncomfortable. I could almost hear the thoughts that were going on in my mind. I text my pastor and was telling him where I was and how I was feeling. He responded in a very aggressive manner; at least that is what I felt at the time. I then replied, "Never mind." He then said okay and good luck. I thought that was odd and could not figure out what that meant. I sat there a few more minutes and then gathered my things and went to the lobby. I called the conductor and told him I was in the lobby and needed to leave. He immediately told me to stay where I was and that he was coming. He arrived with his male friend, introduced us, and then picked up my things. I followed him back to the room and we began to talk.

He stated again that I should be by myself and that he should not be there with me. This time I asked why he keeps saying that. He mentioned that his mother was "one too." He said she was with God as well. She was a very spiritual woman and had special gifts. I just listened with astonishment. He let me know that he was not a spiritual person but did believe in God. He also stated that he was just doing what he felt he should do. As I was receiving what was being said, he said I was very special. I smiled and said, "Okay."

All of a sudden I felt that power like I felt before I left home. I began talking about so much. A lot of knowledge was coming out of my mouth that I had no clue I even knew. I had explanations for things that were happening and was going to happen. He stated again, "I should not be here."

After our conversation, I was very tired. We both said we were going to sleep and would see each other in the morning. He had to return to the train that next morning and assured me that I could stay in the room until I was picked up. It was a good thing because I wanted time to myself briefly before leaving out.

That next morning, we said our goodbyes. I thanked God he was a perfect gentleman. I expected it actually since he was old enough to be my father. He told me to call him when I was leaving so that he could get me a seat on the way back.

Sitting there alone I began to reminisce on the events of the night before. Everything that was said and my actions had me a little confused, but I thanked God for the safety and let those thoughts go. I called my girlfriend, but got her voicemail so I left a message. After waiting about 20 to 30 minutes, I called a taxi. As I walked down the hall, confidence entered my mind. I was beginning to wonder about when I got to my girlfriend's house what would happen. That quickly faded and I was outside loading my bags in the taxi.

I arrived at her house and went straight in. She had given me a key which was lovely because otherwise I would have been standing at the gate for quite some time being she did not answer her phone when I called again while on the way. Once I entered, I did not see or hear anything. I peeked in her room and she was asleep. I smiled and let her be until she awoke.

I sat on the couch for maybe 10 minutes and here she came out her room down the hall toward me. With a sleepy look on her face she smiled and said, "Hey friend", and laid her head on my shoulder. It was a different feeling when I hugged her. She had always been the dominant one, yet I felt as if I had more authority than she. I rubbed her head and said, "All is well."

So we sat and chatted for a bit then I opted to take a shower and get comfortable. While showering I began to feel a fear as I did once before and then it went away. I was not sure what that was about, but I ignored it. I got out of the shower, dried off, and went into the living area to lotion up. I was pretty comfortable around her, so being in just a towel was nothing. She respected my space and never violated it. As I began greasing up my legs, she started talking about something. I cannot remember because the next thing I know, I saw another person when I looked at her. I do not know who or what it was, but it was not her. I immediately stood up and paused for a minute. She went to the kitchen, picked up a knife, and began to open a package of water. As soon as she picked up that knife and looked at me again, I headed toward the door, opened it and went outside. With just a towel covering my naked body I hurried to the building next to hers. A woman was coming out and I ran toward her frantically. I asked her, "Do you believe?" Puzzled, she answered, "Yes." She started walking me back to her building and as we walked, my girlfriend came rushing outside. I was scared out of my mind.

My girlfriend began to get close to me; she looked like herself, but I knew what I just saw. I extended my arm and yelled in a deep tone, "NO!" The lady was telling her to get back and they began to argue. Someone else came out of the building and she asked her to call 911. Meanwhile, I am sweating profusely. The woman was rubbing my back trying to call me down and next thing I know is I see an ambulance. I remember being questioned about drugs and then being guided to the inside of the ambulance. My pressure was taken and said to be tremendously high. The technician told me to think of something calming and as she was talking, I asked the other technician, "Do you believe?" He looked at me with an upset look on his face and said, "I am not where I should be but I am trying . . . at least I am trying." I looked at him and said, "Of course."

Because my pressure continued to be high, they were taking me to the hospital. I was repeatedly asked about drugs and if I was being abused. I stated to the officer who came on the scene that I was a certified Domestic Abuse Facilitator and was fully aware of all she was about to run down to me. That stopped her in her tracks and went on to ask me what may have caused this. My girlfriend was sticking her head in the vehicle giving her two cents on the matter. She let them know that I had been fasting for five days. They immediately said I was dehydrated or suffering from malnutrition and probably was hallucinating. I knew different and did not say anymore because nobody seemed to understand what I was experiencing. The more I tried to explain, the crazier I appeared. My lips were sealed from that point on.

When I arrived at the hospital, fear began to set in again. There were so many police officers there that I could not count them all. The lady technician from the ambulance said to me, "God reveals things to His great prophets in many ways." I just looked at her like, what does that mean? I was rolled over to an area to be treated and was hooked up to an IV. The first nurse to attend to me was not very pleasant. As she got closer to me, I felt an extremely bad energy. Another nurse came in and the energy changed. I was noticing many things, but said nothing and showed no emotion. I focused on the light that was above me and thought about God.

There were a couple of officers that were standing right in front of my bed staring at me. I could hear them talking to each other and I smirked at something one of them said. They looked at me with a mean mug, yet I continued to smile. With them in my peripheral vision, I looked back at the light and thought about God. The next thing I know is I could hear one say, "If she makes one move I am going to put one in her head." Now what really disturbed me is not what was said, but the fact that neither of their lips were moving. I continued to look into the light. Something strange was happening.

A doctor entered the closed off area I was in and pulled the curtain so no one could see in. He began to take my pulse and listen to my heartbeat. He then asked me, "Why are you nervous"? I told him hospitals made me nervous. He clearly knew it was him I was nervous about. My pulse continued to rise as he touched me. He made the statement, "You waited until you got up here to do this?" I immediately relaxed. It was as if he understood what was happening without me saying anything. He told me that he would take good care of me and everything would be alright. He smiled and left out. I then heard him telling the officers that everything was fine with me and there was no problem. I heard footsteps moving past me and traveling away from me. The energy changed again.

The next thing I know my girlfriend was coming through the curtain with a big smile on her face. I actually was glad to see her by this time. She brought me something to put on and then went to get me something to drink. Not too long after she arrived I was discharged. When I walked outside everything appeared brand new. I had a recollection of what and where everything was, but there was a newness to it all.

We went to a restaurant and ate because she believed I now needed to eat something of great substance. As we sat across from each other she kept telling me how scared she was for me because of how I was acting. I told her I did not have an explanation for her and I was glad it was over. She then stated that I had a different look. She said it was a glow. I continued to have strange feelings and thoughts, but all went well for the rest of the evening. We were to attend church the next day.

What I remember about the next morning was I did not care to have any jewelry on nor did I do my hair. I was very plain in appearance and did not mind at all. That was very odd for me. When we arrived to the church, she took my hand. I recall feeling very obedient. She spoke to someone as we went through the doors and nothing came out of my mouth. She told me I had to go to the restroom, which I did, but wondered how she knew that. I sat down on the seat only to begin to lose all feeling in my body. I began to fall toward the floor as I yelled her name. Standing right outside my stall, she rushed in and caught me before I hit the floor. I felt like a ragdoll. I had no control of anything. She held me for a moment and then told me to get up, and I was able to stand as she lifted me up. Feeling like I was watching this through a window, I could not wrap my brain around what was happening to me. As I walked out of the stall, there were several women in the restroom. I remember an older short woman looking at me saying I was alright. I felt a bit disoriented yet washed my hands and headed toward the sanctuary.

It all was like a dream. When I walked in this cathedral of a room I saw and heard the choir singing "No weapons formed against me shall prosper" in stands that reached the high side of the back wall. The pulpit was as long as the church and the people were filled in every seat. We sat in the very back row on the very end. No matter where you sat in this place you were able to see. I couldn't take my eyes off the harmonious choir. Those words rang so deep within my soul at that moment. I felt they were singing to me and for me. I began to sing along with the choir with much emphasis. Each word I sang rang deep within my being. I felt confident and believed every word that melodiously flowed from my mouth.

When they finished singing, I saw a man at the top of the choir stand gesturing to come on up. As one of the clergy began to speak to the congregation, I began to walk to the front. Feeling as if I was called to the enormous pulpit with all the other anointed and appointed individuals, I arrived at the entry way to security. I remember looking at him and thinking, "What am I doing up here. Don't think I am crazy. I was lead up here." All sound had left my ears and then I heard, "Kristine, come on sweetie. You can't be up here." My girlfriend was reaching her hand to mine as I turned around. I gazed at her and said, "Okay'. I was in a daze.

I returned to my seat feeling very relaxed. I took a deep breath and leaned back in a slouched position. As I continued to breathe deeply, I lost all ability to sit up and fell to the side. The next thing I remember is a woman holding a tissue to my mouth wiping the saliva that was falling from it. She helped me up as another woman was fanning me from behind. I did not say a word. I watched and listened. Out of nowhere, a man came over to me and sat down beside me. He began telling me about myself. I recall him saying I was blessed and favored. He also said there was a song out here waiting for me to sing. There were so many other things he shared with me that fluttered my heart with amazement. All I could think is "why is this happening to me"?

Sitting on the back row on the end, we were able to see everyone who passed by. My girlfriend introduced me to several people who were on the clergy. The pastor and his son walked by in their long robes and shook my hand. The man that told me all those things about myself was a part of the clergy as well; a prophet. When he got up and left, my girlfriend was saying, "Kris, you are anointed. You are special Kris," while smiling from ear to ear. I shrugged my shoulders and said, "Wow that is something." The rest of the service was pretty mild compared to these events. The message was very relative to what was transpiring; Trust God.

I do not remember how the next day began but I do remember feeling very submissive. I began professing to her all the wrongs I had done; some that were to her and some that were not. I told her about different guys I had slept with and where I did it at. I felt so compelled to tell all that I had done wrong. I remember she had my mother on the phone telling her I was confessing. All I remember is feeling so remorseful. The next thing I know, I was urinating on her floor. I recall having a feeling of being free.

I then went and laid in her bed. After about ten minutes, I urinated in the bed. She called the police.

When they arrived, they remembered me from the last incident and told me to walk with them outside to the squad car. Reminiscing on the vibe I got from the officers at the hospital, I was terrified to get in the car. The officer did not put me in cuffs, but she did put me in the back seat. With a frantic look on my face, she consoled me through the rearview mirror. I was trying to find a light to focus on but could not find one. I had no clue where we were headed, but I knew I was alright.

Pulling up near the jail made my stomach do flips. "I did not commit a crime", I started thinking. As we walked through the doors it seemed as if everyone was staring at me. They put me in a room and told me to sit and wait. I still had no idea where I was. A few minutes went by and a tall man came in and began talking to me. I got down on my knees. He told me to get up and come with him. I sat in another room that appeared to be a semi-office. A woman of Asian descent came in and asked me to explain what happened. I immediately knew I was in a psych ward of the jail. "I don't know" I told her. She began going over what looked like a statement from the police report from the previous day. "Why were you outside with no close on wrapped in a towel?" I said, "I had a spiritual experience." Looking at me like I was nuts she said, "Did God tell you to go outside with no close on?" Something told me to be quiet!

Another person came in and started speaking to me. This guy asked me questions about myself and what I liked to do. We began a conversation without including anything that happened. He smiled, looked me in my eyes, and told me to write down the Lord's Prayer on a piece of paper. I said I didn't know it all by heart. He handed me a Bible he had with his pad.

I told him I did not know where it was in the Bible. He smiled again and turned right to it.

As I began to write, my hand shook like crazy. That was not my writing that was on that paper. It was very scribbly but legible. I instantly thought of a time I saw this writing before. I was very angry and wrote a very hateful poem. I looked at the guy and he looked at me with a straight face as if to say, "Yeah, I just wanted you to see." I kept writing until the last word; AMEN. He then said you'll be just fine and gave me a name of a place where I could get information on being a counselor. I shook my head and smiled.

The Asian lady came back in and said she had spoken with my mother. "You cannot go days without eating. It is not healthy." The next thing I remember is sitting in a chair with a severe case of the shakes. I was not cold, but was shaking uncontrollably. I requested a blanket and just observed where I was and who was in this place.

Another man walked over to me and began speaking to me. All I remember him saying is I need to ask for help when I need it because that is something that I do not do. And then he walked away. I wanted him to come back and tell me more. I thought to myself really hard . . . HELP ME! He turned around immediately. Quickly I said, "Jesus." He came back over to me and said, "Go back home and get things started for your children. You have lived your life and had your fun." I had no clue what that meant, but I held on to it like it was gold. I was given meds to help me sleep and recall waking up the next day being told I would be leaving. I felt refreshed and ready to go.

My girlfriend had come up there behaving like a madman. The therapists along with the officer was not going to let me leave with her until she calmed down. She told them she was upset that I was there and only wanted me out of there. After a while, I was released.

I do not recall how I ended up at a clinic, but I do know I was very afraid once we pulled up. I told my girlfriend I did not want to go in there. She said I needed to so I can get some meds to help me sleep because I was not getting adequate rest; which was true. When we walked up to the building, I saw the entire building wobble like it was a cartoon and then roared like a monster. I desperately asked her not to take me in there. I looked up at the sky and heard the thunder roll. It was beginning to rain. She grabbed my hand and said that it would be okay. When I got to the counter I had to sign in. I looked at the sign-in sheet and saw that I was the sixth person and ran out of the door. She came outside to get me and as I looked around it was as if everybody was looking at me; which they probably were. She grabbed my hand again and took me inside.

As we waited to be seen, the security guard gave me a look and then rolled his eyes at me. I thought to myself, "These people think I am crazy." I did not care. They had no clue what I was experiencing. Under the circumstances I believe I handled it very well. I began praising God non-stop. "Thank You Jesus, Praise Your Name Lord, Thank You Jesus" is what I kept saying all the way to the doctor that was prescribing the medicine. As I looked around her office, I saw a few religious artifacts and began to feel a bit at ease. My girlfriend began to tell her what had been happening and then stated that I was praising God too much. As I was still praising God, I boldly said, "I CAN PRAISE GOD AS MUCH AS I PLEASE. YOU CANNOT TELL ME HOW MUCH I CAN PRAISE HIM!" She said, "I know Kris, but you are doing it a lot." "I CAN PRAISE HIM HOWEVER AND WHENEVER I WANT TO. YOU OR NOBODY ELSE CAN TELL

ME DIFFERENTLY." The doctor offered me a snack she was eating. Although I was very hungry, I declined. I believe she was trying to help me, but doing it the wrong way. Medicating me was not the proper solution, yet she had a kind enough spirit to make me feel comfortable after being afraid the whole time while in that building. After I proclaimed my loyalty to God, I stopped praising Him consecutively. It became every 15 to 20 minutes. We left with the prescription, retrieved it on the floor below, and was on our way back to her house. Once we got to the entrance of the clinic area, everybody was smiling and waving bye to us. Mission accomplished I thought to myself.

When we got to her house all I wanted to do was write. I grabbed my pad and started writing things down. My girlfriend was working evening shifts and invited me to go with her because she was concerned with leaving me alone. I assured her I would be fine. I did not want to chance being around any bad energy. It seemed I was very sensitive to people's spirit. I opted to stay in.

It was a long, long night for me. I took the medication that was prescribed, but it did not have an effect on me. After the third day, I did not take them anymore but told my girlfriend I was. I had a few more experiences while I was alone, but it would be very difficult to explain. I believe this to be things I only needed to know.

My girlfriend had spoken to one of my sons and asked him to come by and be with me for a while. I felt a little nervous about it initially, then was overwhelmed with comfort. As she was leaving for work he was just arriving. We all chatted a bit before she left. I stood up and made a statement to my son that was so random but profound at the same time. I made a reference to him and his father. He looked at me and said, "Wow ma!" I wondered to myself where that came from.

We said our good-byes to my girlfriend and we began to talk about God. He mentioned he wanted a Bible at one time and informed me that his girlfriend had gotten him one. This made me very happy being that I always would talk to him about the goodness of God and to read at least a little a day. He continued to tell me how he was feeling spiritually and things he was doing to assist with his curiosity.

I had been receiving spiritual paraphernalia in the mail and brought one of the writings with me on this trip. I would get encouraging, spiritual letters from a well-known church that included a prophetic message in it. I sent seed offerings to this church countless times and took a liking to their letters. They always seemed to fit exactly what was going on in my life. I grew to look forward to them. Lately, I had been receiving two of the same. I knew the second was for someone, only I did not know who.

Once he began talking, I knew instantly it was for him. I told him to hold on a minute that I had something for him. When I returned, I handed my son a sealed envelope. As he began to open it, there was knocking on the wall. We both looked at each other wondering what that was. As he went to open it again, the knocking continued. He said, "Ma, do you hear that?" I immediately had a sensation of calmness run through me and I said to him, "He is knocking, let Him in." He was looking frightened and I assured him he was fine. I told him to open the envelope because it was a word for him. When he opened it, the knocking stopped. As soon as he started reading, I went to the restroom. While in there, I thanked God several times and let out a huge sigh. Once I sat back down next to my son, he was in total disbelief. He stated that the letter was very much on point. He asked me again if I heard that knocking. I told him yes and let him know all was well. My son and I just shared an experience we will never forget. I did not mention what happened to my girlfriend when she got home.

I was looking forward to going home. I tried to get in touch with my friend who works on the train so he could get my ticket to return home as he promised me. I did not get a response from him. I didn't get alarmed but did wonder why. I called my mom and asked her to call him for me. I waited patiently. As I was holding on to hope, I was compelled to write. I grabbed my book and started writing without pause line after line. I had filled 14 pages front and back of unsystematic phrases and words before stopping. I looked at it when I was done and thought, "What is this?" A little after I finished, my mom called and assured me that my friend would call me soon. Once he did, everything was set up for me to return home.

Seven days I will never forget!

I was looking forward to going home. As I pondered on what had occurred during this visit, I was very puzzled. I knew I would have understanding later, but was overwhelmingly curious right now. As I exhausted my thoughts, I realized seven days had gone by. Knowing that this is the number of completion eased my inquisitive cognizance.

My girlfriend was glad I was "feeling" better. She had bought me some spiritual and encouraging reading material for me to take home. I was anxious about reading these materials and eager to know if they would help me in my quest to gain understanding of what has transpired.

Once I returned home, I did not want to think about leaving again any time soon. I realized I was supposed to be right where

I was, so my back and forth days were over. Being with my mother now felt like a blessing. I felt at peace with my situation that once had me frustrated. I was in a new place for a new reason and I wanted to seek why.

I confided in a couple people at the church I was attending at the time about the events that had taken place. What they told me was something I pretty much knew already. I was looking for answers that they were unable to provide. It should have been evident to me that I was not going to receive an answer from them as we continued to be interrupted while I was explaining what happened. I counted it all joy and continued seeking.

Time had gone by yet nothing forgotten about what I had went through. I continued praying and waiting for my answers to be revealed.

My habits began to change as I took on new ones. I no longer smoked cigarettes, I was not drinking, and I was not seeing anyone. I was alone with the Lord the majority of the time. I believed once I took time out to notice, my answer was being given to me through my actions. Everything I did was in and about the Lord; willingly. I wanted nothing more than to seek His face and know Him better. I was still puzzled, but continued to hold on to His hand tightly.

I came to understand that the only voice I was attracted to, the voice I heard the loudest was God's. I yearned for Him day and night.

There was a time at church where I was unable to participate in a song being sung by our choir because I was not provided with the words. I stood on the front row along with my choir but was unable to praise my Father through song. This hurt me to my core. I cried afterward and realized I desired a lot more than I realized but did not understand why.

God was showing me through these events His power, my faults, my purpose, my desires, my gifts and talents, the ways of the world, my faith, and how powerless people really are. God allowed me to see things like Jonah in the belly of the whale; crazy to everyone else yet very true and real to me. God allowed me to see Him at the peak of my life. Like many, I was tested and stayed true despite how unbelievable the circumstances were. He saw me through as I went through the process of being called.

I could understand when Jesus was in the wilderness being tested a little more. Satan used all kinds of tactics to throw Jesus off because of the weakness He displayed at the time. I too was weak, yet continued to praise my Father in Heaven. He was acknowledged despite the uncertain circumstances. I had no clue what was happening, but kept Him as my focus.

As He called me, I continued in the direction I was being called. I did not try to turn away. I kept going through that unimaginable maze of circumstances. I had no understanding of what was happening, yet did not turn away from Him. I did not curse Him, I did not blame anyone, nor did I want to quit. I held on to the sweet sound in my ear as I followed the melody pounding in my heart. He called me and I had to answer no matter what.

Matthew 22:14

For many are called, but few are chosen.

NOW I AM FOUND
Chapter Fifty-two

✠ SCRIPTURE ✠

Ephesians 2:8-9
For by grace you have been saved by faith. And this is not
your own doing; it is the gift of God, not a result of works,
so that no one may boast.

Being lost for so long has been a reward in itself. It has shown me things I would have otherwise not been able to see. The experiences I have encountered were all for my good for God's sake; not my own.

Although I had a better understanding of what had just transpired in my life, there was still a question of, "What now?" What was I supposed to do with this knowledge? I had no immediate answers. I kept doing as I was told. I became frustrated at times, but for the most part I was obedient to His Word.

I continued attending Bible study and other programs at church. One in particular comes to mind being it was the one that extended me further into my ministry.

My mother and I attended a World Prayer Day service. It was where many of the "heads" of the church came together and prayed for the world about an array of issues. When I walked in the church I could feel the realness of it all. It felt unlike any other time I ever entered the Sanctuary. I sat on the row my mother and I usually sit on. As I sat close to the wall, I was taking in all the folks gathering together in Jesus's name for one cause. It was actually overwhelming.

As people began to come in and be seated, a few people came to the row I was on. My mother was not seated yet, so I opted to come out from the comfort of the wall and sat on the aisle seat. This was alright with me because I had a clear view of what would be taking place.

While sitting there, I thought about all I had been through and my recent experiences. I still had many questions and felt I could ask in prayer along with the many prayers that were going to go forth. I waited in great expectation.

The Sanctuary was now full and the service began. There was a world map that selected women that were placing ribbons on it to designate the area being prayed for. As places were being pinned, prayers went forth. I could feel the power within the room and began to embrace each word of the prayer. On about the third prayer that went forth, I began to feel overcome by something. I was not sure what was happening. I felt dizzy and all of a sudden I heard myself loudly praise Jesus and I went blank. I remember leaning forward, shaking, and murmuring sounds I have never heard. My voice was in a tone I never heard. I could not stop it. I had no control over it.

I believe I was toward the end of this occurrence because I was able to see others around me. I noticed people coming from behind me, touching my back saying a quick prayer and walking away. Others were fanning me and praising God. I was still rocking back and forth still uttering this sound. I heard someone ask me if I wanted some water and I felt the air from a fan blowing against my face. I looked up and praised Jesus and then said, "Yes please."

My mother was sitting in front of me staring at me asking was I alright. Just as I wondered what was happening to me, one of the attendees whispered in my ear, "You can't do nothing about that Holy Spirit can you?" I looked at her in wonder. I received my answer immediately. I drank my water and sat in amazement.

Afterward, many people came to me and hugged me and just smiled. I did not know what this experience meant exactly except I had been blessed with the Holy Spirit. But why now at this moment?

I read and read to see what I could find that would explain what happened. All I could find is descriptions of what I went through. I wanted an explanation. I knew what happened, but I wanted details. I prayed and prayed. I knew not to ask anyone because of what happened the last time I inquired from someone. I felt I needed to wait on the Lord, but was being very impatient.

I remembered when I was locked up years ago, while in one of the Bible study classes we said a prayer to receive the Holy Spirit. I received then and heard the same sound, but this seemed a bit more drastic. I was surprised then as well, but was expecting it. This time I was just sitting still with no thought of the Holy Spirit and He took over out of nowhere.

Time went by and still no answer. My quest for this knowledge began to lessen. I figured God knew my prayer and I would get my answer soon enough.

Not until I went against His Word did I learn of what I was looking for.

It was Thanksgiving time and, my mother, two of my sons, daughter in-law, and grand-daughter, and myself went down to my brother's house where my oldest son was living at the time. When we arrived we all greeted each other and began to settle in. Music was playing, aroma was lurking in the air, and laughter was all around.

My brother and I went to the store and picked up some wine for the evening. Now, this did not bother me because I knew I had not drank in months and was so out of touch with thoughts of drunkenness. I believed I could handle a glass or two and be just fine while mingling with the family.

As we were enjoying one another with a few glasses of cocktails, aggression broke out between my two sons. Unsure of what it was about, I held my wine in my hand and continued drinking as my brother handled the situation. It seemed as if it were going to escalate into more, so I put my glass down and grabbed my granddaughter. I was attempting to keep myself calm. I could feel the rise in me because of the changed atmosphere along with the persuasion of alcohol. I silently prayed to myself.

As my brother talked my sons down, I stood beside him adding a word here and there. I did not want to say much of anything so I would not get worked up. I became nervous because I was known for getting emotional when I drank. Keeping the peace is what I needed to do for me; my brother had a grip on their situation.

After calming one son, the other continued his battle. It was a personal issue that had now disrupted the evening. I could no longer contain myself and began to speak with my son to gain some understanding. He was so far gone in his past, I and everyone else could no longer see his issue. This frustrated my brother and me. I grabbed my glass of wine and filled it up. As I drank, I became more and more upset. I began to yearn for a cigarette which I had not smoked in about a year. I was falling apart.

The situation went from my sons to my brother and me yelling at each other. I became agitated with my mother about our past which was crazy because it really had nothing to do with the situation at all. I was no longer present; the alcohol had taken over. I was lost.

My brother had me up against the wall trying to calm me down and I would not back down. I remember picking up a glass and trying to hit him with it. He kindly rejected that thought and pinned me up against the wall. In that moment I was very frightened. This was something of my past that was in my present. As I began to let go, my body did too and I urinated all over myself. Yelling for him to let me go, it became apparent to everyone else what I just did. He let me go and I went upstairs embarrassed and ashamed.

Once I got cleaned up, I laid on the couch in the room where I was to sleep. From this room I could hear a small chatter from everyone downstairs. It seemed everything had settled down. I think my act stole the show. I stayed upstairs the rest of the night feeling very remorseful. While I isolated myself, each person from downstairs came to pay me a visit. It was interesting because each one of them mentioned the positive change in me and knew I had a lost moment. It was as if God sent them to verify the feelings I was experiencing. Love was shown through each of them. God was comforting me through them.

As I laid there, I realized I messed up. God had cleaned me up and allowed me to step into a drunken stupor to show me where I was. He brought me to a place of newness, freedom, and cleanliness. All my shame, guilt, and sins were washed away and I fell right back in it. How could I allow myself to go back to that place again after so long? I was doing so well. I became weak and became embraced with negativity. My focus was lost very quickly.

God showed me once again how much I need Him. In all situations I need Him. When I think I am able to handle something, God shows me how strong I am not. I made the choice to focus on God and not the things of this world. I decided when I was hurt, I would turn to Him. I turned to alcohol when I felt fragile. I leaned on alcohol when I knew things were getting out of control. I turned to everything else but God. He allowed me to see how lost I am without Him.

This is something I had been through time and time again. The thing is, I thought "I" was able to deal with circumstances because He strengthened me.

I needed to see it is always God who is there to provide the strength I need in every situation. I never need to fly solo. I am never strong enough to handle anything alone. I always need to turn to Him no matter how well I am doing or how long I have been doing well. I am only doing well because He has never left me. However, He will allow me to see how much control I do have when I try to take it . . . None!

Although I had this new life of walking right by God, I have to continue to walk with Him. God taught me that I can get lost at any time although I am a Holy Spirit filled woman of God. I can never think I am capable of dealing with anything without Him. If I need to fall to my knees all day long to keep me from losing His light, then that is what I must do.

Up until this moment I was still lost because of the way I was thinking. It was not a bad thing. It was what I had to go through just like everything else in my life in order to know who I am. I realized someone can be saved and still be lost because of lack of understanding. I continue to pray for knowledge, understanding, and wisdom. I pray for eyes to see and ears to hear God with. I pray for continued guidance and leading from the Holy Spirit into His truth each day. I pray that God's Will is fulfilled each day and not my own. I pray I become more and more like Him and less of myself each day.

After so many years of being lost, now I am found!

SCRIPTURE

2 Timothy 4:17-18, 22

But the Lord stood with me and strengthened me, so that through me the proclamation might be fully accomplished, and that all the Gentiles might hear; and I was rescued out of the lion's mouth. The Lord will rescue me from every evil deed, and He will bring me safely to His heavenly kingdom; to Him be the glory forever and ever. Amen.

The Lord be with your spirit.   Grace be with you.

To God Be the Glory,
I pray that through my journey you were able to grab hold
of something that will lead, guide, or direct your path
toward or closer to God.

CPSIA information can be obtained
at www.ICGtesting.com
Printed in the USA
FFOW03n0531201016
28603FF